THF

Butterworths

History of a Publishing House

Butterworths

History of a Publishing House

H. Kay Jones

London
Butterworths
1980

England
Butterworth & Co (Publishers) Ltd
88 Kingsway, London WC2AB

Australia
Butterworth Pty Ltd
586 Pacific Highway, Chatswood, Sydney, NSW 2067

Canada
Butterworth & Co (Canada) Ltd
2265 Midland Avenue, Scarborough, Toronto M1P 4S1

New Zealand
Butterworths of New Zealand Ltd
T. & W. Young Building, 77–85 Customhouse Quay, Wellington

South Africa
Butterworth & Co (South Africa) (Pty) Ltd
152–154 Gale Street, Durban

USA
Butterworth & Co (Publishers) Inc
10 Tower Office Park, Woburn, Boston, Mass 01801

ISBN 0 406 17606 X

Layout by Hilary Norman
Typeset and printed in Great Britain by Cambridge University Press

Foreword

During the years 1976 to 1978, a white-haired figure wearing a surgical mask could frequently be seen emerging from closets in 88 Kingsway and 4/5 Bell Yard, Butterworths' two London offices. He would be clutching ribbon-tied files from which he would smack off the dust; then, mask set aside, he would commandeer a conference room and riffle eagerly through each forgotten archive.

This was Kay Jones's idea of the way a man should spend his retirement. No company history has had a more assiduous researcher than this one; and few company historians can have had as rich a lode to mine as Kay, for successive generations of Butterworth managers, with a sub-conscious yearning for immortality which modern managers are too cynical or busy to entertain, had preserved everything they wrote.

The interplay of strong and stormy personalities is normally pictured as confined, in the world of publishing, to best-selling authors, high-stake publishers and editorial geniuses. The Butterworth story reveals that the cloistered retreats of publishing have their share of drama.

Although the story substantively covers the years from 1818 to 1978, it also reaches back to the beginnings of legal publishing in England with which Butterworths can trace a connection; and points forward to the emerging form of publishing in which the computer complements the printed word. In this sense, it is a case study of how any publishing house has to adapt its product, its style, its territorial span, its ownership, in order to survive. The times when Butterworths failed to innovate were the times when it became flaccid, comfortable and vulnerable.

My own contributions have been, firstly, to become possessed with the story to the point of commissioning the book; and, secondly, to act as Kay's editor. My most repeated exhortation to him was to write about the people more than the product, because they would bring the product to life. Kay has done this nobly. He has also shamed me in his unfailingly graceful accommodation to the brutality of my ex-newspaperman's pencil. How much careful research has been discarded, only Kay and I know.

The author and publisher are grateful to Peter Cochrane, who not only edited the final manuscript, but drew our attention to defects in structure and sequence which, with his skilled diplomatic help, we have been able to ameliorate.

Gordon Graham
Chairman of Butterworths
January 1980

Author's Preface

From my earliest days in Butterworths, I listened with interest and respect to the reminiscences of my older colleagues, and in time I amplified them by collecting background material in a desultory way. The information was useful for the enlightenment of visitors, particularly after Butterworths had become part of the International Publishing Corporation, and I also drew upon it when I addressed induction courses for new employees. Inevitably my friends began to ask me if the results of my researches would be published.

When I was commissioned to write this history, it was partly no doubt due to the fact that I had already amassed a good deal of information on Butterworths. But the project was now official, so many more people had to be consulted, and the archives of the company offered an additional and formidable mass of material. It was soon obvious that the major problem would be one of selection.

So, in thanking my friends and colleagues for all the trouble they have taken, I ask them to forgive me that so much has to be omitted. To name all who have helped me would be tedious, and might lead to unfortunate omissions, but this omnibus word of thanks is none the less sincere. This is not just my book – I am the scribe for my colleagues living and dead, and it is their book as much as mine.

But the problem has been not only one of quantity, but also one of purpose. One friend suggested that all I could do was to write my own reminiscences – but that was not my brief. The book could have been primarily about the Butterworth list – a sophisticated catalogue, adding perhaps biographical notes and recollections about authors. It could have been primarily about the staff, whereas in the final book names appear and disappear without any attempt at biographical completeness. With my love of figures I could have made it a sort of internal audit, assessing financial trends and problems of profit and loss.

My editor, however, kept the prime task clearly before me. The book was to be an account of what made Butterworths develop as it did. Publications, people and profits enter and leave the stage as they illuminate this overall design. The selection may sometimes seem arbitrary; it has but one end, to give a picture of Butterworths as experienced by those who worked in it.

Old Butterworthians are a closely knit and loyal fellowship. Gordon Graham presided in July 1976 over the first function of 'Butterworth 25', a new society formed to honour the old tradition, of which I am proud to be Chairman. It is open to all who have worked for the company for twenty-five years, or who have retired with ten years service. There are over 100 members. The veteran as I write is Gus Calcutt, who joined the firm in 1910. The oldest in years, Miss Gosden, joined in 1916, and the youngest, Eric Spalding, has now twenty-nine years service.

Retired Butterworthians have handed over the leadership to a new generation of managers who are both forward-looking and tradition-conscious. My former colleagues, old and young, with whom the future lies, will carry the name and traditions and achievements of Butterworths into the seventeenth decade since Henry Butterworth set up his business at No. 7 Fleet Street.

H. Kay Jones
Reigate, Surrey
January 1980

Contents

Acknowledgment

The author and publishers have endeavoured to trace the photographers and the copyright owners of the photographs used in this book (apart from those taken specially). They regret their lack of success in a few cases. The names of the photographers are stated in the captions where known, and permissions have been obtained where appropriate.

Chapter 1

Prologue

Amateur Butterworth historians have long claimed that their company dates back to the reign of Edward VI, if not earlier. Whether history or legend, this tradition has been a source of pride and inspiration to many Butterworthians.

Credibility was lent by the fact that the firm was founded in 1818 at No 7 Fleet Street, believed to have been the same building 'within Temple Bar' at which one Richard Tottel had published 'at the sign of the Hand and Star', which was the Butterworth trademark for many years. Tottel opened his business in 1553. According to the Butterworth tradition he had learnt printing from his father-in-law, Richard Grafton; the printing press which he inherited from Grafton may even have belonged to William Caxton, from whose workman, Wynkyn de Worde (from Wörth in Alsace) Grafton is supposed to have acquired it.

The Hand and Star, from the colophon in Year Book, Henry vi, year 4 (published 1556). Reproduced by permission of the British Library Board

Tottel's eminence as a law publisher during the latter part of the sixteenth century is firmly established. He was granted licences to print books on the common law by three sovereigns – Edward VI (12th April 1553); Mary (1st May 1556); and Elizabeth (12th January 1559). The first two were for seven years; Elizabeth's licence was for life. Tottel was granted what was in effect copyright protection, for Edward VI's licence states 'that none other shall imprint any book which the said Richard Tottel shall first take and imprint during the said term upon pain of forfeiture of all such books'.

With the aid of Pollard and Redgrave's *Short Title Catalogue*, 1475–1640, over 400 separate books or editions published by Tottel can be identified.

At least 225 out of Tottel's output consisted of issues of the *Year Books* – the equivalent of law reports today. Very few of these had been printed before 1500. This was a period of transition from law French to English, and not all printers were equipped to print law French. G. D. Painter writes*:

---

* *William Caxton: a Quincentenary Biography of England's first Printer*, 1976, p. 173, fn.

'After Caxton's death Wynkyn de Worde kept the monopoly of the *Statutes*, which he continued to print in English, while Pynson, who was trained as a specialist in law printing, produced the annual law reports or *Year Books*, and other works for which law French was still compulsory.'

Tottel, in the second half of the sixteenth century, published both *Statutes* and *Year Books*. More than half the issues of *Year Books* recorded between 1475 and 1640 were published by Tottel during the forty years of his licence. He reprinted most of the 'parts' of the Year Books three or four times, thus keeping them in print.

About two-thirds of the remainder of Tottel's output were law books, but he also ventured into general publishing, including religious controversy. His first such book, published in 1553, was Sir Thomas More's *Dialogue of comfort against tribulation*, followed in 1554 by Dean Richard Smith's *A bouclier of the catholike faith*. Less dogmatic works of those years included Boccaccio's *A treatise...shewing...the falles of sondry most notable Princes*, and Hawes's *The history of graund Amoure and la bel Pucell called the Pastime of Pleasure*.*

His best-known general venture came to be known as *Tottel's Miscellany*. Tottel published six editions of this poetic anthology between 1557 and 1574, under the title 'SONGES AND SONETTES, written by the right honorable Lorde Henry Haward late Earle of Surrey and other'. *Tottel's Miscellany* provides an early example of diligent publishing. The first issue appeared on 5th June 1557. A second issue on 31st July 1557 corrected numerous errors, and changed the selection (30 poems were omitted, and 39 new ones added). The subsequent four editions were less commendable in that new errors gradually crept in.

Jasper Heywood, whose translation of Seneca's *Troas* was printed twice by Tottel in 1559, took his translation of *Thyestes* to Berthelet (1560). In his preface (in verse) to the latter work he writes of Tottel's slovenly printing:

'For when to sygne of Hande and Starre
    I chaunced fyrst to come,
To Printers hands I gave the worke
    by whome I had suche wrong,
That though my selfe perusde their prooves
    the fyrst tyme, yet ere long
When I was gone, they wolde agayne
    the print thereof renewe,

* This is described on the title-page as 'Invented by Stephen Hawes, grome of Kyng Henry the seventh, his chamber'.

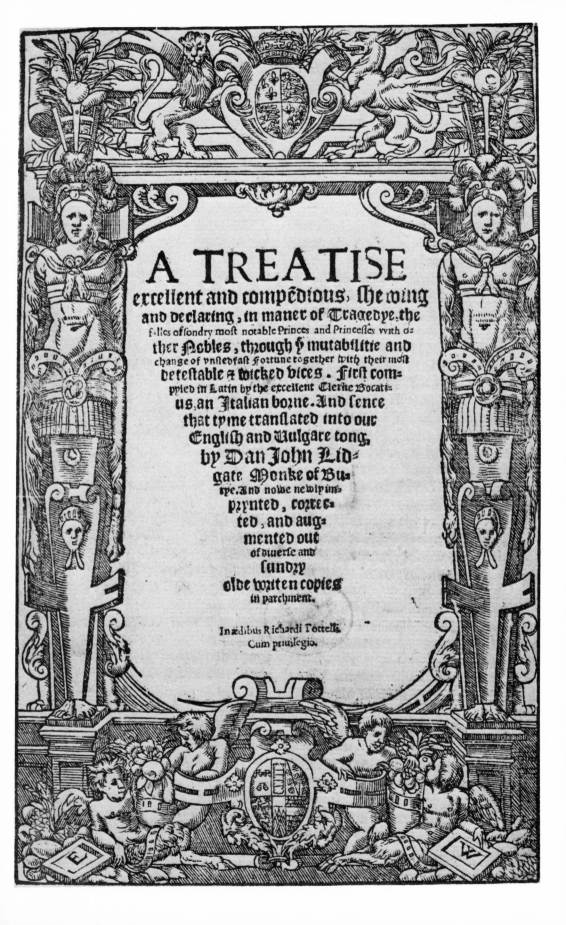

A TREATISE

excellent and compēdious, shewing
and declaring, in maner of Tragedye, the
falles of sondry most notable Princes and Princesses with o=
ther Nobles, through ý mutabilitie and
change of vnstedfast Fortune together with their most
detestable & wicked vices . First com=
pyled in Latin by the excellent Clerke Bocati=
us, an Italian borne. And sence
that tyme translated into our
English and Vulgare tong,
by Dan John Lid=
gate Monke of Bu=
rye. And nowe newly im=
prynted , correc=
ted , and aug=
mented out
of diuerse and
sundry
olde written copies
in parchment.

In aedibus Richardi Tottelli.
Cum priuilegio.

> Corrupted all: in suche a sorte
>   that scant a sentence trewe...
> And to the printer thus I sayde:
>   within these doores of thyne,
> I make a vowe shall neuer more
>   come any worke of myne.'

But Tottel was first and foremost a law publisher. From the beginning of his career he published editions of standard legal works: Fitzherbert's *La Nouuelle natura brevium* (1553), Fitzherbert's *New boke of Justices of peas* (1554); Littleton's *Tenures* (1554); Glanville's *Tractatus* (1555). Further printings of these and similar works followed. He was the first publisher ever to produce a collection of the Statutes of Ireland (1572). In 1585 and 1588 he published reports by Sir James Dyer, the Lord Chief Justice.

Tottel was a member of the Stationers' Company in 1557, at the time of its incorporation by Royal Charter as a Livery Company. He held various high offices in the Company, and was Master in 1578 and 1584. After this he gradually retired from active life, so much so that on 30th September 1589 the Court of Assistants of the Company passed the following ordinance*:

> 'Forasmuch as the affairs of this Company are often hindered, by reason of the continual absence of Mr Richard Tottell, who dwelleth in the furthest parts of the realm [i.e. in Pembrokeshire]...It is now therefore for the furtherance & more speedy execution of the business of this Company ordered at a full Court holden this day (being the quarterday) That the said Mr Tottell...from hence forth shall stand discharged and removed from [his] assistantship in this Company...Nevertheless as touching the said Mr Tottell (having been always a loving & orderly brother in the Company, & now absent [not] for any cause saving his infirmity & far dwelling from the city) it is agreed that always whensoever he shall resort hither, he shall [in] regard of the offices he hath borne in the Company, sit with the Assistants of the Company at their meetings. And his name to be still entered in the book amongst the said Assistants.'

At the same Court two others were removed without qualification.

After Tottel's death in 1594 his patent was granted to Charles Yetsweirt, who continued to trade at the house known as the

---

* Greg and Boswell's *Records of the Court of the Stationers' Company, 1576 to 1602*, p. 33.

To the right honorable ſir Nicho-
las Bacon knight, lord keeper of the
great ſeale of Englande: Richard Tottel
wiſheth health and long lyfe,
with encreaſe of
honour.

Ot long ſythens, right hono-
rable, and my eſpeciall good
Lord, there was deliuered to
mee A collection of the kinges
prerogatiue, whiche Maiſter
Staunforde had gathered and
dedicated vnto your honour: which woorke by-
cauſe it is thought well of by the Sages of the
lawe, and well worthy to be printed, I am therefore the bolder to put it in print, and publiſhe the
ſame. And although the ſaide Maiſter Staunforde verie ſhortlye after that hee hadd dedicated the ſame booke vnto your Lordſhip, were
for his wiſedome, grauitie, learning, integritie, &
ſyncere dealinge, aduaunced to be a Iudge in the
chiefe Court of this Realme for common plees,
and for his good ſeruice therein was by iuſt de-
ſert made knight, and albeit that your Lordſhip
alſo ſythens that tyme haue achieued the place,

A ii.   title

The dedication from Stanford's *King's Prerogative*, published by Tottel in 1567.
Reproduced by permission of the British Library Board

Dick's Coffee Shop (No. 8 Fleet Street, behind No. 7), reputed to have been part of Tottel's original printing-house

Hand and Star. It appears that he did not long survive Tottel, and that his widow carried on the business for a period.

From 1599 No 7 Fleet Street (but no exclusive licence) was held by the printer and publisher John Jaggard, who had been Tottel's apprentice. John's brother, William Jaggard, had been apprenticed to Henry Denham, the printer of *Holinshed's Chronicles*, from which Shakespeare took so much of his historical matter. William's son, Isaac Jaggard, was one of the four publishers of the First Folio edition of Shakespeare in 1623. This tenuous link between 7 Fleet Street and Shakespeare has excited Butterworthians.

From 1629 until 1779 7 Fleet Street was occupied by a series of law printers and publishers of whom little is known.* From 1779 till 1818 there was a break in the law publishing activities at No. 7. The customers, and probably the stock and staff also, moved to No. 43 Fleet Street, at which Thomas Whieldon began to trade as a law bookseller and publisher in 1776. No. 7 Fleet Street was let to a firm of haberdashers. In 1790 Thomas Whieldon took into partnership one Joseph Butterworth, aged twenty. Whieldon retired in 1793, and Joseph Butterworth became the sole partner.

The Dictionary of National Biography describes Joseph Butterworth's business as large and lucrative, and quotes Timperley's statement that his fortune was 'the largest ever known in bookselling'. He was also a man of great religious, philanthropic and political interests. His house was a gathering place for the reformers of the day. He was a member of the first formally appointed committee of the British and Foreign Bible Society. A mission was founded in Cape Province in his memory, and it is from this that the town of Butterworth, the oldest settlement in the Transkei, takes its name. He was a Member of Parliament – first for Coventry (1812–18), and then for Dover (1820–6) – in which capacity he is described in Cobbett's *Rural Rides*.

The business at No. 43 continued under Joseph Butterworth until his death in 1826, and thereafter under his son, Joseph Henry. His son died two years later and the business was sold.

But in 1801 Joseph Butterworth had taken in his fifteen-year-old nephew as an apprentice. Seventeen years later, back at No. 7 and the Sign of the Hand and Star, this nephew, Henry Butterworth, founded his own business – the one which this history describes.

---

* The names are listed as a peg for further research: 1629–69, Richard Meighen, followed by Gabriell Bedell in partnership with Mercy Meighen; 1669–90, Thomas Collins, Gabriel Collins; 1691–1723, Thomas Bever; 1723–65, Joel Stephens; 1765–73, Hugh Edmonds; 1773–9, Norton.

Chapter 2

The Butterworths
and the Bonds

Henry Butterworth, the founder of the firm, was born on 28th February 1786 in Coventry. His father, also Henry, was a wealthy timber merchant in the town; his grandfather, the Rev. John Butterworth, was a Baptist minister who had been appointed pastor of Cow Lane Chapel, Coventry, in 1753 and remained there till his death in 1803. He was the author of *A New Concordance and Dictionary to the Holy Scriptures* (1767).

Burke's Landed Gentry (1939 edn.), supported by pedigrees held by a descendant of the Rev. John Butterworth and by a descendant of his brother James, describes Henry Butterworth's great-grandfather as Randal Butterworth of Butterworth Hall, Rochdale, Lancashire, with an ancestry going back to Reginald de Boterworth, who lived there from 1135 to 1154. *The Dictionary of National Biography* gives him a more modest descent, saying that the Rev. John Butterworth's father, also called John, was a blacksmith in Rossendale (i.e. in the Forest of Rossendale area, north of Rochdale).

The Rev. John Butterworth had three other sons, of whom the youngest, Joseph, was the one who went to London in 1790 at the age of twenty, joined up with Whieldon, and became a law bookseller and publisher.

Young Henry was educated at the Grammar School at Coventry founded by John Hales (later called King Henry VIII School).* At the age of fourteen he decided that school had nothing more to offer him, and proposed to seek his fortune. His Uncle Joseph, called in to help with the family problem, arranged for Henry to live in Bristol with his friends, Mr. and Mrs. Stock, whose daughter Marianne (or Mary Anne, the spelling varies) subsequently married Joseph's son, Joseph Henry. A picture of the Bristol household and of the friendship between Thomas Stock and Joseph Butterworth is given in Marianne Butterworth's *Portraiture of a Father* (1859). This

---

* A portrait of John Hales, by Holbein, was bequeathed by Henry Butterworth to the school on his death in 1860. It was destroyed by bombing in 1941.

Henry Butterworth from
a photograph in the
Butterworth Board
room

includes family letters, but does not mention Henry's sojourn
in Bristol.

There young Henry attended the school of a Dr. Johnson, but
after a short while Mr. Stock took him into the counting house
of his sugar refinery. This, too, bored Henry. Once more Uncle
Joseph came to the rescue, and took him into his law publishing
business, when the boy was fifteen; Henry arrived in London
on 5th December 1801.

Henry was a very active apprentice and employee. He
worked and hoped for a partnership, so it is not surprising that,
at the age of thirty-two, married and a father, he preferred to
set up on his own, rather than play second-fiddle to his younger
cousin (born in 1792). After his cousin's death in 1828 he wrote
to a potential customer:

'By the death of my Uncle and lately of my Cousin the business carried on by them at No. 43 Fleet Street towards the success of which I contributed near seventeen years the best portion of my active life & for which I was actually promised a share of their business, has actually been disposed of to Strangers at a price which I considered far beyond its actual value.'

(It may well be that the executors were willing to sell to Henry, but were obliged to take the highest bid.)

On 25th February 1818, Henry opened a bank account for his new business at Hoare's Bank (an account operated by the company for 160 years). He acquired a lease of the historic premises at No. 7 Fleet Street, formerly The Hand and Star, and so associated himself with a tradition dating from at least Edward VI's reign.

During the early months he was building up his stock and by May he was ready to issue a prospectus to customers. A letter book (1823–53); a bundle of incoming letters (mostly 1818–20); a binder's account book (1818–21); a stock book (1818–35); a messenger's book (1818–26); and catalogues dating back to 1820, are still extant. There is a long gap in the archives after these early documents. The letter book starts again in 1884. The Publishing Ledger is continuous from 1st July 1828.* There also exists an invaluable 'Price Book', started in 1861, and kept up to date thereafter, recording the publisher and the price of all legal books currently in print.

Henry not only sold his own publications, but also built up a stock of books and reports from other houses. When he was asked for a book not in stock he 'borrowed' or bought at a discount from other booksellers, especially during his first ten years from Joseph Butterworth. From time to time there was friction over payments to Uncle Joseph. After his uncle's death in 1826, followed quickly by that of his cousin Joseph Henry in 1828, the premises at 43 Fleet Street, and probably the goodwill, were sold to Messrs. Saunders and Benning (described

---

* The first entry, in respect of *Archbold's Forms*, reads 'To balance bro. from blue ledger page 7...£21.4.–'. This debit balance was turned into a credit by the end of the year by the sale of 173 copies for £111.0.2. The first Publishing Ledger contains three books which were still in print after World War II: *May's Parliamentary Practice*, *Oke's Formulist* and *Stephen's Commentaries*. The second Ledger contains *Coote's Probate Court Practice* (1858 – the forerunner of *Tristam and Coote's Probate Practice*), *Kelly's Draftsman* (1873), *Mozley and Whiteley's Concise Law Dictionary* (1876), *Powell on Evidence* (1865), *Seaborne's Vendors and Purchasers* (1872), *Underhill on Torts* (1874) and *Underhill on Trusts* (1878).

7, FLEET-STREET, LONDON,
May   1818.

HENRY BUTTERWORTH respectfully announces to his Friends and the Public in general, that he has just commenced Business on his own account as a LAW BOOKSELLER, at No. 7, FLEET-STREET, between the TEMPLE GATES, and being determined to deal on moderate and liberal Terms, he hopes to merit their support; and they may rely on his utmost diligence in executing their Orders with punctuality and dispatch. In addition to an extensive Collection of the best Legal Publications new and second hand, he intends to keep an Assortment of the most approved Works of Miscellaneous Literature, in various appropriate bindings.

Periodical Works will be regularly served.

Libraries or smaller collections of Law Books purchased, valued, and arranged.

A general Catalogue of recent Law Publications is now in the Press, and may shortly be had, as above, gratis.

by Henry as 'Strangers'). The following year he sold at auction
'the law library at Chancery Lane', as noted in his stock book.
The family tradition is that this was Joseph Henry's stock.
Possibly Saunders and Benning did not want it, or Joseph
Henry's widow thought this would be more profitable. The
public sale on 27th May 1829, fetched £1,623 19s. At this Henry
Butterworth purchased books amounting to £163, having
already retained books worth £118 18s. before the sale.

Surviving letters indicate that some of today's problems
existed when the firm was founded. Objections to assumed
'standing orders' (or was it even 'unsolicited goods'?) appear
early. Charles Waller writes on 30th October 1819:

> 'You will much oblige me by not sending any more Reports
> until you have further orders from me & shall expect an
> account of what is owing you by Tuesday's or (the furthest)
> Wednesday's post.'

Delayed deliveries produced this letter dated 10th April 1820:

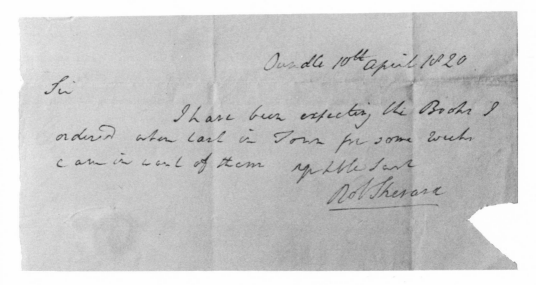

Reminders of overdue accounts were courteously phrased.
This one is dated 11th March 1824:

> 'We have supplied a considerable quantity of Law Books to
> your partner Mr. C. Ward Gravesend, and for the use of the
> firm. I request therefore to be informed, if it is convenient to
> you now to pay the account delivered to Mr. Ward up to
> Christmas amounting to the sum of £235. The favour of an
> immediate remittance will much oblige Sir Your obdient
> servt   H. Butterworth.'

In 1826 Henry was having copyright troubles. A letter is copied into the book, dated 14th September 1826, but is endorsed 'not sent'. The abandoned letter starts:

'I see by the Mornings paper that the Chancellor has granted an injunction against your Publication of which I am the unfortunate Publisher...'

and refers to a discussion. The author seems to have anticipated the abandoned letter, for the next day Henry Butterworth writes:

'I have just received your consolitary [*sic*] letter, but I feel more than I am able to express the disappointment and vexation of seeing my name held up to the world as the medium of publishing a piratical work to the alleged injury of the other Party. You surely ought to have made some defence. Have you seen Mr. Gunnell & made arrangements with him for the printing your Book & what steps do you mean to take to pay me? What you intend doing should be done quickly to relieve my anxiety on the subject. Waiting your answer, I am Sir Yours obedty   Henry Butterworth.'

On 14th September 1831 Henry Butterworth wrote to the representative of one of his authors, Mr. Chitty, regarding his liability as a warehouseman with respect to stock stolen from his warehouse. He refers Mr. Chitty to his own book on Commercial Law, Vol. 3, page 68. The theft of sheet stock had been a considerable one – *John Bull* for 18th July 1831 gives the value as £4,000. The thieves had hired a cart from a Mr. Jupp who was told to report in Carey Street; he was then asked to back down Bell Yard, where 7 cwt were loaded. The shafts then broke and the paper was transferred to another cart. Eventually 2 tons of paper were removed from the Butterworth store in Apollo Court. The greater part was recovered from a number of traders, including a tripe seller and a snuff manufacturer; the thief evidently knew what he was about. Henry wrote to Mr. Chitty's representative:

'I regret on my own account that so much quire property has been stolen out of my warehouse, & I equally regret it in regard to Mr. Chitty's respective works entrusted to my care & to which he or his assignees will become liable of such books as have not been or cannot be recovered from the Receivers.'

The earliest Butterworth catalogue to survive was 'A Catalogue of Law Books in general use of the Best Editions; intended as a Guide to Purchasers of Legal Works'. This was the second edition, 'corrected and enlarged', and appeared in 1820. This catalogue, like the whole series up to 1850 and later, is not confined to books published by Henry Butterworth. It bears on the back cover a list of nine books which 'shortly will be published, printed for H. Butterworth'. Four of these had not appeared three years later: 'the remaining volumes' of *Chitty's Commercial Law* were also outstanding. The third edition, 'corrected and much enlarged', appeared in 1823; it had

A
GENERAL CATALOGUE.
OF
Law Books,

INCLUDING ALL THE REPORTS.

LONDON.
HENRY BUTTERWORTH.
Law Bookseller & Publisher,
Nº 7. FLEET STREET,
Adjoining Middle Temple Gate.
1850.

grown from 130 pages (6½ × 4 in.) to 208 pages (7 × 4¼ in.).

The fourth edition (1826) is the first to bear an engraving on the front cover, depicting the Butterworth premises. A fifth edition appeared in 1836; the title page of this contains the motto *Per ardua Deo favente*. The picture was slightly changed before the 1843 edition, but thereafter the same plate was used, merely altering the date. The Butterworth section at the back of the 1843 edition is headed 'Henry Butterworth has recently published the following Law Books', and it contains eight pages. By 1850 there is appended a sixteen-page list of 'Law Books published by Henry Butterworth, Law Bookseller and Publisher, and Publisher to the Public Record Department'. On 23rd November 1852 Messrs. Butterworth became 'Law Booksellers and Publishers to the Queen's Most Excellent Majesty'.

The stock book does not distinguish the books published by Henry Butterworth from those which he stocked as a bookseller.

7, FLEET STREET, LONDON.
January 25th, 1848.

Sir,

Mr. OKE *having handed your name to me as a Subscriber for* one copy *of his forthcoming Work entitled* "A SYNOPSIS OF SUMMARY CONVICTIONS," *I beg, as Publisher of the same, respectfully to inform you that it will be ready for delivery on Saturday next, the 29th Instant, price 14s., neatly bound in cloth and lettered.*

Allow me to add, that the Work may be ordered through your regular Bookseller, or on receipt of a Post Office Order for the amount of such number of copies as you may require, they shall be forwarded to you, carriage free, by

Sir,

Your very obedient Servant,

HENRY BUTTERWORTH.

[*Turn over.*

George C. Oke published *A Synopsis of Summary Convictions* at his own expense, having first obtained subscriptions, as shown in this announcement

Henry used a private shorthand to value his stock. The names of the books are in long-hand, but the code concealing the amounts has not been deciphered. A variant in January 1821 and January 1822 gives the amounts in figures, in a different hand, but not the names of the books. The stock was classified according to its location: Reading Room (with a pencilled footnote: 'The 2nd Hand Books in Shop Window included in the above'); Old Law Books in Shop; Stock in back shop; Stock in Warehouse. Each location was subdivided into sizes: folio, quarto, octavo, twelvemo. Henry ran his business carefully.

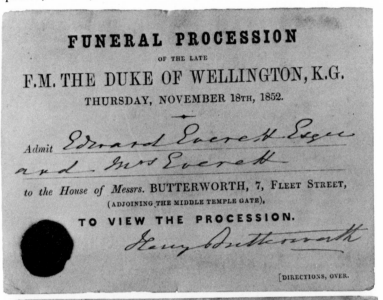

FUNERAL PROCESSION

OF THE LATE

F.M. THE DUKE OF WELLINGTON, K.G.

THURSDAY, NOVEMBER 18TH, 1852.

Admit *Edward Everett Esqre and Mrs Everett*

to the House of Messrs. BUTTERWORTH, 7, FLEET STREET,
(ADJOINING THE MIDDLE TEMPLE GATE),

TO VIEW THE PROCESSION.

Henry Butterworth

[DIRECTIONS, OVER.

DIRECTIONS.

THIS CARD OF INVITATION to 7, FLEET STREET, may be *shown* to the Police, if required, at the Barriers, but should only be *parted with* to the Servant on entering the House.

The required number of *Pass Tickets*, to enable the Visitors specified on this Card to pass the City Barriers on foot between half-past Six and Eight o'Clock in the Morning, are enclosed herewith, and must be produced to the Police at the Barriers.

Extract from the Regulations of the City Police.

"The Barriers at Southwark and Blackfriars Bridges, Temple Bar, Chancery Lane, Holborn Bars, and all other Streets running Northward from thence to Finsbury Pavement, and all Streets from the Eastward giving access to Moorgate Street, Princes Street, King William Street, and Upper Thames Street, will be closed at *half-past Six*, A.M., and no Carriages will be permitted to enter or remain in any of the Streets enclosed within the Barrier after that hour.

" Inhabitants of and *Visitors* proceeding to houses in St. Paul's Churchyard, Ludgate Street, Ludgate Hill, or Fleet Street, will be *permitted to pass the Barriers*, on foot, North and South of these Streets to the hour of 8 A.M., *upon producing a Ticket*, to be obtained by the inhabitants of those Streets.

" Holders of these tickets will be required to proceed without delay to their destination."

Henry had married in 1813 Elizabeth, daughter of Captain Henry Whitehead, of the Dragoon Guards and of Espley-in-Mitford, near Morpeth. She was evidently a woman of some attainments; a volume of her *Poems and Songs* was published by Pickering in 1848. The marriage was a very happy one. They had three sons and four daughters. The eldest daughter, Elizabeth, died at the age of sixteen; the others survived their father.

Henry Butterworth was active in the affairs of the Stationers' Company, and in the affairs of his parish church, St. Dunstan's-in-the-West. He was on the building committee for the new church of St Dunstan's, and 'earnestly supported the architect, Mr. Shaw, in introducing many novel features as to church architecture in that building'.

Soon after the death of their eldest daughter in 1836 the Butterworths moved to Upper Tooting, then a rural area six miles from the city. This led to an increase in Henry's social and public activities. In London he had been a Vestryman, a Guardian of the Poor, and a Common Councillor. Although in 1841 he declined nomination as an alderman, and resigned from the Common Council, he was made a Commissioner of Taxes for the City. He also became a Captain in the Royal London Militia, and rose to the rank of Colonel; his portrait in uniform hangs today in Butterworths' Board room. In 1849 he became a Fellow of the Society of Antiquaries. In Surrey he became a Commissioner of Roads, but declined to become a magistrate.

His church building activities continued. In 1853, as a

Henry Butterworth in the uniform of the Royal London Militia from a portrait in oils in the Butterworth Board room

churchwarden of Streatham Parish Church, he was a prime mover in the plans to build a new church at Upper Tooting. After the new edifice was consecrated on 26th June 1855 as Holy Trinity, 'the Bishop, the clergy and members of the Committee retired to the residence of Mr. Butterworth, Churchwarden, on whose invitation they there partook of an elegant collation', according to a contemporary report.

Henry Butterworth continued to visit the business in Fleet Street regularly, though not every day, until his death on 2nd November 1860. The *Gentleman's Magazine* records:

> 'Active in mind and purpose to the last, he persevered, against advice, in taking a walk of nearly two miles on the 1st of November, in company of his son, which walk produced symptoms of fatigue of unusual character, although by dinner-time he became refreshed, and dined heartily; retired to rest, and, very early in the morning of the 2nd, tranquilly and unconsciously even to his son who was with him at the time, he had entered that sleep which knows no waking.'

He was buried at Kensal Green, beside his wife, who had died in 1853, and his daughter Elizabeth.

There was a proposal for a memorial window at St. Paul's Cathedral, but instead the Cathedral accepted the gift of a silver-gilt almsdish. The stained glass window was erected in St. Dunstan's Church, with which he was associated for so long, as well as a memorial tablet to him, his wife and daughter.

* * * * *

Joshua Whitehead Butterworth, Henry's second son, became the sole proprietor of Henry Butterworth & Co. in 1860 at the age of forty-three, and remained so until his death thirty-four years later. He had been effectively running the business for some time, during his father's declining years. A letter in 1847, addressed to their prolific author, G. C. Oke, ends 'In the meantime I am for my Father Sir your very obed. Servant Joshua W. Butterworth'. Another to the same author in 1850, signed by Henry, starts 'My son has laid before me your letter...'. The last letter in this book, dated 3rd December 1853, starts 'I have mentioned to my Father your proposal...' and ends with a variant 'I am for my Father & Self...'.

Joshua made few changes in the business. The preface to the 1864 catalogue announces:

> 'In compliance with repeated applications...the compilers have issued the following GENERAL CATALOGUE OF ALL

Joshua Butterworth
from a photograph in
the Butterworth Board
room

MODERN ENGLISH LAW BOOKS now in the course of sale and not rendered entirely obsolete by changes in the law, with, in nearly every instance, their dates, prices and sizes annexed. The latest General Catalogue issued by the compilers bears the date 1850, and its greater bulk over the present production arose from the indiscriminate enumeration of all Legal Works published during the last century and even earlier, whether obsolete or even obtainable. It is hoped, however, for the reason stated, that the present Catalogue may be found suitable for its purpose, namely, as a suggestive guide to Purchasers in all branches of Legal literature.'

This was the only 'General Catalogue' issued by Joshua Butterworth. Thereafter only Butterworths' own publications were catalogued.

The 1864 Catalogue also contains the first known appearance of the Butterworth 'Hand and Star' colophon, the history of which is described in Appendix IV.

Joshua Butterworth conducted detailed investigations into the history of No. 7 Fleet Street, in company with his friend Edmund Waller. The latter was a fellow-executor of Henry Butterworth's will, and subsequently became an executor of Joshua's will. They were both active members of the Stationers' Company, and both Fellows of the Society of Antiquaries. Joshua Butterworth and his friend not only studied the leases for No. 7, going back to Henry VIII's reign, but they also explored the accumulations of years in the cellars. They claimed to have found links with Shakespeare and with Caxton, but no written account was prepared by them.

In 1872 Trübners published *Shakspere and Typography* by the eminent typographer and Caxton scholar, William Blades. This 'attempt to show Shakspere's personal connection with, and technical knowledge of, the art of printing', specifically as employed by Thomas Vautrollier between 1585 and 1589, has been described thus*:

'A *jeu d'esprit* of another kind had been published in 1872, whimsically connecting Shakespeare with the printing profession, a jest which amused [Blades] all the more that it was taken *au grand serieux* by some sober-minded correspondents.'

Whether Joshua Butterworth's researches preceded or followed the publication of Blades's book – whether or not either knew of the other's activities – Joshua Butterworth would surely have taken *Shakspere and Typography* seriously. But neither the

---

*   Talbot Baines Reed in the Memoir prefixed to Blades's *Pentateuch of Printing*, 1891, p. xvii.

Shakespeare nor the Caxton associations with 7 Fleet Street are history.

In 1888 a monument to the Butterworth/Waller enthusiasm was erected in the form of five windows in the west wall of Stationers' Hall. One of these – the Shakespeare window – was presented by Joshua Butterworth. The other four (three of them given by Edmund Waller) depict St. Cecilia, William Caxton, Archbishop Cranmer and William Tyndale.

The Caxton window in Stationers' Hall, reproduced by permission of the Worshipful Company of Stationers and Booksellers. The window depicts Caxton showing his work to Edward IV and his Queen, Elizabeth Woodville, surrounded by the devices of seven Masters of the Company and of Wynkyn de Worde.

In 1889 Joshua was nominated to the Court of the Company. He became Master in 1894, and in that year presented the great Caxton window in the north wall of Stationers' Hall.

Joshua Butterworth, like his father before him, gradually withdrew from the day-to-day management of the business. All letters in the letter book from 1884 to 1895 are signed 'per

W. O. Greenwood'. One dated 24th November 1884 suggests that the business was ripe for take-over:

> 'I saw Mr. J. W. Butterworth on Friday evening last and conveyed to him your courteous request, and I am desired by him to say, that, while reciprocating your courtesy, he most positively declines to sell.'

On 5th January 1895 Joshua Butterworth put his mark on a codicil, making his only personal bequest: 'to my manager William Orsmond Greenwood for long and faithful service to my late father and myself a legacy of £1,000 free of legacy duty'. He died of pneumonia three days later.

*   *   *   *   *

Joshua was the last surviving child of his father Henry. He appointed Edmund Waller, and a solicitor, A. E. James, as his executors, instructing them 'as soon as possible after my death to sell and dispose of' the business and the residue of the estate, and divide the proceeds among those 'who would be entitled thereto if I were to die intestate'.

On 25th June 1895 Shaw & Sons sent the following letter to the executors:

> 'We are willing to buy the business of the late Mr. Butterworth as carried on at No. 7 Fleet Street including the goodwill copyrights & stock of every description (furniture & fixtures excepted) as on the 1st July 1895 for the sum of £5500 (Five thousand five hundred pounds). A proper contract to be prepared and approved by our Solicitors.'

The executors' solicitors replied on the same day accepting the offer. The formal contract was executed on 30th July 1895 – solicitors moved quickly in those days. In it the purchasers were described in full as 'Charles Bond and Richard Shaw Bond carrying on the business of Printers and Publishers at 7, 8 and 9 Fetter Lane in the City of London under the style of Shaw & Sons'.

Shaws had been founded in 1750 by Henry Shaw, a Scotsman from Nairn who migrated to London after Culloden. The business flourished, and descended through his son and grandson to his four great-grandsons. Only one of the four had a son, and his health would not stand up to a business life. So the surviving two great-grandsons brought in as their partner Charles Bond, husband of their sister Jane, in 1852. Before 1868, when this Charles Bond died, all the Shaw brothers had died or retired, and Charles's three sons, Charles, Richard and Henry, were partners. Henry had indifferent health, so in 1895 Charles and Richard Bond, the purchasers of Butterworths, were in command.

The scope of Shaw & Sons' business was much as it is today – local government printing and stationery, and the publication of books and journals, mainly on magisterial or local government subjects.

Shaws had made light work of placing a value on Butterworth & Co. In June 1895 Charles Bond made an 'Estimated valuation of Law Books' on a single sheet of foolscap. (See reduced reproduction overleaf.) This started as a list of twenty-one books, each separately valued and totalling £2497. To this was added £100 for 'waste'. Subsequently nine books had their value increased by a total of £1395 and finally £1000 was added for goodwill, making a total of £4992.

Most of the document is written in red ink by a single hand; some black ink corrections are possibly in another hand. There are also some red ink rough workings, and two figures, £300 and £1000, in blue pencil at the side. Charles Bond wrote at the bottom: 'say £5000'. The settlement statement says 'To stock and Copyrights as at 30th June 1895 sold to you for £5,300'.

The statement for July 1895 includes 'Managers Salary 1 month to 1st August £54'. The words 'portion of' are added in pencil and the figure is altered to £40. W. O. Greenwood continued to sign all letters up to the end of July, and there is one letter signed by him on 6th August 1895. Thereafter he was presumably pensioned off. The accounts for the six months to 31st December 1895 show 'Mr. Greenwood £176 16s.'.

The assignment of 30th July 1895 did not deal with the premises at 7 Fleet Street, though it imposed two conditions on any sale of the lease by the vendors to another party: (1) that the premises would not be used in the book trade before 29th September 1900; (2) that a notice might be affixed to the premises 'or to the site thereof in the event of the present buildings being pulled down' announcing the transfer of the business.

Butterworths remained at 7 Fleet Street for another four years. George Doe, one of Joshua Butterworth's staff who stayed on, recalled afterwards that he tried to persuade Charles Bond to buy No. 7 Fleet Street, but he thought it 'too big'. It was George Doe who eventually found the smaller premises at 12 Bell Yard to which the firm moved in 1899. No. 7 was shortly afterwards occupied by the law publishing business of William Clowes & Son, until the building was demolished in 1907.

The year 1895 might have seemed, to the contemporary

		£			1800	440
					720	180
Bainbridge		21			2520	
Brown Copyhold		140 + 70	100	500		
Coote		100 + 100				
Fisher		30				
		20				
Grant		12				
Hunt						
Kelly		5				
Okes Sam		7				
Okes formula		180 + 250				
Synopsis		200 + 300				
Okes Fishing		5				
Powell		70 + 100		£1000		
Steam Carl		1760 + 250				
Stevens Nat L		40 + 25				
Serven		10				
Underhill Nat		175 + 150				
" John		175 + 150				
De Colyar		10		1395		
Daly		5				
Judson		20				
Whitelaw		12				

West Say	2487
	100
	2597
	1395
	3992
Goodwin	1000
	4992

Say 5000 £

June 1875

observer, the low point of Butterworths. Joshua Butterworth had died a lonely death, with no one to succeed him. But in fact it was the beginning of a new upsurge.

Shaws brought in their own staff to run Butterworths, including Charles Bond's young son, Stanley Shaw Bond, whose eighteenth birthday was on 8th July 1895. Stanley's initials first appear in the letter book on 27th August of that year, when he wrote to Hobbs, Hart & Co.:

'We expected the Safes on order, long before this, and are disappointed that we have been kept waiting so long. The bar for the padlock on the street door has not yet arrived...'

Stanley was impatient. He was also a sickly youth. In 1928 he said: '...my father put me into Butterworths, as, owing to illness, the idea was that I should have a quiet and easy life. But things happened otherwise.' He was called by his family, at one period, 'Paddle your own canoe Stanley'. He was anxious to get on.

Stanley Bond had been working on the journal *The Justice of the Peace* at Shaw & Sons before the acquisition of Butterworths. Later the *J.P.* became his personal property. To the day of his death he liked to open *J.P.* mail himself: he said that it was 'Butterworths in miniature'.

There were others who came from Shaws to No. 7 (which Stanley Bond described as 'sleepy, dark and dreary'). A. W. Temple was brought in as Manager in place of Mr. Greenwood. His name appears on a letter dated 14th August 1895. He was Showroom Manager at the time of his retirement early in 1939; he returned to 'help out' during World War II. He was born in 1867, and was still alive in 1961. A photograph dated 1957 shows him standing in front of the Temple Bar in Theobald's Park, Hertfordshire; he had seen it being pulled down in Fleet Street in 1877. Some senior employees today still remember his pointed white beard and sharp temper. Temple was a Plymouth Brother, and set very high standards of behaviour. One typist whose initials were D.A.M.M. was instructed to abbreviate them on letters to D.M., as some people might construe the initials as a wicked word.

Another transfer from Shaws, book-keeper W. G. Whelham, became Counting House Manager. He too retired in 1939 but helped out during the war.

One new-fangled device was immediately introduced by Butterworths' new proprietors. From 1st August 1895 letters began to be *typewritten*. Carbon copies came much later – the typed letters, like the hand-written ones, were transferred onto the damp tissue of the letter book by means of a hand press. The first letter of 1st August, addressed to his Honour Judge Emden, whose letter of March had gone unanswered, contains this revealing statement of policy:

'We dislike as a rule the system of royalties and have rarely found it to work satisfactorily, very often a royalty on a book hinders its success, whilst it is liable to be a fruitful source of

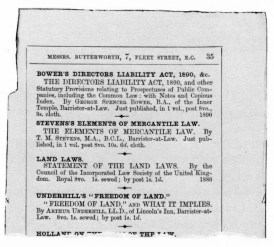

Extracts from Butterworth catalogues of 1894, 1895 and 1907 (the latter with a telegraphic code, both for ordering and for legal business)

irritation both to the Editor and Publisher.

We prefer either bringing out a Book at an Editor's own risk and expense, he taking the profits, if any; or at our own risk and expense, paying the Editor a fee for his work either on publication or after a certain number of copies are sold.'

Other changes calculated to rejuvenate the old firm and establish the new proprietors included a complete re-styling of the catalogue.* The Royal Warrant was re-issued to the new

.....emy 8vo. 1894. Pi..... .....ell, with order, post free,
18s. 6d.

Stephen's (Sir James) Digest of the Law of Evidence.
SIXTH EDITION. By Sir J. F. STEPHEN, Bart., formerly Judge of High Court of Justice. Crown 8vo. 1893. Price 6s. ; for Cash, with order, post free, 5s. 5d.

Stevens' Elements of Mercantile Law.
The Elements of Mercantile Law. By T. M. STEVENS, Esq., M.A., B.C.L., Barrister-at-Law. 1890. Post 8vo. Price 10s. 6d.; for Cash, with order, post free, 9s.

Stone's Justices' Manual.
Justices' Manual, or Guide to the Ordinary Duties of a Justice of the Peace, with Table of Cases, Appendix of Forms, and Table of Punishments. By the late SAMUEL STONE, Esq. TWENTY-SIXTH EDITION. By GEORGE B. KENNETT, Esq., Town Clerk, late Clerk to the Justices of Norwich. 1895. Post 8vo. Price 25s. ; for Cash, with order, post free, 20s. 8d.
   "We say without hesitation that every reliance can be placed on it. Always welcome to the profession. It has superseded all other books on Magisterial Law, and it is now by far the most comprehensive of the treatises on the subject."—*Justice of the Peace.*
   "In all the instances in which we have checked the notes of recent decisions we have found the effect of the cases accurately and tersely treated. We think the present a well-preserved edition of a standard work."—*Solicitors' Journal.*
   "Will retain its high position in the estimation of the profession. Its reputation is necessarily well established. Complete to date. Found to satisfy all the requirements of the practitioner."—*The Law Times.*

Law Libraries and Reports Purchased.

1895

BUTTERWORTH & Co., 11 & 12, Bell Yard, W.C.   33

yle and Davies' Principles of Rating.   DEPREHENDO
Second Edition. By E. BOYLE, K.C., and G. HUMPHREY-DAVIES, F.S.I.   1895
Price £1 5s. ; for Cash, post free, 20s. 9d.   (*Third Edition in preparation.*)

yle (E.) and Waghorn's (Thos.) Railway   DEPRIMUNT
and Canal Traffic.
Three vols.   1901.   Price £2 10s. ; for Cash, post free, 40s. 10d.

yle (E.) and Waghorn (Thos.) on Compen-   DEPUDESCO
sation.
1903.   Price £1 17s. 6d. ; for Cash, post free, 30s. 9d.

acton's Note Book.   DEPURGATUM
A Collection of Cases decided in the King's Bench during the reign of Henry III. By F. W. MAITLAND, LL.B., Barrister-at-Law, etc.   3 vols.   1888.   Price £3 3s. net ; postage extra.

amley on Death Duties.   DERCEARUM
1904.   Price 3s. 6d. net ; postage 3d. extra.

....'. ....

* In a temporary return to an earlier practice, the catalogues of 1895 and 1907, and a later one of 1924, included books not published by Butterworths.

proprietors on 15th February 1896.* The Hand and Star device
was registered as a trade mark in 1898.

Some old brooms were kept on. George Doe wrote to Stanley
Bond's widow in 1943:

> 'The old firm was just an ordinary one employing four
> people. Mr. Greenwood, Manager, Mr. Barnes, Salesman,
> Mr. Burtt, warehouseman, and myself. I do not remember
> anything unusual occurring while I was there, each day was
> the same as the one before very quiet.'

W. G. Burtt, the warehouseman, who was born in 1847 and
joined Henry Butterworth & Co in 1870 (one account says
1860), was still employed by Butterworths up to his death in
1929 at the age of eighty-one. By this time he had become an
embarrassment, but successfully rejected inducements to retire.
An obituary in the March 1929 issue of the *Butterworth Magazine*
relates that on his eightieth birthday he was given a clock by
the firm, and at the presentation recalled that from 1885 to 1894
he had lived on the premises. He attributed his late marriage
to the fact that he was required to do this. Stanley Bond told
his cousin, Morton Bond, that Burtt was a rough diamond who
would have made an excellent manager if he had possessed more
education and polish, for he had 'the brain and knowledge' to
be a publisher.

One important newcomer to Butterworths in the early Bond
years was George Charles Bellew. His application for a post at
Butterworths, dated 22nd February 1906, stated:

> 'In response to your advertisement in today's *Daily Telegraph*,
> I beg to offer my services, and ask for the favour of an
> interview.
>
> I am 19 years of age, and for the past 18 months have been
> engaged at Sir Isaac Pitman & Sons Ltd. (Incorporating
> Isbister & Co.) of 1 Amen Corner, E.C., where I think I have
> gained the experience required to fill adequately the position
> you advertise. I have the knowledge which will enable me to
> manage the production of a book from the commencement
> of the printing until it is quite ready for publication. The
> whole time I have been at Sir Isaac Pitman & Sons, Ltd. I
> have worked in the department where this part of the work

---

* This warrant was endorsed in 1901 for use by reference to 'the late
Queen Victoria' (as shown in the reduced reproduction opposite). A
new grant for appointment to King Edward was refused on the grounds
that it was only available to those supplying goods and services for the
personal use of the monarch, and this was repeated in the 1950s when a
fresh approach was made.

These are to Certify that I have Appointed

Messrs. Charles Bond & Richard Shaw Bond
trading as Messrs. Butterworth & Company.

into the Place and Quality of
Law Publishers to Her Majesty —

To hold the said Place so long
as shall seem fit to The Lord Chamberlain
for the time being. This Warrant is strictly
personal and will become void on the Death,
Retirement, or Bankruptcy of the persons
named therein.

Given under my Hand this
Fifteenth day of February 1896 in the
Fiftyninth Year of Her Majesty's Reign.

Lathom

Lord Chamberlain.

has been done. I have had experience regarding printing, binding, indexing and revising books, and I also have a good knowledge of process engraving.

I may say that I am well educated, and have a good knowledge of literature; and I feel sure I could do good work for you. The salary I require is about £2 per week.

If you see your way to grant me an interview, I will bring with me a reference from my present chief, and shall be glad to supply you with any further information you may desire to have. Let me add in conclusion that I am not afraid of work.'

The letter is endorsed 'fairly good & would suit by & by no doubt'. Pitmans, who had employed Bellew for twenty months and were paying him 25s. a week, gave him a good reference, and said they were sorry to lose him. He was duly engaged.

Four years later, when Bellew was still not more than twenty-four, the following notice was issued, signed by Bond:

'Owing to the extended ramifications of the business, I have thought it desirable to appoint a General Manager of the business, and Mr. George C. Bellew holds that position as from 1st July 1910.'

Bellew used to recall with amusement that this notice was on black-edged paper. The mourning was not for him, but for King Edward VII. G.C.B. was to be around for a long time.

Between 1895 and 1908 the brothers Charles and Richard Bond divided their printing and publishing interests between their respective families, and between the two businesses they owned – Shaws and Butterworths. Richard Bond carried on the printing and law stationery business of Shaw & Sons in Fetter Lane, and left it to his four sons. The law book publishing activities of Shaws were transferred to Butterworths. Richard retained an interest in Butterworths until the end of 1901, when the balance on his capital account was transferred to Charles Bond. The complexity of the family arrangements was such that there exist to this day Butterworth publications with obligations to Shaws and the Bonds. *Lumley's Public Health* and *Stone's Justices' Manual* still have the name of Shaws on their title pages in addition to that of Butterworths. Charles Bond retained personal possession of some titles and bequeathed them to Stanley and others of his sons;* these are published by Butterworths on a commission basis.

* One of these other sons, Frank Bond, was the proprietor of the Abbey Press in Westminster, which had, until the late 1940s, a virtual monopoly of the printing of publicity material for Butterworths.

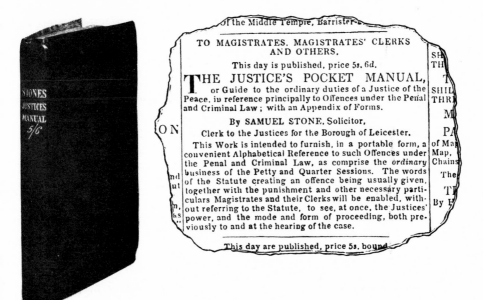

The first edition of *Stone's Justices' Manual* and the announcement in the *Justice of the Peace*

The transfer of the Shaw list to Butterworths is said in Shaws' bicentenary booklet, *A Good Name Endureth (1750–1950)*, to have been finalised in 1905 'when Charles Bond retired'. It would seem, however, that Charles Bond's retirement was a very gradual process. He retained an equity in the business until 1st January 1908. As at that date his capital in the books of the business was £17,703; Stanley's capital account stood at £12,232. Most of Charles Bond's capital account was then converted into a mortgage, bearing a fixed interest. He also drew a variable profit from the few titles he retained as his personal property. The mortgage was still outstanding on his death on 18th May 1932.

This financial set-up contributed greatly to the firm's strength. Stanley Bond was for all practical purposes the sole proprietor. Competing companies such as Sweet & Maxwells and Stevens & Sons had many family shareholders to whom profits were distributed on a generous scale. Stanley Bond was risking his own money.

The date of Charles Bond's retirement is not precise. In 1910, when L. H. (Gus) Calcutt, a pensioner still living seventy years later, joined Butterworths, Charles Bond still retained a room at the Bell Yard offices. He was 'Mr. Charles', and his son 'Mr. Stanley'.

A personal letter from Charles to his son dated 19th September 1912, written on a hillside at Pitlochry, said:

'Your mother was very pleased to receive your letter yesterday from Menaggio. I notice you expected to return to town this week, so I am sending this line.

Mr. Bellew saw Mr. Guthrie & doubtless has told you the result of the interview. I have written to Guthrie and await his reply. It is not of course reasonable to expect him to be bound not to write for any other paper when he is only receiving £2.0.0. per week, I think this was one of the conditions of his appointment, when I get his answer I shall see exactly where he stands at least I hope so.

<u>Will you meanwhile send me up here the original agreement with him that I may see its terms</u>, or, if you think better a copy of it, but I hardly think the document is now of sufficient value to trouble to make a copy.

I hope you will find everything in order on your return & not have a lot of arrears to pull up so as to undo somewhat the good of your rest.

Mother noted you said nothing about your eyes yesterday. I told her no news is good news. Is it so?

This is not the letter of one who had retired. The underlining in the third paragraph is in Stanley Bond's familiar thick blue pencil, and he wrote in the margin: 'Guthrie agree^t sent to Pitlochry, Sept. 21st 1912'. He used registered post.

From 1908 Charles Bond's income from the business remained constant at £750 plus the profit on the few books he retained, while Stanley Bond's increased steadily. Stanley had started with an 'allowance' of £40 a year in 1896, 1897 and 1898, to which was added in 1898 the sum of £17 12s. 6d for lunches. In 1899, being then of age, he had a salary of £120. The next year his salary had risen to £175 plus 'a share of profit', £37 10s. It was not a life of riches for the boss's son. But industry and enterprise had their reward, for by 1903 Stanley Bond's salary was £1437. He also derived in that year a profit of £1842 from one publishing project which he kept for himself. Stanley had taken over Butterworths in his own mind, long before his father let go, and was injecting into the business the seeds of its future success.

Chapter 3

Stanley Bond's 'Major Works'

Stanley Bond's unique contribution to legal literature lies in the great encyclopaedias which became, and remain today, authoritative and indispensable works of reference wherever English law is practised: the *Encyclopaedia of Forms and Precedents*, *Halsbury's Laws of England*, the *English and Empire Digest*, and *Halsbury's Statutes*.

John M. Lightwood – a Chancery barrister, who contributed to the *Encyclopaedia* and to *Halsbury's Laws*, and who became Editor-in-Chief of the third edition of the *Encyclopaedia* and Editor of the *Law Journal* – wrote to Stanley Bond's widow in 1945:

'...though he was not the founder [of Butterworths] it was by his foresight, energy and capacity that it secured a position of special prominence among law publishers...He was not in the law, but he was nearer to the heart of it than most practising lawyers. Only so could he have realised what sort of publications they really wanted. He supplied the profession with a set of Conveyancing Precedents, with a statement of the whole of the law of England, and with a digest of the cases on which that law is very largely based.

None of these publications was the first of its kind. There had long been precedents for the use of conveyancers; there had also long been digests of cases and there had been statements of the whole law which were widely used and appreciated by lawyers. But Bond had a vision of something still more complete and still more useful in each of these three classes...

I remember in particular one occasion when a question had arisen whether the new forms of conveyances under the Birkenhead Act submitted by a contributor were really drafted with a view to the simplication which was contemplated by Lord Birkenhead or too closely followed the older and more technical precedents. A large number of contributors assembled with Mr. Bond in Sir Arthur Underhill's chambers to discuss the matter and Mr. Bond showed great interest in this discussion... Mr. Bond had a way of quiet dignity and determination which showed that he expected work done for him to be efficient but his expectation was shown in such a way that no contributor ever thought of giving less than his best.'

Nearly thirty years later, Maurice Maxwell, a director and past Chairman of Sweet and Maxwell, Bond's most noted competitors, wrote:

'Stanley Shaw Bond introduced professionalism into law publishing, and it took the other law publishers nearly half a century to catch up with him in this respect.'*

Ron Watson, a later member of the Butterworth staff and himself certainly a professional, observed that Stanley Bond had no experience or training outside Butterworths. Watson never met Bond but felt able to sum up his achievements in terms less respectful but more detached than those of Bond's contemporaries:

'[Bond] had a brilliant idea; an idea perfectly suited to the needs of lawyers and perfectly in tune with his system of organisation and method. He realised that lawyers worked by precedent and books were the fundamental tools of their trade, especially books of reference and publications which would keep their law up to date. He published *Forms and Precedents* and *Halsbury*, examples of his reference books, and *All England Law Reports*, an example of "current awareness" publishing. Each of these two aspects was capable of spawning, or expanding to, an infinite number of supplements, "noters up", glossaries and so on. Then came the second brilliant idea. Each subscriber to *Halsbury* or whatever must undertake to subscribe to all supplements "as published". He receives this literature automatically, with an invoice: Butterworths' "Catch 22". It was almost the perfect publishing ploy.'

Bond realised that it was not enough to produce the right books: he had also to sell them. The counterpart of his editorial genius was to send, knocking on lawyers' doors, representatives who were respected and welcomed. They worked on commission: if they sold the goods, they reaped their reward. Aitcheson, who started life in Australia, and went to Canada in the 1930s, was reputed to be the best paid man in Butterworths – better

---

* In a contribution to *Then and Now*, p. 133, published by Sweet and Maxwell, 1974.

paid than any director (save Bond). His reputation was world-wide. Lawyers' doors were wide open to him in the West Indies and in the Far East, as well as in Australia and Canada.

Another legendary salesman was R. A. Allen, of whom Owen Elliott, the Manager of the Canadian office, wrote:

'London had sent us...a man who had made a name for himself in every part of the British Dominions, as a wizard at making sales. His name was Robyn Alan Allen. He landed in Vancouver, from Japan, and swept through Canada from coast to coast, like a whirlwind. In the year he was with us he made about 800 sales, approximately 600 *Digest* and 200 *Halsbury*.'

When Allen telephoned to make an appointment he ran his own name and that of his employer together: 'This is Mr. Allen–Butterworth'. Alan really was his Christian name; soon he had become to the outside world 'Mr. Butterworth'. He finished as London Sales Manager.

Every territory has its recollections of 'wizards at making sales' – Schneider in Southern Africa; Peter Barton in England in the 1960s. One early representative was the brother of a bishop. Their strength lay in Stanley Bond's concept of direct selling. The representatives were his personal ambassadors.

*   *   *   *   *

In 1902, seven years after S.S.B. first entered that 'dark and dreary' office in Fleet Street, the first volume of the *Encyclopaedia of Forms and Precedents* was published. Sir Arthur Underhill, the Editor-in-Chief, wrote in 1938:*

'I think that it was early in the twentieth century that Mr. Stanley Bond, then a very young man who had recently acquired the goodwill of the ancient law publishing business of Butterworth & Co., called at my chambers and expounded a project of his own which seemed to me very ambitious, viz., to publish in a set of twenty large volumes, a complete library of legal forms and precedents other than Court forms. Of this heavy work he was so good as to offer me the General Editorship. I was considerably alarmed about the project, particularly on his account; for I saw at once that the outlay would be extremely heavy, and (as I told him) I considered that the members of the Bar were wedded to the precedents

---

* *Change and Decay: the Recollections and Reflections of an Octogenarian Bencher*, p. 103, published by Butterworths.

of Key & Elphinstone (the authors of which were both Conveyancing Counsel of the Court), and that the solicitor branch of the profession were equally attached to Prideaux's precedents. He, however, said that before he embarked on the speculation, he was going to circularize every solicitor on the Roll, and that unless he got at least enough subscribers to obviate loss, he should drop the idea. On that understanding, and also on his promise that I should have a choice in the selection of authors who were to draft the precedents and notes, I agreed to be the general editor.

To my astonishment, he turned out right, and within (I think) a month, he had obtained contracts for the sale of 1,500 sets of twenty volumes each at 18s. per volume, and the sale very soon ran up to several thousands at a fifty per cent increase in the price – a wonderful triumph of commercial foresight.'

At this time Arthur Underhill was fifty years of age, and Reader in the Law of Real and Personal Property to the Council of Legal Education. He was appointed a Conveyancing Counsel of the Court in 1905, after accepting the editorship of the *Encyclopaedia*. His selection by Stanley Bond was clearly inspired. He lived to be one of the conceivers and drafters of the Birkenhead Property Legislation of 1922 and 1925 (in connection with which he received a knighthood). He also lived to edit the second edition of the *Encyclopaedia of Forms and Precedents* published twenty-three years after the first.

E.F. & P. (to use the house abbreviation) was a resounding commercial success. The net profit was transferred to Stanley Bond's personal account, the firm retaining the difference between the trade and retail price, and receiving a commission which increased from 5 % in 1902 to 10 % in 1908. Stanley Bond himself thus reaped the main financial benefit from his brainchild – £1051 in 1902 rising to £5581 in 1908. One might say that he was careful of both the law and the profits.

Although E.F. & P. was by no means confined to conveyancing or even Chancery matters, these were of paramount importance. When therefore the property legislation, associated with the name of Lord Birkenhead, was passed in 1922, due to come into force in 1926, it was clear that the *Encyclopaedia* would become virtually useless.

To appreciate the wide scope of the legislation it is only necessary to remember the names of the six general Acts (all still in force) constituting the new property code

Settled Land Act, 1925
Trustee Act, 1925

Law of Property Act, 1925
Land Registration Act, 1925
Land Charges Act, 1925
Administration of Estates Act, 1925

It was necessary to rewrite all the portions of the *Encyclopaedia* directly concerned with this legislation, bearing in mind the revolutionary nature of some of the proposals and their consequent unfamiliarity. It was also necessary to revise and bring up to date the portions of the work not directly affected. And it was necessary to complete the work after the changes were finalised, and in time for the practitioners who needed guidance.

The Acts listed above were passed on 9th April 1925, and came into force on 1st January 1926. The effect of the changes had been known since the passing of the Law of Property Act, 1922 and the Law of Property (Amendment) Act, 1924; but the final form of legislation awaited the 1925 consolidations. It is one of Stanley Bond's greatest triumphs that all the twenty volumes of the new edition of the *Encyclopaedia* were published in the course of the two calendar years 1925 and 1926.

Having launched in 1902 his first and, for the family solicitor, his most popular work, Stanley Bond turned his energies to his most ambitious project – a complete restatement of the Law of England, case law and statute law, in a single consecutive narrative. He had learned from reading its report that a government committee had found this an impossible task, which fired him to try to do it.*

The first volume was published on 14th November 1907; Stanley Bond was then thirty years old. The *Daily Chronicle* observed: 'It is the sort of project that the State might be expected to undertake. But no Government in this country has shown, or is likely to show, much zeal for such a project. Where the State hesitates private enterprise has stepped boldly in.'

Having conceived his great project Stanley Bond had four tasks: to prepare an outline scheme; to assemble an Editorial Board; to secure a worthy Editor-in-Chief; and to get the work written.

He approached Lord Halsbury, who was Lord Chancellor until 1905, with a request to become Editor-in-Chief; and T. Willes Chitty, a Master of the Supreme Court, to be Managing Editor. Chitty's contribution to *Halsbury's Laws of England* and

---

* An account of the workings of the committee is given by the Earl of Halsbury in his Introduction to the first edition of *The Laws of England*, pp. ccxii–ccxiv.

other Butterworth encyclopaedias was only equalled by that of Arthur Underhill on the Chancery side.

Simon Partridge, the present Legal Publishing Director, heard as a young man from Stanley Bond's own lips an account of the engagement of the Earl of Halsbury:

> 'I decided I must have the support of the top men if the idea was to succeed. I determined to invite the Lord Chancellor to be Editor in Chief and I obtained an interview with him. He was obviously interested but said he must have time to think it over. I waited for a while and then hearing nothing, I made enquiries to find, to my consternation, that Lord Halsbury had gone on holiday to Nice. As I needed to start as soon as possible, I took myself to Nice and finally ran Lord Halsbury to earth in an hotel.

The Earl of Halsbury

I accosted him in the foyer and in surprised tones he said, "Hello Bond, what are you doing here?" I replied, "I've come for my answer, my Lord." "But I'm on holiday," Halsbury replied. "I'm sorry, my Lord," I said, "but I must have a reply one way or the other." "Well, Bond," he said, "I admire you for your cheek...and, yes, I'll do it. Only, Bond, the labourer is worthy of his hire...eh?" "Name your fee, my Lord," I replied. He named it and it was a stiff one. I pulled out my cheque book and wrote him a cheque for the lot. "Done, my Lord," I said.'

The work took ten years to complete, and it was not an immediate success. Stanley Bond recalled that after a few volumes the work was running at a loss, and his friends and relatives implored him to stop before he was ruined. He determined to hang on a little longer. Suddenly the tide turned and orders began to flow in. Stanley Bond dramatised this by saying to Simon Partridge: 'You could say that one night I went to bed facing blue ruin and awoke the next morning to find myself a wealthy man.'

By 1910 ten volumes had been published, and no one knew how many were to come. In the 1910 order form the subscriber agrees 'to take all subsequent volumes as issued', although in 1908 letters had been sent as follows:

'We have received your letter and note with pleasure that providing the number of Volumes in the above work does not exceed 22 or 23, you will have no objection to taking the extra volumes. We are therefore accepting the order on these conditions, and are sending the volumes to you at once.'

The work in the end consisted of twenty-eight volumes of text and three volumes of Tables of Cases and Index.

Manuscript delays were a continual bugbear. In June 1912 Owen Elliott, sent to see J. M. Lightwood who was writing 'Real Property', reported:

'He states he is making good progress but that he will not be able to let us have any portion of it until the title is in an advanced stage, as he constantly has to refer to parts of the title. Mr. Lightwood was rather annoyed at our worrying him and especially resented us asking him what particular portions of the title he had completed. He states he is working as fast as possible and we shall have the MS as soon as he can part with it, but that it is impossible to give any idea whatever of the date.'

Elliott was at that time on the publishing staff of *Halsbury*. Four months later he was sent to Canada, where he was in charge until 1957. In his retirement he wrote a frank picture of the *Halsbury* set-up in 1912:

'The Halsbury Editorial group comprised nine members: Mr. P. M. Henderson, Press Editor (who was a solicitor from Berwick-on-Tweed, and nephew of Dr. Maclagan, the late Archbishop of York), myself as number two, Mr. Whitmore (a solicitor) who read proofs, Mr. Wilcox (also a solicitor) who compiled the Index; Miss Dipple, Miss Smallwood and another girl compiled the Tables of Cases and Statutes. Mr. Roberts, who had a desk in No. 9, compiled the annual cumulative Supplement. A young boy named Moore, who ran messages, completed the group. (He was killed in the first World War.)

My particular task, if it can be so designated, was to organise the contributors and editors of the First Edition of *Halsbury*, so that there was a constant and unimpeded flow of manuscript and proofs (both galley and page) from the original contributors, through editors and revising editors, and ultimately through the Press Editor to the Printers.

...Master (later Sir) T. Willes Chitty was the Managing Editor, with whom we were in direct touch daily. His office, or chambers, in the Law Courts, was just across Bell Yard and I could reach him in less than five minutes, which I did several times a day. Master Chitty was in every possible way a perfect gentleman, with emphasis on the word "gentle"; he was never cross or put out no matter how hard was the going. He worked tremendous hours, and if any one individual was outstanding as both the architect and builder of the first and basic edition of *Halsbury*, it was T. Willes Chitty....'

Of Lord Halsbury Elliott wrote:

'...he was outstanding in every way; his length of life, his reputation as a lawyer and a judge, his length of tenure of the Chancellorship, his ability to fight for what he wanted. On occasion, he would put in an appearance at Bell Yard, without warning, with a batch of page proofs in his hand, having walked from the House of Lords, or even his house at Kensington, to Bell Yard. He had "a point" and before that point was cleared up, Mr. Bond's room was full of texts and reports, with Master Chitty and two or three other interested authors or editors called in. By the time Lord Halsbury stalked out with his point won, the rest of the group were in a state of near collapse.'

The monthly reports use the expression 'Big Men', to signify the search for prestigious authors. One note lists the state of the search as follows:

Name	*Result*
Lord Justice Collins	His nephew, Mr. Darby is considering the question of approaching Collins, L.J.
Mr. Justice Hamilton	Mr. Baker Welford promised to approach him.
Lord Macnaghten	Lord Halsbury may approach
Mr. Justice Neville	Considering the matter

The overall scheme for the first edition of *Halsbury's Laws* was a printed document of seventy-six pages, with manuscript

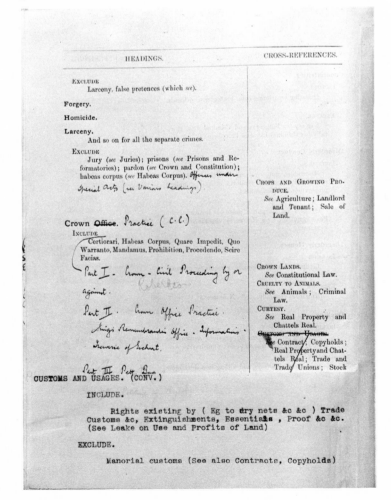

An extract from the working scheme for the first edition of *Halsbury's Laws of England* (reduced)

additions. Bellew's copy is marked as having been revised on 2nd January 1908 and 12th August 1909, but alterations were clearly being made continually. Every page of this document contains evidence of both flexibility and improvisation. The title 'Deeds and other Instruments' did not appear at all in the printed scheme. 'Colonies and Dependencies' is altered to 'Dependencies and Colonies' – reflecting the contributor's tardiness, no doubt.

The Butterworth Representatives Manual of 1910 contains sixty-three pages of advice and instruction. The first part is concerned with how to be a successful representative, and the second with the selling points for *Halsbury* and other major works, more particularly the answers to the questions and objections likely to be raised.

In 1912 it was decided to issue a 'Special "Turnover" India Paper Edition'. There was some sales resistance from those who had already bought the thick edition (or an earlier unsuccessful thin edition, of which the pages stuck together). The text volumes in the 'Turnover' edition were advertised as occupying twenty-six inches of shelf-space. Canadian publicity portrays a leather 'Travelling Case and Bookcase combined', with which a purchaser enters a railway carriage and studies his problems as he rolls across the continent.

Stanley Bond suggested to Bellew the use of anecdotes for publicity:

> 'If some Barrister can be found to write up some of those questions prepared by Henry Stephen, so that a short tale may be made of the facts, I think it may be an improvement on a mere list of questions. Attached is the story I referred to the other night. An adaptation of the story might even be used, with the query "What redress had the girl against the hotel?", or some such query. At any rate, this story might be shown as a specimen for style.'

The list of questions has survived, but not, alas, the story, so we shall never know what happened to the girl in the hotel.

Bad publicity was rare. In 1915 the *Daily Chronicle* published a paragraph headed 'Lord Haldane bans Lord Halsbury's book'. The Lord Chancellor had referred to the rule against citing a work by a living author as conclusive authority on a point of law, and stated that in that sense *Halsbury's Laws of England* was 'not to be cited here again'. The newspaper omitted the rest of Lord Haldane's remarks, namely that it was 'edited by a distinguished living author, and that several eminent legal authors had written in it, and that the admirable statements in it might be read by counsel as part of their

19. DEFERENCE TO THE VIEWS OF OTHERS.	SUCH AS RELIGION AND POLITICS.
20. THE ABILITY TO LISTEN WELL.	23. ORDER AND ORGANISATION.
21. THE POWER TO TALK WELL AND NOT TOO LONG.	24. A KNOWLEDGE OF HOW FAR TO GO WITH MEN.
22. THE POWER TO AVOID CONTROVERSIAL TOPICS	25. A READINESS TO HELP OTHERS.
	26. SELF-RESTRAINT.

I. FITTING ONESELF.

The first step in becoming a successful representative is to fit oneself for the work in every way; and in doing this the list of essentials for success given above should prove use

1. Believe in yourself.—Be thoroughly conv
others have done you can do. Be not only dete
success, but be absolutely certain that you can
you have convinced yourself that you can do
already half done it. This is one of the great

2. Believe in the house you represent.—
right to represent a house that he does not b
heart. Feel that your firm is the greatest
then determine that you will make it still
dignity of representing a business that has exi
years, and with which are associated some of
in the legal world. Feel the prestige of
great and notable publishing business.

3. Believe in the dignity of your pr
representative.—Your firm is largely est
you represent it. You can represent it
tion. Your relation to the firm is ver
Ambassador to his country. People w
judge your firm by you, and it is ess
the importance and dignity of such a
success.

4. Believe in the books you ha
believe in them yourself, you have no

---

only by doing your work thoroughly can you be successful in securing orders.

15. Use your powers of observation.—When you go into a man's office, you can, without appearing to be inquisitive, gain a great deal of knowledge about the man and his business and his methods by simply keeping your eyes open. Train yourself to see a great deal at one glance. Then, again, when you talk to a man, by watching his face you can read his mind to a large extent. Cultivate this power of observation, for there are few qualities more useful to a representative.

16. Recognise the value of time.—Do not waste your own time, and do not waste the other man's time either. Remember that time is money. Get straight to the point. Don't affect to have come on some matter that is not business. Don't spend time
        rks about the weather and kindred topics. Explain
                        to say, but do it as concisely as possible.

                    dge.—Don't neglect
                    pers. Remember
                    man who knows,
                    f the world and of
                    t a loss for a phrase
                    at fault when some
                    ness conversation.

                    aw, and lawyers.—
                    ssion, you should cer-
                    ld. It is particularly
                    s to the positions and
                    wyers, especially those
                    orks you are carrying.
                    Who's Who," and other
                    f the various technical
                    d understood, and these
                    y's "Law Dictionary."

            you are talking to.—
            ogmatic. But if he makes

BUTTERWORTHS'
REPRESENTATIVES' MANUAL

PROLUSION.

THERE is no profession or business where a man's own personality—his ability and determination and manner—count for so much in the making of success, as in that of travelling representative for a high-class publishing house. Genius and brilliancy are not the pos-sessions of all men, and fortunately they are not necessary to success; but it is essential that a man have perseverance, tact, push, principle and enthusiasm, if he is to do justice to himself and to the firm he represents. Given these qualities, all of which may be acquired by any man who is diligent and determined, and success as a travel-ling representative is assured. To go into greater detail, we might tabulate the essentials of success in this way:—

1. BELIEF IN YOURSELF.
2. BELIEF IN YOUR FIRM.
3. BELIEF IN THE DIGNITY OF YOUR PROFESSION.
4. BELIEF IN THE BOOKS YOU HAVE TO SELL.
5. A THOROUGH GRIP OF THE BOOKS YOU HAVE TO SELL.
6. PUNCTUALITY.
7. AN EVEN TEMPER.
8. DETERMINATION AND PER-SEVERANCE.
9. PATIENCE.
10. A CONVINCING MANNER.
11. ENTHUSIASM.
12. OPTIMISM.
13. ENERGY.
14. THOROUGHNESS.
15. POWERS OF OBSERVATION.
16. APPRECIATION OF THE VALUE OF TIME.
17. GENERAL UP-TO-DATE KNOWLEDGE OF THE WORLD AND LITERATURE.
18. KNOWLEDGE OF THE LAW AND LEGAL PROFESSION.

---

ends, to which you would be
might arise, and which would
on any subject for which you
your contention and at first si
the expense of purchasing thi
mentioned, but if you consid
the advantages arising from
that the extra expenditure w

"IF I SUBSCRIBE TO
MUST ALSO HAVE
SUBJECTS."

I see your point, but
say is not quite the case
branch, he will of course
to that subject; but if
quickly it will be found that a lar
suited to instantaneous reference. "The Laws
a great advantage in this respect, as it is produced in such a ma
that information with regard to any particular point can be secured
with scarcely a moment's delay. It may be necessary to buy one
or two text-books on very special subjects, but, generally speaking,
the possession of "The Laws of England" will render unnecessary
the purchasing of everyday text-books.

"I HAVE HAD A PROSPECTUS AND SEVERAL LETTERS
IN CONNECTION WITH THE MATTER, BUT I HAVE
DECIDED NOT TO SUBSCRIBE TO THE WORK."

(No reason may be given for this decision.)

This statement should be tackled along these lines:—

"I hardly like to take up more of your time after you have made
such a decisive statement, but it does occur to me that when you made
your decision with regard to the work, you might not have been
fully conversant with all the advantages that are secured by sub-
scribing to it." A sentence such as this might be used as a peg
to hang a conversation upon with regard to the whole work, and to

---

s mentioned in this Manual. A
r who makes the above objection
onsider the work favourably.

K IS A COMPLETE STATEMENT
OF ENGLAND, I SAY IT IS NOT.
WN STATEMENT YOU SAY IT IS
HAVE THE LAW REPORTS, ETC.
S COMPLETE, IT WOULD NOT BE
TO HAVE THE LAW REPORTS.

d deal with this objection along these
be under rather a misapprehension as
statement 'The Entire Law of England.'
entire Law of England' is a complete
aw of and of all the English Statutes, and
decided under them.

al with the statutes fully, and we set out
ided under them, and the principles the
we have done this, we claim to have given
you an   uld be impossible to set out in extenso, the
complete reports of all the cases cited, as the work would then run
to anything from 500 to 700 volumes, and there are some people
who suggest that the work is more than large enough now, when
it is within the humble limit of 28 volumes.

THE WORK IS AN ENCYCLOPAEDIA, AND I OBJECT TO
ENCYCLOPAEDIAS BECAUSE THE EXPENSES INVOLVED
IN PURCHASING THESE ARE CONSIDERABLE, AND
THEY DEPRECIATE IN VALUE, AS WITNESS THE
"TIMES" ENCYCLOPAEDIA BRITANNICA.

"The Laws of England" is not an encyclopaedia at all, it is
a series of 168 treatises, which treatises comprise the whole of the
law of England. It will not go out-of-date, as it will be kept

argument'. An apology was drafted, including the omitted words of praise.

The second edition of *Halsbury's Laws of England* started in 1931. Plans for the new edition had been in hand for some time, and at one stage Lord Birkenhead was expected to act as Editor-in-Chief. It is difficult to imagine so erratic a genius in that capacity. Ill-health prevented him, and he was replaced by Viscount Hailsham (father of the present Lord Hailsham of St. Marylebone), who was invited as the then Lord Chancellor.*

The second edition of *Halsbury's Laws* was similar in literary and typographical style to the first edition. The substance of the law was revised, but the smallness of the qualified internal editorial staff would amaze today's editors. At the beginning of 1938 it consisted of three barristers only.

The thin edition had a new 'leather-cloth' binding, discovered by Stanley Bond in America; unfortunately the rubber base perished in time and the spines cracked badly with use. But this again shows Bond as a bold innovator.

The third of Stanley Bond's encyclopaedias was the largest, and the least successful. The text of the *English and Empire Digest* consisted, in the end, of forty-five volumes; selling in 'about twenty-four volumes' had started in 1913, but World War I delayed preparation. The first volume was published in 1920; in the following year a memorandum sets out 'Plans settled 27th June and 7th July 1921, for reducing the length of the *English and Empire Digest*'. Publication was completed in 1930.

The plan was to set out summaries of all the case law of England and the Empire, fully classified, together with exhaustive annotations indicating the subsequent cases in which each case had been referred to and whether approved, distinguished, over-ruled, etc. This was to be done from the original sources, which involved the clerical assembly of all relevant material and its preliminary assessment by legal staff. For the first time Butterworths were involved in a publication on which the bulk of the work was done by a large internal team of qualified and clerical staff.

The raw material consisted of pasted-up or typed copies of headnotes from published reports, and the 'Great File', a card

* His tenure of office was short on this occasion (1928–9, though he held office again in 1935–8), and at the time the first volume appeared he was not Lord Chancellor. In fact it was not until Viscount Simonds in 1952 that the Editor-in-Chief was Lord Chancellor when Volume 1 appeared – a distinction he shares with Lord Hailsham of St. Marylebone.

being without his legal library pressed hardly upon the lawyer appearing in a Court at some distance from his own headquarters.

Now all this is changed. HALSBURY'S "LAWS OF ENGLAND" can now be carried in a leather case, placed in an ordinary railroad train, and taken from place to place as readily as a suit case.

The busy lawyer, travelling to the town where his presence is required, can now work up his brief in the train, confident that he has with him the most authoritative, the most complete, and the most up-to-date treatise on his subject, whatever that subject may be.

Truly "multum in parvo" might now well be rendered "the whole law in a travelling case."

Working up his Case en route.

AN INVITATION TO BELL YARD

FROM time to time, a good many Members of the Legal Profession, particularly those resident in or near London, take an opportunity of calling at our Show Room on various matters, principally to consider and examine the latest Legal Works. Particularly of recent times has this facility been very much availed of and appreciated.

As the Show Room has recently been enlarged and remodelled, it is desired that it should be taken advantage of still more extensively. Under these circumstances, we are enclosing an Invitation Card, which it is hoped will be used at an early date.

Great developments have been made in the production of legal works during the past few years, and a visit to our Show Room will demonstrate what a great help a well-equipped library can be in bringing about the smooth working of the vast number of matters that have to be dealt with in a lawyer's office.

Within the past few months the Publishers have completed one of the greatest—if not the greatest—enterprises ever undertaken by any law publisher, and have thus conferred a lasting benefit upon all members of the profession, who, until the appearance of the ENGLISH & EMPIRE DIGEST—which with its Comprehensive Index casts, as it were, light upon the dark and obscure perplexities of Case Law—were compelled to make their own researches under conditions that were almost too arduous to support.

It is particularly hoped that practitioners may find time to examine the volumes of this really remarkable work and test for themselves how easily the Index guides them to a point and, when that point is found, how clearly and completely the sum total of the experience of the Courts on a particular topic is set before them.

Another enterprise which has already earned high praise and congratulation from the legal profession in this country and the Dominions is Halsbury's Statutes of England. For a long time it had been represented to the Publishers that much valuable time would be saved if a practitioner could summon to his aid at a moment's notice the exact wording of any statute on any subject without having to search through volume after volume and then, perhaps, only to miss the all-important amendment which would have the effect of nullifying all that he had previously found.

By the publication of HALSBURY'S STATUTES OF ENGLAND it has been possible to achieve a great ideal, because henceforward it is within the power of every practitioner to be able to set his doubts at rest as to whether any particular Act or section of an Act has been revised or repealed. Every year, by the Halsbury System of Supplements the whole work is brought up-to-date, and a single reference to the original work, confirmed by a glance at the supplement, will enable the practitioner to keep himself always up-to-date on the question of Statute Law.

The Butterworth Show Room

index of all decided cases with contemporaneous references in other series of reports and annotations from later decisions. Endeavours were made to obtain permission to reproduce headnotes verbatim, but some had to be re-written for copyright reasons, or because they were unsuited to the overall style. Many cases were relevant to more than one title, and the headnotes had to be differently slanted to the purpose of each title.

Stanley Bond's attention to detail is exemplified in relation to this redrafting. He wrote on 14th September 1920:

'When a headnote has been so altered that it is desirable for a copy to be taken so that it may be clear for the Printer, it is essential that the original manuscript should be pinned to the fair copy that has been typewritten. At the same time it is essential that the original should be crossed through with a pencil so that it may be perfectly clear that the original is not for the Printer, but that the fair typewritten copy has been prepared for that purpose.

Please regard this direction as most important, and that it is imperative that it should be carried out without fail.'

This is Memo No. 1 in a new series, and ends with the words: 'I am taking over the Administration of the DIGEST myself as from the present time.'

The *English and Empire Digest* included, as its name indicates, cases from Scotland, Ireland and the Dominions. An impressive list of consulting editors throughout the Empire appears in the volumes, and it seems from a letter from the Australian Manager, Herbert Page, that sheets were sent out to the Dominions for revision by local editors. The *Digest* did not attempt to include all overseas cases, but gave precedence to those which were parallel to English decisions. Exceptionally full treatment was given to Canadian cases, and Owen Elliott spent eight weeks scouring the provinces for all available series, and contacting copyright owners.

By the outbreak of World War I work on 'labelling' or 'placing', and on the typing of cases, had made good progress, and some re-writing of headnotes had been done. 'Placing' could be done piecework by editorial staff in their spare time. One editor who commuted from Bournemouth is said to have earned more in the train 'placing' than he did for his work during office hours. Another, who took work home, laid sheets on the floor and at the end of one evening found that his cocker spaniel had eaten them.

Instructions issued during 1923 and 1924 show an elaborate hierarchy of editors, sub-editors, and 'polishers'. One of But-

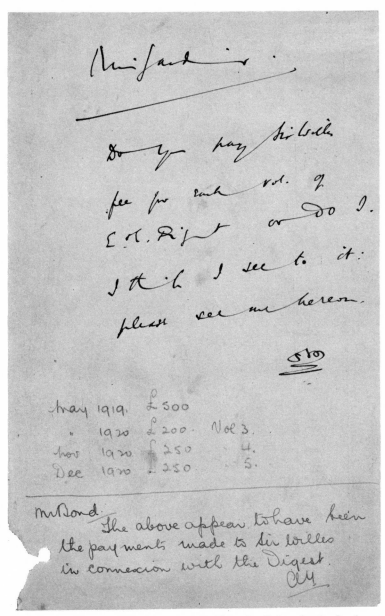

This memo (written on the back of a discarded letter-head) from Stanley Bond to Bellew's secretary (A.G.) apparently resulted in a request for figures. Sir T. Willes Chitty was an Editor of *Halsbury's Laws* and of the *English and Empire Digest*

terworths' most valued editors, W. J. Williams, who died in harness at the age of eighty in 1968, retained till the day of his death the name 'Polisher Williams' acquired to distinguish him from another Williams. (Bellew complained that the *Digest* was staffed by 'bloody Welshmen'.)

The careful back-up procedures to ensure the highest standards are evident throughout the documents; e.g.

'Dicta added by a Polisher must be left in. If a dictum seems too long or not strictly necessary the editor must consult the Polisher concerned.'

Three people assisted in the preparation of the Introduction in Volume I of the *Digest* – Harold G. Meyer (then in charge of the internal editors), his assistant, Arthur Pritchard, and Sir Willes Chitty. They all produced drafts, which were read aloud in conference to Mr. Bond 'who presided like a university tutor listening to the feeble efforts of his undergraduate pupils'. In the end the Publishers' Announcement on p. xix of the original Volume i was based on Chitty's work, and the Introduction on p. lxxxvii was based on the other two drafts.

The *Digest* editorial staff in the early days worked behind locked doors, and were called 'Jurisprudence'. They formed a separate community, with their own legends. 'Do you remember old – – – – – ?', Polisher Williams once asked the author. 'He was the last of the "two hat men". When he went out for his morning coffee, he wore one hat, and left the other on the peg. When Bellew rang up, he was told: "He's not in his room, but he must be somewhere about the building – his hat's here".'

Top management (i.e. Bond and Bellew) kept a close watch on time-keeping. A social historian would have a happy time with the daily reports sent to the Chairman's secretary during 1928 and 1929. The briefest excuse for lateness reads 'Gas and plumbers'. An editor 'telephoned to say that an explosion had taken place in his house completely wrecking the bath-room and breaking through six-inch walls. He did not know what time he would be able to get here'. Two went to the Boat Race on Saturday 31st March 1928. One of them 'Will be here soon. Will make up time after hours'. The other had already arrived by 11 a.m. Illness varies from '. . .is very queer and is in bed' to '. . .had a running cold and was sneezing constantly'.

In one respect the *Digest* staff made regrettable history; because of the large numbers involved, there were more dismissals on the completion of the work than on any similar occasion in the company's existence.

The *Digest* did not have the same appeal to the profession as its predecessors. Many lawyers, if they wanted fuller details than *Laws* could give, preferred to go the full Reports. Hard selling pushed the number of subscribers up to an acceptable figure. Sales in India helped, but led to considerable bad debts. The sales force contained some rogues as well as some sterling workers. At one stage rumours of serious errors led to a brave challenge from Butterworths, offering to pay for every error pointed out; was it a coincidence that the same error came repeatedly from one representative's area?

Publicity exhibits the florid style of the period. An explanatory announcement starts:

> 'The Publishers of the ENGLISH AND EMPIRE DIGEST request all their subscribers to give their earnest attention to this announcement, which explains the full significance of the two accompanying volumes.'

The two volumes were entitled the 'Instantaneous Desk Index' and the 'Combination Supplement'. Both were fully described in the announcement, but neither the words 'instantaneous' nor 'combination' were used except in the titles; one can deduce that a good index will produce instantaneous results, but it is only a guess that a 'Combination Supplement' is used *with* the main work.

Rhetoric reached a peak in 1924:

> 'But it is still well-nigh impossible for an individual, even though he may be conscious of the brains, energy, and organisation that are being devoted without stint to the compilation of the great DIGEST, to realise its value to the full. Just as a spectator who gazes at some vast edifice arising with stately majesty is conscious of its beauty and grandeur but can only faintly surmise its ultimate glory, so today the full magnificence of the ENGLISH & EMPIRE DIGEST can only be imperfectly comprehended.'

The full title of the fourth major work was 'The Complete Statutes of England Classified and Annotated in Continuation of *Halsbury's Laws of England* and for ready reference entitled *Halsbury's Statutes of England*'. Here Stanley Bond's determination to build up a complete and coherent system of legal research is for the first time fully revealed. The new work is to be used with *Halsbury's Laws*, and therefore bears the name of Halsbury.

Its preparation, like that of the *English and Empire Digest*, depended largely on internal staff. The design was based on the earlier *Butterworths' Twentieth Century Statutes (Annotated)*, a work in five volumes covering the Acts of 1900 to 1909, which had been kept up to date by annual volumes. Like the other major works it was arranged according to subject matter.

Just as with the *English and Empire Digest*, it was determined to go back to original sources. Butterworths prepared their own texts of the statutes in force, comparing them afterwards with other official and unofficial compilations. The annotations were, as they still are, adequate but not exhaustive. Special attention was paid to mechanical aids such as the authority for amendment, cross-references, definitions, etc., rather than to matters of interpretation.

This work, like the second edition of the *Encyclopaedia*, was produced with commendable speed. All twenty volumes appeared during the calendar years 1929 to 1931. The second edition, in twenty-eight volumes, appeared between 1948 and 1951; and the third edition, in forty volumes, between 1968 and 1972.

These four works are the central pillars of Stanley Bond's publishing achievement. While immersing his publishing self in these and other ventures, he was also taking steps to change Butterworths from an English house into a multi-national one.

Chapter 4

Butterworths in the Empire

Stanley Bond applied the same speed and decisiveness to his overseas marketing that he showed in his publishing. In 1907, when the first volume of *Halsbury's Laws of England* was published, a Canadian agent was appointed. By 1910 Bond had determined to open offices in India and Australia. The Canadian office was established two years later. J. J. (Jerry) Holme, who was put in charge of the correspondence with these overseas offices, maintained that the promotion of *Halsbury* and other Butterworth works in the Dominions significantly delayed the development of legal systems different from that of the mother country. Even to this day their availability makes a positive contribution to such uniformity as still exists in the common law. Holme remained in charge of the Overseas Department (often known as the Dominions Department) for twenty-five years, assisted (and in due course succeeded) by another Butterworth mainstay, Martha Clark. She joined Butterworths in 1910, and succeeded Holme as Company Secretary of the overseas companies when he joined the army in World War I. She and Holme were among the trusted few who received personal legacies from Stanley Bond.

Stanley Bond believed in control. His management style was monolithic and paternalistic. The management of the overseas offices was sent out from England. Representatives, particularly the more successful ones, were assigned to undertake tours abroad, sometimes to stimulate flagging local effort. Overseas managers were dispatched for spells at other offices, on which they were expected to report. Whether they went to teach or learn was never spelt out.

Such freedom as the overseas companies attained came slowly and painfully. Owen Elliott, manager of the Canadian office from 1912 to 1957, records:

> '...all books of original entry such as Sales Book, Cash Received, Cash Paid etc. were in duplicate, and the carbon copy of each completed sheet was sent to London each week. Carbon copies of all letters written to customers were also sent

to London, which were often commented on or criticised by the Overseas Department.'

Limited companies were incorporated *in England* to trade in each dominion. They purchased their stock at a discount from Stanley Bond, trading as Butterworth & Co. The first two companies, Butterworth & Co. (Australia) Ltd. and Butterworth & Co. (India) Ltd., both incorporated on 2nd September 1910, had initial issued capital in each case of 1000 shares of £1, of which Stanley Bond subscribed for 999, the thousandth being in the name of a solicitor. The Canadian company, incorporated on 14th November 1912, had the same initial shareholding, as did also Butterworth & Co. (Africa) Ltd. incorporated on 14th August 1934.

Australia

Stanley Bond visited Australia and New Zealand early in 1911, when he arranged for the opening of the original Sydney office, with a local man as manager, assisted by a typist, a clerk and a boy. Two years later Herbert Page was sent out from England to become Manager. He was the leader of the Australian enterprise (except for the years 1922 to 1927) until his sudden death in 1932, and was responsible for laying the foundations of the Australian business.

By the time Bill Nichols* – to retire as Resident Director in Australia and New Zealand in 1965 – joined the Sydney office in 1916, the staff had grown to nine, as well as about four travellers. (The staff turnover during World War I must have been considerable, for ten members enlisted at one time or another.)

The original dingy little shop at 76 Elizabeth Street was acquired by the University of Sydney in 1914; on its site they built the University Law School and barristers' chambers. Butterworths moved to an old colonial house at 180 Phillip Street, on the site of which now stands the present Wentworth Court, home of the Sydney bar. The next move was in 1920, to 170 King Street, which was renamed Halsbury House. This building in its turn had to be vacated in 1928, when offices were found at 8 O'Connell Street; there Butterworths stayed for over thirty years. The new Australian High Court and New South Wales Supreme Court Building, opened in 1977, includes the

---

* Nichols died on 18th June 1978. Much of the early material about Australia and New Zealand is derived from correspondence with him extending up to the onset of his final, eight-week illness.

site of Halsbury House. Butterworths moved from building to building, but always in those early days in the legal quarter.

Although the marketing of London books was the object of the Sydney office, and remained so at least until 1927, Herbert Page was responsible for a number of early ventures into local publishing.

In 1914 he bought the *Federal Law List*, which he redesigned and issued as *The Law List of Australia and New Zealand*. This was published annually until 1975, though a corresponding medical directory only survived for two years.

For three years starting in 1917 (until the Government produced an official series) Butterworths published annual volumes of *New South Wales Statutes, Rules and Regulations*. These included chronological lists of earlier statutes, indicating amendments by new legislation. *New South Wales Statute Law Decisions, 1825–1918* followed two years later. These publications provided valuable experience for later developments in both Australia and New Zealand.

A book on the *Commonwealth Income Tax Acts* appeared in 1918, only two years after the first of those Acts was introduced. *Hammond and Davidson's Landlord and Tenant* (1919) was notable for having, in four editions, four editors who were subsequently appointed to the bench. In 1921 and later years Butterworths published a number of books written by Norman Rydge, who subsequently established *Rydge's Business Journal*; he was later a director of the Reserve Bank of Australia, and received a knighthood. In the early 1920s *Joske's Law of Marriage and Divorce* appeared; the author of this too became a Judge of the Australian Supreme Court. The text-books of the period were not numerous, but their authors were highly distinguished.

The most important development during this period was the appointment in 1918 of Butterworths as publishers of the *Victorian Law Reports* on behalf of the Council of Law Reporting. The series had started in 1875, but Butterworths were only able to purchase from the previous publishers back volumes from 1895. This laid the foundations of a close connection between Butterworths and the legal profession in Victoria, which has continued until today.

The problems of representatives in those early days were formidable. Many towns had but one lawyer and one doctor; trains went once a day or less; roads were often impassable – chains were necessary and stranded cars were rescued by farmers with horses. To help representatives make full use of their time, Stanley Bond established in 1919 the Muston Company as general exporters, whose diverse goods the representatives peddled. Bill Nichols recollects Londovus Rat

Poison, Maisie Tooth Paste, The Jiffy Ladder Platform, My Own Haircutter, and an antiseptic ointment called Iglodine. Only the last named had much success, but the agency for it was sold in 1923. The Muston Company faded out soon after, except for its letterheads, which were used for many years by Butterworth executives to obtain discounts on their personal purchases.

In 1922 Herbert Page returned to London and resigned from Butterworths. The senior sales clerk, H. H. Barton, was made Manager. He was able to increase the sales of major works, but he fell out of favour in 1924 when he advised that the Australian company relied too much on sales of London publications. George Thomas was sent from London and put over him. Thomas's term of office lasted three years, and in 1927 Herbert Page returned as Resident Manager for Australia and New Zealand; he became a director of the Australian company in January 1931. Barton was vindicated, for Herbert Page came back with specific authority to extend local publishing in both his territories. Barton continued as Manager of the Sydney office, and Bill Nichols (by then senior sales clerk in Sydney) was sent to Wellington to extend local publishing in New Zealand. Herbert Page died unexpectedly in December 1932, and Barton retired early in 1935 after a nervous breakdown. (He came back during World War II to act as stock clerk.)

Within two months of Page's death Edward Lawrence Jones* was engaged as Resident Director. He had been the Dunlop Rubber Company's manager in India. He had no experience of publishing, but his dynamic personality and his strength in negotiation compensated for this. To him must go much of the credit for the Australian publishing successes of the next few years.

In 1934 Lawrence Jones received a new lieutenant from England, Harry Henry, a chartered accountant, twenty-five years of age, who had been employed in the Accounts Department in London for about two years; he had also had a short spell in India. On Barton's retirement Henry succeeded him as manager in Sydney. He and E.L.J. made an effective team: Lawrence Jones's dynamism complemented the accountant's industry and attention to detail. Henry found working with E.L.J. exciting and rewarding, and said that he learnt more from him than from any other man.

---

* In private life he was Mr. Jones, but he was called Mr. Lawrence Jones in the office, to distinguish him from other Joneses. Similarly when the author joined the company two years later, Bond asked that he should be called Mr. Kay Jones.

Before his death Page had been in negotiation with the Governments of Queensland, Tasmania, New South Wales and South Australia for producing reprints of their respective State Statutes. Lawrence Jones brought the first two to completion, and they were published in 1935. Bill Nichols, fresh from producing the *New Zealand Statutes*, was brought back in 1934 to advise the Editors of the Tasmanian reprint. He recalled that during that visit he conceived a proposal for a series of law reports to cover the whole Commonwealth.* He put the proposal forward in due course but nothing came of it. It was not until 1973, as a consequence of discussions about the future of the *Australian Argus Law Reports*, that the *Australian Law Reports*, covering all matters in Federal jurisdiction, were started.

The contracts for the New South Wales and South Australian reprints were awarded to the Law Book Company of Australasia (a company associated with Sweet and Maxwell). A project for the Statutes of Western Australia was also discussed, but the Government of that state decided to publish for themselves.

The failure to obtain the contract in New South Wales, the state in which Butterworths had their headquarters, was particularly galling. Lawrence Jones recommended publishing a rival series, without government support; Bond accepted this advice and the first volume was produced in 1937. It was wholly loose-leaf in form – an innovation used here for the first time in the British Commonwealth. The New South Wales Government, having given the Law Book Company their contract, planned to defeat the Butterworth rival by an action for breach of copyright in the text of the statutes. They relied on the fact that there existed in New South Wales no equivalent to the Treasury Minute in the United Kingdom which authorises the reproduction of statutory material without specific permission. Butterworths lost the case; they had to withdraw Volume I and abandon the project. As a result of what can now be seen as a precipitate step by Butterworths, Australian Government printers in both the States and Commonwealth have jealously guarded their copyright, thus depriving publishers of the opportunity to produce works like *Halsbury's Statutes*.

Meanwhile the sale of English major works was stimulated by local supplements (called 'Pilots') to *Halsbury's Laws of England* (second edition) and by Australian supplementary volumes to the *Encyclopaedia of Forms*. Stanley Bond in 1941 congratulated Harry Henry on his efforts to prevent the length

---

* This was about the same time as Stanley Bond was planning the *All England Law Reports*, which started publication in 1936.

of the four volumes of *Australian Forms* from exceeding plan. He implied that it should have been planned as a five-volume work, but added to Henry: 'The responsibility is *not* on your shoulders'. The Australian volumes were not profitable but, as Henry pointed out, the profit from additional sales of the English *Encyclopaedia* could be regarded as compensation for the loss on the Australian work.

Developments in other fields during the 1930s included the *Australian Income Tax Reports* and a number of text-books, of which the most notable were *Baldwin and Gunn's Australian Income Tax Acts* and *Pilcher, Uther and Baldock's Australian Companies Acts*. Both these works succeeded in combining Commonwealth and State Law, always a difficult problem with overlapping systems. *Baldwin and Gunn* was transformed in 1943 into *Gunn's Commonwealth Income Tax Law and Practice* (the Commonwealth Government having taken over the States' powers to legislate on taxation). A single subscription covered the quarterly loose-leaf service to Gunn and the *Australian Income Tax Reports*. It is indicative of the growth of the company that *Gunn* (now called *Australian Income Tax Law and Practice*) is now a multi-volume encyclopaedia with a fortnightly updating service. It is the largest single revenue earner in the Australian company.

In 1939 Lawrence Jones was called to London to become Sales Director. Bond decided to leave Henry in charge for a trial period. Before long he had formed a high opinion of his work, and thought him the most promising of his generation. Henry returned to England in 1945 to become Sales Manager under Lawrence Jones.

By 1945 the Australian company had ceased to depend solely on the sale of English works: in that year local publications produced 47·5% of the total Australian turnover. Moreover, local publications were profitable. The gross profit from them averaged 43·6% over the period 1918 to 1945. Australia was standing on its own feet.

New Zealand

An office in Wellington was opened by Butterworths in June 1914.* It was under the control of a 'travelling manager', Alan Allen, the same whose selling prowess has been referred to in the previous chapter. The office was run by Miss Butt, who had been sent out from London, and who used the title 'office

---

* A fuller account of the development of the New Zealand office and list is to be found in the *New Zealand Law Journal*, [1962]73; [1964]241.

manager'. The operating company was 'Australia Ltd.', and from 1919, if not earlier, the Wellington office was clearly controlled through Sydney.

By 1919 Allen was in Canada, and Miss Butt had returned to London. Managers were appointed to Wellington by Sydney (subject to London's approval): George MacArthur (1919–25) and Hugh Jenkins (1925–8).

W. H. (Bill) Nichols succeeded Hugh Jenkins. He had joined the Sydney office as an office boy in 1916 and had risen, as has been noted, to become senior sales clerk. He had been involved from about 1922 in the inter-office correspondence between Sydney and Wellington, and was in sympathy with Herbert Page's brief to extend local publishing in both Australia and New Zealand. In selecting Bill Nichols to be his lieutenant as New Zealand Manager, Page both made sure that New Zealand would be a publishing base and put Nichols firmly on the management ladder, to the great benefit of Butterworths as a whole. Nichols was to stay in Wellington until 1945, and to remain responsible for New Zealand from Sydney until 1965.

Bill Nichols

Bill Nichols was a tough character and got results. This did not always endear him to his superiors. Correspondence has survived which makes it surprising that he lasted until retirement. He himself believed that it was Lawrence Jones who first dubbed him a 'rough diamond', in the hope of getting him withdrawn from Wellington, so that he could use him in Sydney. The two were never on good terms: London did not help. One episode is recalled by Nichols in these words:

'My resignation in 1936 was because E.L.J. had persuaded the Wellington accountant not to take a better position with another firm and offered him subject to London approval an increase in salary, instead of which, when in London, E.L.J. cabled me to dismiss the accountant, as a London man was coming out. I resigned as a protest, but on the advice of Charles Wheeler, the firm's Auditor and Attorney in N.Z., I withdrew my resignation. However in the meantime, Owen Elliott from Canada was sent to Wellington to investigate, but there was nothing for him to do and after a few days he went to Sydney.'

This was one of many clashes between London and Nichols. There were other threats of resignation, and talk at times in London of dismissal. Despite all this, Nichols was made Resident Director in New Zealand in January 1939. Bond told him that he hoped in due course to make him Resident Director for Australia and New Zealand, but this did not happen until after Bond's death.

Distance seldom lends enchantment to a business relationship. Remarks which are acceptable face to face can be intolerable in writing. The able and forceful rough diamond is a trial to a dictatorial home office. But the company often benefits, and New Zealand did in the case of Bill Nichols.

Local publishing, which Nichols was to intensify, had started as early as 1916 when Butterworths became the publishers of the *New Zealand Law Reports*, which were produced by the Council of Law Reporting for New Zealand. In 1932 Butterworths took over the editing and production of the Reports. In 1925 the *New Zealand Law Reports* from 1883 to 1924 were reprinted by Butterworths, much of the stock of the earlier volumes having been destroyed by fire before Butterworths' involvement. (Butterworths bought what was left, and shipped it to London, where sets were completed by reprinting.)

In the same year, 1925, *Butterworths Fortnightly Notes* started, to be renamed the *New Zealand Law Journal* three years later.

The Law Book Company of New Zealand Ltd. was acquired by Herbert Page for Butterworths in 1918. It was intended to operate this company as a separate entity. It had a number of local publications, including several by Professor Garrow, issued on commission at his expense, as well as being agents for Sweet and Maxwell books. But Sweet and Maxwell transferred their agency elsewhere; and when the manager of the Law Book Company moved to Ferguson and Osborne, Professor Garrow went with him.

In 1920 the Law Book Company was moved from Wellington to Auckland. It was quite successful in selling Butterworth books there, and continued its major annual publication, *Rules and Bye-Laws*, 1908 to 1935. This was superseded in 1936 when the Government Printer started *Statutory Regulations*.

Before this, in 1929, Butterworths had opened a branch in the Law Book Company's office in Auckland, and from then on the operations of the Law Book Company were gradually phased out – though as late as 1960 it had a turnover of £791, and a net profit of £279!

The first two text-books under the Butterworth imprint appeared in 1928, the year Bill Nichols took over. *Maunsell's Licensing Laws of New Zealand* was published at the author's expense. *Ferguson's Conveyancing Scale of Charges* was the property of Whitcombe and Tombs, the printers, to whom Butterworths had given work; Butterworths published the second edition in 1928, and purchased the copyright later.

In the same year editorial work started on *Butterworths' Annotations to the New Zealand Statutes*. Both conception and execution of this publication were the joint work of Nichols and

Herbert Page, the Resident Director for Australia and New Zealand. The two volumes were published in 1930, at the high price for those days of 10 guineas a set. A representative, Sid Cooke, was seconded from Australia, and he signed up 700 pre-publication orders, out of a market of 1040 solicitors. This work was kept up to date by annual supplements.

Meanwhile a bargain with Professor Garrow put local publishing on its feet. Bill Nichols describes how:

'During 1929, having heard that Professor Garrow had a new book in preparation, I approached him about B. & Co. publishing it and suggested terms, and later in the year, when Herbert Page visited New Zealand, he confirmed to Garrow that we would publish at our expense and pay him a royalty, and a contract was signed. Later I suggested to Page that we should buy Garrow's stock of his publications: *Real Property* (2nd Edn.), *Personal Property* (2nd Edn.), *Law of Trusts, Crimes Act* (2nd Edn.), and *Notes on Evidence*. A sum of £900 was offered to Garrow, and as he had never made money out of his books, he gladly accepted. This purchase laid the foundation of real local publishing in New Zealand, and most of Garrow's books are still current, having run to a number of editions.'

Campaigns to sell English major works led to local publications. A campaign in 1930 to sell *Halsbury's Statutes*, conducted by Roland Hill, another Australian representative, met with little success until Nichols produced tables comparing the sections of certain English and New Zealand Acts. These led, in discussion with Herbert Page and with the Chief Justice of New Zealand, to an even more ambitious proposition, to publish a complete annotated reprint of the New Zealand Statutes, 1908–31. This was published under contract with the Government, and Wellington was the first Butterworth overseas office to publish such a work. It involved close co-operation between the New Zealand Parliamentary Law Draftsmen and Butterworths in London as well as in Wellington. One of the editors of *Halsbury's Statutes*, H. A. Palmer, was sent out to New Zealand to work on the publication.

New Zealand 'Pilots' were published to adapt the second edition of *Halsbury's Laws* for New Zealand use. Two New Zealand supplementary volumes of forms related to the second edition of the *Encyclopaedia of Forms and Precedents* enabled sales of that edition to continue, at a time when the new third edition was of limited application in New Zealand.

New Zealand dominated local publishing faster and earlier than any other Butterworth company. The combination of Bill

Nichols and a 14,000-mile communication line was formidable. In 1944 Nichols was able to write to Stanley Bond's widow:

'The policy of issuing local publications has been carried on to a greater extent in New Zealand than in any of the other Dominions. Today there is a wide range of books covering nearly every possible subject a lawyer needs for his everyday requirements. Mr. Bond was a believer in giving the profession what they wanted. It was on this policy that he built Butterworths up, and today the name of Butterworth stands high in New Zealand. In New Zealand Butterworths are known to every practitioner and every legal clerk. One of the reasons is of course that we have no really active opposition, but the main reason is that we have given the profession books that they needed.'

Canada

In August 1912, on return from holiday, Owen Elliott, a twenty-six-year-old clerk who had joined Butterworths in 1910, was called to the General Manager's office and asked whether he was prepared to go abroad to an unknown destination. When he asked for how long he was told 'probably for the rest of your life'. After consulting his wife, Elliott accepted the offer. He was instructed to tell no one, not even his departmental head.

All subsequent discussions took place at Bellew's private flat at 5 South Square, Gray's Inn. Stanley Bond took no part in the discussions, but came to say goodbye when the couple left by train for Liverpool. Elliott and his wife had kitted themselves out, knowing neither what the climate nor what the living conditions would be. He had thought he might be going to China, but was assured that the inhabitants were mostly white, and that the climate was colder than England.

He was to leave on 4th October 1912. He received his tickets on 2nd October, and thus learned that his destination was Winnipeg. It is a Butterworth legend that Stanley Bond sent for a map of Canada, and stuck a pin in the middle, thus choosing Winnipeg. But Owen Elliott records that Bond, returning from Australia to London, had once stopped at Winnipeg. He found it to be a flourishing town (the third largest in Canada), and was assured by local businessmen that it was the ideal centre. Bitter experience was to prove that, while Winnipeg was the commercial centre for destinations west, it was a country town to the conservative easterners of Ontario, Quebec and the Maritime Provinces.

Elliott was told the names of three others who would follow in a few days: a secretary, a salesman (F. W. Walkerdine*) and a junior clerk (Holley). Those three also did not know their destination, nor did any of them know that the others were going. Elliott was to tell no one in Winnipeg why he was there. The Elliotts were due in Winnipeg on 13th October. Bellew said he would follow, arriving on 24th October.

On arriving at Montreal, the Elliotts found they were faced with a forty-eight-hour train journey of 1,400 miles. No sleeper had been booked; there were no berths on that or the next night.

The junior clerk sent to Canada, Holley, is standing second from the left. This group also includes L. H. Calcutt, standing on the right, and W. G. Whelham, seated centre. It was taken in 1912 on the occasion of the move to 4–6 Bell Yard.

Elliott describes their journey:†

'We were, however, fortunate enough, or thought we were fortunate, to find two young ladies who had purchased a berth each, one lower and one upper, and were prepared to sell us the upper. We grabbed at the opportunity and considered our troubles were at an end.

To those who have travelled 1,400 miles in an upper berth in a tourist car in 1912, no description will be necessary. But we were sleeping *two* grown adults in a berth built for only one person and not built on generous lines. Comfort and

* Walkerdine retired in 1959, two years after Elliott.
† *Reminiscences of a Law Book Man* (unpublished), by Owen Elliott. Other quotations of Elliott's words in this book are from the same source.

pleasure were to be entirely absent during the two nights we spent on that train. In the intervening years, I have spent dozens of nights in an upper berth (only when I had to) but I look back in horror on those first two nights when in our ignorance we endeavoured to pack two full sized persons, with their hand luggage, into one upper berth.'

Having found some sort of accommodation for himself and his wife in Winnipeg, Elliott set out to seek offices for Bellew's inspection. Winnipeg was a boom town and premises were hard to get. The night of 24th October produced a blizzard; Bellew's train was late; Elliott struggled home on foot at 3.30 a.m., leaving Bellew installed in the C.P.R. Hotel, next to the station.

Next morning they hired a sleigh, complete with driver and buffalo robes. Their exploration of the town was not without incident:

'Mr. Bellew, struggling along a wooden side-walk, stepped off and rolled on his back in a deep drift. To see the usually immaculate and debonair Mr. Bellew lying on his back half-buried in a snow drift must have brought a smile to my face, because he shouted "Don't stand there laughing you damn fool, help me out." I got him out, dusted him off, but it was quite a while before he would speak to me civilly.'

They found offices at 191 Hargrave Street, a house with a shop attached. It had a kitchen, and they were able to allocate one room to Walkerdine and the boy for sleeping accommodation. They bought some furniture, including a two-sided desk which Elliott kept to the end of his career, forty-five years later, and which Bellew christened 'The Throne'. They managed to get a sign-writer to prepare, under oath of secrecy, a sign, 8 ft × 2 ft, which was to be hung from a projecting bar when the day came.

In the three weeks that followed, covert preparations for the launching of a campaign for the new 'Turnover India Paper Edition' of *Halsbury's Laws of England* were pursued feverishly.

'London had prepared a very elaborate brochure 11″ × 9″ consisting of about 40pp which amongst other things included photographs and biographies of the distinguished top rank authors of the First Edition. However, because of the secrecy, the title page had been omitted, printed separately and sent over by express. These had to be tipped in by hand, an Order Form, announcement and an envelope included and enclosed in envelopes that had been addressed in London and shipped out by express. With only a limited number of days to deadline, number 191 Hargrave Street was a busy place, and it was not unusual for some of us to put in 48 hours at a stretch, without sleep. Mr. Bellew even recruited my wife to help and she joined the "hundred hours a week" group. There was one occasion when Walkderdine and I commenced work on Thursday morning about 9 a.m. and we did not quit until Sunday morning about 2 a.m., almost 80 hours without a real break. A day or so before he died, Mr. Bellew wrote me a final letter in which he spoke of "the Winnipeg days and nights" and he finished his letter with the words "Oh, how we toiled". [After an all night session, Bellew visited the barber and fell asleep in the chair. When he woke up he was presented with a bill for everything the barber could offer – hair-cut, shave, shampoo, face-massage.]

However, on the day fixed for the despatch of the booklets, they were all ready; they were packed on a truck (four loads) and taken to the Post Office; the die was cast. There was one for each lawyer in Canada, be he a Judge of the Supreme Court in Ottawa, or the latest graduate to the Bar, together with all the Libraries – Law, Legislative and University, from Coast to Coast. All we had now to do was to await the results of our efforts.'

Four representatives were poised to take the road the next day: Thomas Dalziel, Percy Lightfoot, and Wilford Wood from England, and one locally recruited. The launching of the campaign on the 14th November (one month after Elliott reached Winnipeg – a triumph of hard work and determination) was an immediate success. Fifty orders were recorded in five days, and the pace continued. Elliott records that one firm of five partners ordered eleven sets, one each in the office, one each at home, and one for the office library. The orders were such that there were temporary shortages of stock.

But the reason for the secrecy was also revealed. A writ arrived from the Canada Law Book Company claiming an injunction and damages for breach of contract. The plaintiffs maintained that they had an exclusive right to sell *Halsbury* in Canada. Stanley Bond maintained that their concession for *Halsbury* had been for five years beginning on 14th November 1907. Hence the launching of the campaign on 14th November 1912: hence the incorporation of Butterworth & Co. (Canada) Ltd. in London on the same day. The issue of a licence to a 'foreign company' to trade in Manitoba took a little longer; it followed on 21st January 1913. (A reduced reproduction appears overleaf.) Bond and Bellew would have made good military men.

The sales campaign did not falter in the face of the writ.

Lieutenant-Governor

Canada:
Province of Manitoba

George the Fifth, by the Grace of God, of the United Kingdom of Great Britain and Ireland, and of the British Dominions beyond the Seas, King, Defender of the Faith, Emperor of India.

To all to whom these presents shall come—GREETING:

WHEREAS it is provided by Chapter 10 of the Statutes of 1909, being "An Act respecting the Licensing of Extra-Provincial Corporations," that any Company, Institution or Corporation, duly incorporated as mentioned in said Act, upon complying with the conditions in said Act set forth, may obtain a License authorizing it to carry on its business within the Province of Manitoba:

Attorney-General

AND WHEREAS

Butterworth & Co (Canada) Limited

is a Corporation duly incorporated by _Memorandum and Articles of Association under the Companies (Consolidation) Act 1908 of Great Britain_

AND WHEREAS the said Corporation has applied for a License, under the provisions of the said Act, to carry on its business in the Province of Manitoba.

NOW KNOW YE that, by and with the advice of Our Executive Council, and under and by virtue of the provisions of the said first-mentioned Act, and of all others powers and authority in Us vested, We have granted, and hereby grant, License unto and authorize the said

Butterworth & Co (Canada) Limited

to carry on its business, as authorized under the said _Memorandum and Articles of Association except to act as Trustees_ within the Province of Manitoba, subject to the provisos, limitations and conditions in said Act, or in any other Act or Acts of the Province of Manitoba already passed or hereafter to be passed, contained;

IN TESTIMONY WHEREOF WE have caused the Great Seal of our Province of Manitoba to be hereunto affixed. Witness His Honour Douglas Colin Cameron, Esquire, Lieutenant-Governor of Our said Province of Manitoba.

AT OUR GOVERNMENT HOUSE, AT OUR CITY OF WINNIPEG, this _Twenty first_ day of _January_ in the year of Our Lord one thousand nine hundred and _thirteen_ and in the _third_ year of Our reign.

BY COMMAND.

Provincial Secretary.

Elliott recalled that the proprietor of the Canada Law Book Company was not popular, and many lawyers hoped that Butterworths would successfully resist their claim. But Butterworths took the case with the utmost seriousness. In spite of the rigours of the prairie winter Bond himself came out. On 31st December 1912 Butterworths obtained an interim injunction restraining the Canada Law Book Company from circulating comments on the case, with extracts from their Statement of Claim. The case came up for hearing at Winnipeg in February 1913. The decision, on 10th March, was against Butterworths. Selling of *Halsbury* had to cease immediately. All that was left to sell was a few text-books not taken up by the Canada Law Book Company.

Bond and Bellew returned to England, but only to re-group. An appeal was promptly lodged in the Manitoba Court of Appeal. Butterworths won this appeal on 25th April 1913. Leave was given to the plantiffs for a further appeal direct to the Privy Council. There, too, Butterworths were successful, the appeal being dismissed on 24th January 1914. It was held by the highest court that, by virtue of a letter of 14th June 1907, the Canada Law Book Company's agency expired on 14th November 1912. The Winnipeg staff celebrated with a dinner at the St. Regis Hotel, followed by a visit to the opera to see *Tales of Hoffmann*.

Stanley Bond felt secure enough to lift the embargo on sales of *Halsbury* during the autumn of 1913, at a time when he was starting to take orders for the *English and Empire Digest*, for future delivery. The team of representatives was redeployed in Canada on a temporary basis. But the momentum had been lost and was scarcely restored before the outbreak of World War I.

During the 1920s the Canadian office developed as a successful outlet for the English major works, particularly *Halsbury's Laws* and the *English and Empire Digest*. The inevitable move from Winnipeg started in 1923, when a small branch was opened in Toronto, and was completed in 1925.

But the Canadian office remained a selling outlet rather than a publisher of Canadian publications. As in Australia, articles other than law books were sold, through the operations of the Muston Company which consisted of Stanley Bond acting as a general exporter and agent. Legal expertise was irrelevant and the business obtained its wares where it could, and sold them as best it could, through Butterworth channels.

A firm which made sectional bookcases, sold by Butterworths to hold their encyclopaedias, diversified into gramophones and other furniture. The Muston Company sold these successfully, but other lines less so. Owen Elliott wrote:

'One which I remember clearly emanated from Cleveland; it was an oil can with a flexible neck that enabled one to oil in awkward places. The drawback, which we ultimately found, was that the necks leaked as much oil as they pumped through.'

Meanwhile, competing Canadian law publishers were making hay. The year of Butterworths' entry into Canada, 1912, saw the commencement of the *Dominion Law Reports* by the Canada Law Book Company, and of the *Western Weekly Reports* by Burroughs of Calgary, who had broken away from the Canada Law Book Company to set up his own business. Burroughs started a more ambitious project in 1919, namely *Canadian Encyclopaedic Digest (Western)*, but foolishly imitated *Halsbury* so closely that he was forced to rewrite and reprint the first issue when challenged on copyright. This episode did not, for some reason, energise Bond to do himself what Burroughs was attempting.

In 1921 Richard de Boo joined the staff as a representative, and proved very successful in that role. He stayed with Butterworths until 1928, when he transferred to the American Law Book Company (later to be taken over by the West Publishing Co.) and sold the *Corpus Juris Secundum* for them in Canada. Along with another successful representative of the 1920s, Harold Vetter, de Boo spear-headed direct sales of the *Complete Reprint of the Reports of the Supreme Court of Canada*, 1876–1922. This, together with a two-volume index published in 1934, was Butterworths' only Canadian venture into local publishing prior to World War II, other than the *Fortnightly Law Journal*, issued from 1930 to 1948.

It is difficult to avoid the conclusion that Bond regarded Canada as an extension of the home market. In 1930 he visited Canada to discuss the selling of the second edition of *Halsbury's Laws*. It was held by many in Canada (as well as in the U.K.) that they had been promised that the Cumulative Supplement would render a new edition permanently unnecessary. One Canadian representative, C. E. Fisher, maintained vehemently that the sale of the second edition in Canada would be a fraud on subscribers. He expected dismissal, but Bond respected an honestly held opinion. Fisher found himself able to accept the contrary judgment of his superiors, and sold the second edition in Canada until 1932, when he returned to England. The sales force needed strengthening and Owen Elliott persuaded de Boo to return to Butterworths early in 1931, and Vetter, who had disappeared from the Butterworth scene for a period, two years later.

But salesmen need product, and these men pressed for more. Stanley Bond obviously was aware of the proposals for Canadian publishing. In 1930, in the United States, he picked up ideas for the work which ultimately became *Words and Phrases*. De Boo had been working independently on a similar idea, which he offered to Butterworths when he rejoined in 1931. Bond rejected it. Two years later de Boo was called to London for briefing. He and Elliott had produced a plan for developing local publishing, and de Boo was asked by his superior to present it. The plan had a cold reception, in fact so cold that de Boo again resigned, though Elliott was permitted to re-engage him on his return to Canada.

All these plans, which Elliott continued to work upon, were for Canadian major works. In 1936 Elliott, on his mission to New Zealand, had observed Bill Nichols's achievements and the virtual monopoly there. He added, however, 'There was nothing [in New Zealand] in the way of major works, in which I was more interested'. There is no doubt that the missed opportunities of the inter-war years left Butterworths in Canada with leeway to make up. However, all the other dominions started with text-books and graduated to major works. For some reason, Elliott wanted the reverse order.

Those missed opportunities were compounded in 1940 when, on the instructions of Lawrence Jones, then London Sales Director, de Boo and Vetter were dismissed. The company de Boo then founded is today one of Canada's leading legal publishers. His first publication was the one which Stanley Bond rejected in 1931.

It may have been Elliott's preference for major works which caused Stanley Bond to reject his plans. Bond may have thought Elliott lacked the qualities of a publisher. Whatever the reason, Canada must rank as one of Stanley Bond's less visionary enterprises.

South Africa

If the failure to develop Canada showed lack of foresight, the decision to open an office in South Africa displayed a lot of courage, for the differences between the English common law and the largely Roman-Dutch system of South Africa meant that the sales of English major works, the staple income of the overseas companies, were, and would remain, small.

Butterworth & Co. (Africa) Ltd. was incorporated on the 14th August 1934. Kenneth Sheppard, a member of the accounts department, was appointed first Manager. The office

was, after much discussion, set up in Durban. Probably the
'Englishness' of Natal appealed to Bond. Like Winnipeg, it was
not an obvious choice. Unlike Winnipeg, it proved to have
advantages which enabled it to survive. As early as 1937 the
company was showing a cumulative balance of profit. Furthermore, a start had been made with local publishing, and a report
by the Publishing Director to the Board listed five books already
published. These were all written by South African authors in
English and printed in England. In addition Butterworths
published in July 1939 a prestige translation into English, by
Mr. Justice Gane, of the Roman-Dutch classic *Huber's Jurisprudence*. This was published with a financial contribution by
the judge, and a sufficiency of pre-publication orders.

Kenneth Sheppard laid the foundations, in the few years
between the South African company's formation and World
War II, from which a premier position could be, and was, built
in the post-war years.

India

Butterworth & Co. (India) Ltd. traded from 1910 to 1946, when
it was closed – a sorry end to a bold enterprise. Of the years of
expansion until 1929 little is known. The period of decline is
fully documented.

Offices were established in Calcutta (the headquarters),
Bombay and Madras. During the first ten years the company
just about broke even, although at the end of 1920 it owed over
£20,000 to London, covered by receivables. Local publishing
had made a start, and twenty-seven legal books, eighteen
medical books and seven 'general interest' books had appeared.

Between 1921 and 1928 each year showed on paper a net
profit averaging £4,365, with a peak of £13,750 in 1926. But
the indebtedness to London had also increased to £75,000; and
receivables stood at £90,000. There was no profit in cash terms.

In all the company published, during its life, seventy-three
new books and twenty-seven new editions in the legal field, and
thirty-four new books and twelve new editions in the medical
field. Legal publishing reached its peak between 1927 and 1930,
a period during which there were thirty publications. The
medical peak was earlier, nine books being published in 1920
alone.

Many of the legal works ran to several editions, and often to
several volumes. The various Codes of Indian Law led to
exhaustive annotations. In 1929 two mammoth books on the
Code of Criminal Procedure appeared (by two different authors
with the same surname).

Just after World War I Butterworth & Co. (India) Ltd. spread its wings into general publishing. *Three Temples* was published in Hindi in the Devanagari script. The most learned of the series, *Hellenism in Ancient India*, went into two editions. *Midst Himalayan Mists* was by R. J. Minney, temptingly described as 'Author of *Night Life of Calcutta*'. (At a later date he would have been described as the author of a book on Clive of India, first published in 1931.) *An Iconoclast in India* includes a graphic account of a ten-week voyage on a Japanese steamer from London to Madras in 1918. This included a stop at Cape

AN
ICONOCLAST IN INDIA

PLAIN TALES OF THE PLAINS
AND OTHER PLACES

TOLD BY
ASMODEUS JUNIOR.

The Diary of a War Voyage and a Series of
Random Articles

WRITTEN BY
G. MELLANBY GORDON

BUTTERWORTH & Co. (INDIA), LTD., 6, HASTINGS ST.

CALCUTTA :

WINNIPEG :   SYDNEY :
BUTTERWORTH & Co. (Canada), Ltd. | BUTTERWORTH & Co. (Australia), Ltd.

LONDON :
BUTTERWORTH & Co., BELL YARD, TEMPLE BAR.
Medical Publishers.

1919

Town, where the author took photographs of a young lady in the swimming dress of the day, which he entitled 'A budding Venus pausing before taking a plunge at Muizenberg'. This was as far from Butterworths' mainstream as the Canadian oil cans.

In 1929 the bubble burst. There was a net loss every year thereafter, except 1944, until the company ceased trading in 1946. F. W. Shipway, who joined the Indian office in 1920, became a director of Butterworth & Co. (India) Ltd. in 1929. The records of the discussions when Shipway was home on leave that year did not disclose the danger of bad debts. According to Bill Nichols, however, Shipway advised London about this time that further sales of major works were likely to produce bad debts, but Bellew pressed for increased sales.

In 1932 the future Accounts Director, E. C. Leader, was sent to India with Jerry Holme, the Manager of the Dominions Department. They found that the Butterworth instalment terms enabled unscrupulous representatives to pay the first instalment out of their commission, and still make something. Even when they did not resort to such devices, neither representatives nor management made sure that customers were credit-worthy. Holme tried to play down the situation, but Leader sent uncompromising and confidential reports to Stanley Bond. Shipway came home on leave, and died before he could return to India. For Bellew, the India debacle was to prove a first crack in his apparently impregnable position. Doubts arose in the minds of Bond and Leader over this episode.

Stanley Bond visited India himself in April 1934. He summed up the then Resident Director as follows: 'he knows nothing; does nothing; is nothing'. Frank Judson, who had gone to India as an assistant manager in 1933, took command in 1935. He had been Assistant Administration Officer on the *English and Empire Digest*, and, after a short spell as college representative, joined the Dominions Department. In that capacity he and Martha Clark were 'in attendance' at Board meetings of overseas companies between January 1932 and March 1933.

In his 1934 report Stanley Bond commended Judson: 'I found that since he had been in the Calcutta office he had himself arrived at many of the conclusions I had formed during my visit to India.' But otherwise Bond was horrified by what he found.

> 'India, as far as Butterworths is concerned, has been a land of lost opportunities. For the last decade the conduct and direction of the business, we will say in ignorance, has been little short of criminal.
>
> We must start now and build again from the bottom; it

can be done. In this particular class of business the time lost cannot be made up, but nevertheless, we can now proceed to build on sure foundations having regard to my survey of the situation. But the building must be done on the lines that I shall lay down in this memorandum and on no other lines.'

No commission was to be paid to the management; no low-grade books and no books at author's expense were to be published; credit control and collections were to be monitored in detail from London. The lines on which the business was to be run in the future were summarised in paragraphs A to Q, of which these are characteristic:

'N. The responsibility as to (a) the efficient collection of accounts, (b) the resolute and intelligent administration of the Suspended Accounts Department and the suitability or otherwise of the staff employed therein and of the type of correspondence they use and (c) the soundness or otherwise of the granting of credit by Calcutta and Bombay, rests with the Finance Department in London from today's date...

'NN. The Finance Department are to deal direct with Mr. Helps and he is to work under their direction, and they will supervise the letters he writes, and have weekly reports from him as to what he is doing and the results of his work. A letter with complete marching orders must await him at Bombay on his arrival on 14th May or 21st, and let him see who he is working under. Carbons of London's letters can go to Mr. Ellis, if it is desired; if Mr. Ellis does not like London's control of Mr. Helps, he can do the other thing.

'Q. No consent must be given to suggestions by the Management in Calcutta on the grounds that it is not desired to discourage them. The views set out in this memorandum only are to be followed, whether Calcutta is encouraged or otherwise.'

Mr. Helps, sent out from London to deal with credit and the Suspended Accounts Department, took his orders direct from London. The Resident Director, Mr. Ellis, was an impotent spectator for what remained of his tenure of office. Retrenchment and control were Bond's solution. Judson was named Assistant Manager. Against Resident Manager Bond wrote: 'Vacant (I hope indefinitely)'. Discussing a possible office assistant for Judson, Bond writes: 'I understand that Judson is interested in someone in England, and I propose to export her in the Autumn'. Butterworths' man in India was 'to associate with sound European people and not Anglo-Indians; he must aim at being worthy of Butterworths'.

But none of these fiats worked. In the spring of 1936 Judson was transferred to the Sydney office, where he served with distinction, retiring in 1972 after fifty-two years service. The Accountant, a Mr. Potter, became Acting Manager. Potter had given long service to the company, and was due to return to England in May 1937. Bond in his 1934 Report, and Bellew in his instructions to the new Resident Manager in 1937, spoke of him in the highest terms, notwithstanding his share in the mishandling of the previous decade. Like others before and after him he had differences with the Finance Department in London:

> 'I pointed out to him [says Bond] that it was not within his province to dispute with London on the question of policy. I had appointed a Finance Department and their rulings had to be followed. It is always open to him to express his alternative suggestions to any points of policy, but he must not take it upon himself to resist London's policy, as by doing so he only stands in his own light. Incidentally and as a matter of fact, Mr. Potter is exceedingly valuable.'

In January 1937 a new Resident Manager, Lawrence Radice, was sent out to Calcutta, and he was followed within months by a new Accountant, Mr. Sims. When Radice arrived three volumes had been published of the *Acts and Codes of India*, an encyclopaedia in twelve volumes on the lines of *Halsbury's Statutes*. (The earlier proposal to reduce local publishing had not diverted Bond from extending his major work programme to India.) *Acts and Codes* had been suggested and planned by Frank Judson, who had lined up a distinguished editorial board, with the highly respected Sir Tej Bahadur Sapru as Editor-in-Chief. By the time these three volumes had appeared the sales amounted only to 651, half the number expected by this stage. Radice was instructed:

> '...the travellers do not completely understand CODES AND STATUTES. Information has been sent to London from time to time that it has been represented as being an Indian LAWS OF ENGLAND. Upon arrival of the volumes practitioners have found that such is not the case. It would be a good plan for all the travellers to be seen on the matter and their knowledge augmented or corrected as the case may be.'

Before long Lawrence Jones was sent from Australia to help Radice with his investigations. It was too late to get any more volumes ready for publication in 1937, but on E.L.J.'s advice the Managing Editor of *Acts and Codes*, Ram Krishan Handoo, was sent from London to India to get the work going again.

Handoo was a member of the English Bar, who had been one of Butterworths' editorial staff for many years, and Managing Editor of the *Empire and English Digest*.

But even while this was taking place Bond had given up hope of making a success of this major work. A Board minute of the 16th December 1937 recorded:

'The Chairman indicated that there was not much prospect of making a large profit out of the work (it was estimated that this would probably be in the region of £4,000), but that even if this profit were not realised and it were found only possible to recoup the money already sunk in the venture [£19,000], it would, having regard to the present situation of the work, be considered not unsatisfactory to have achieved this.'

In March 1939 the then Deputy Chairman analysed the reasons for the failure:

'1. That the work was not one of which the profession really felt the need.

2. That the price of the work was such that, even had the work really been required, the number of the profession who could afford it was so limited that the capital and work involved could not show the adequate return.

3. That although the name of the Editor-in-chief and the other names on the front page of the volumes are highly respected, the actual contributors do not carry great weight in the profession.'

In 1935, 1936 and 1937 the Indian company made net losses of about 15% of turnover. Prior to those years, the making of sales at any cost (rather than collecting money) had been seen as pleasing to London, as well as advantageous to representatives and executives paid by commission. Greater attention to credit-worthiness might reduce bad debts, but it also reduced sales, and there was a failure to reduce overheads correspondingly.

Kenneth Moore, a chartered accountant who had been appointed a non-executive director of the U.K. company, wrote in 1938:

'I understand that in view of the position and prospects in India some contraction in the Company's establishment there is in contemplation. There is also to be faced at the present time the difficulty and expense of salvaging *Acts and Codes*.

Obviously no effort should be spared to arrest the present trend of results in India, as during the last six years heavy losses have been sustained and the position will soon be reached at which the whole of the accumulated profits of

earlier years (on which the business has been living) will
have been exhausted.'

Bond had been saying all this for at least four years. But he
had been unable to bring himself to be sufficiently drastic.
Memoranda from Leader and Moore led to the appointment
of a sub-committee of the parent Board and to the visit to India
by the Deputy Chairman, whose recommendation, in March
1939, was to reduce overhead by concentrating the business in
Bombay, and by replacing the Manager and the Accountant
by a single Manager-Accountant on the lines of the South
African office.

The Madras office was closed in May 1939. In August,
reduced Bombay and Calcutta staffs were housed in fresh
premises in Bombay. A small office was retained in Calcutta to
finish the editorial work on *Acts and Codes*, and this was closed
on the completion of that work in 1943. Radice had been
engaged on a three-year contract, which expired at the end of
1939 and was not renewed. Authority in the Bombay office was
not exactly clear:

> 'It was reported [said a Board minute of August 1939] that
> it had been decided for the current year that Mr. Sims and
> Mr. Yearsley would retain their present titles while working
> together in Bombay. The Secretary was instructed to write
> to Mr. Sims and inform him that his position in the office
> would be senior to that of Mr. Yearsley, although the actual
> title of Branch Manager would be retained by Mr. Yearsley
> while Mr. Sims would continue to use the title of Resident
> Accountant.'

The following year Kenneth Sheppard was sent from Durban
to India to make yet another investigation. His mammoth
report (eighty-four pages, plus appendices) was a catalogue of
deficiencies, but he still managed to conclude:

> 'While your affairs in India are still not entirely satisfactory,
> they are improving rapidly and given good fortune, exemp-
> tion from military service, and continued *good health*, the
> existing staff can manage these affairs satisfactorily for the
> duration of the war.'

His hopes were not fulfilled. The war with Japan intervened.
Indian independence was coming. By the end of 1946, when the
company ceased to trade, the cumulative loss was £41,723, and
the company owed £48,177 to the London office. The decision
was linked in the public mind with the independence of India,
but it had been inevitable for many years. In 1934 Stanley Bond

had referred to 'the appalling tragedy and mis-management of the business in India'. But he had not been able to correct it. Butterworths' Indian business had been visited too seldom before it went wrong; after it went wrong no amount of visiting could put it right.

*   *   *   *   *

The Moore–Leader report of 1938 had examined the Indian company in the context of all the overseas activities. Moore wrote on 12th July 1938:

'In this Memorandum I have endeavoured to give a broad view of the following matters:
1. The Capital at stake in the Overseas Companies.
2. The extent to which they act as outlets for the sale of London publications.
3. The financial relations between Butterworth & Co. (Publishers) Ltd. and the Overseas Companies.
4. The Trading Results and financial position of each Company, distinguishing in the case of the Australian Company between the Australian and New Zealand trading figures.
5. The more important trends apparent on a study of the various figures.

Even with my very limited knowledge of the various businesses I venture to suggest that many points emerge which merit the active attention of the Directors.

In particular the position in Australia and India seems to call for urgent consideration. Thereafter attention might usefully be given to the affairs of the Canadian Company, which seems to be in the doldrums.

Finally I think it might be useful to weigh up, in the light of the Capital and Managerial effort involved and of the sales effected from London, the whole question of policy in relation to the Overseas Companies.

This Memorandum will have served its purpose if, as I hope, it proves to be of some assistance to my colleagues in approaching these matters and their efforts to improve the efficiency, earning capacity and financial soundness of the main and Overseas Businesses.'

E. C. Leader, the executive director, reinforced Moore's views:

'It follows, from the above, that I earnestly recommend it to the Board for consideration, that the policy which should be adopted at the present juncture is one of strict contraction in the operations of the Overseas Companies. This contraction, in my view, should be applied to both their operations in connection with London-produced works, and also in connection with their local publishing operations.

It is, I submit, emphatically necessary that a halt should be called in the expansion of the activities of the Overseas Companies in order that, over the next three or four years, they may be placed in the position of reducing their book debts so that they may be able substantially to contract the amount of capital, provided by London, which they now find it necessary to employ. It has been demonstrated above that the sale by the Overseas Companies of London-produced works is not really a very profitable matter. It is my conviction that the production and sale of locally-published works is more profitable, but this calls for capital outlay, and this capital, in the final analysis, has to be found by London.

The time, I think, has come when, as a matter of policy, the scope of the overseas operations should be drastically curtailed, and some of the capital which is now spread all over the Empire recalled to London, where in point of fact, even if it were not needed for the purposes of financing London's present extensive business, it could be utilised with a prospect of securing a far greater return than it is securing while it is being utilised overseas.'

By 1938, Bond's twenty-eight years of initiative and highly personal ventures in the Dominions were plainly under fire from his own money-men. Leader, in particular, would not accept that the profits of the London company compensated for low profits or losses abroad. He maintained that the discounts given to the overseas companies deprived the London company of its legitimate profits.

In so doing, he was introducing a new concept – that the whole group must be considered as one, whether the overseas companies were owned by the proprietor of the London company (i.e. Stanley Bond) or were subsidiaries of the London company (as was the case after Bond's death).

In Leader's calculations, the capital employed in the overseas business consisted mainly of profits which could not be remitted until debts could be collected from local customers. There was also capital locked up in London in respect of stocks held on consignment overseas. Any change in the overseas trading policy would have led to the write-off of stock of existing works, and a reduction in the printing number of future publications. Both steps would increase the true unit cost of the copies sold in England. The investigations at this date did not show the result of the curtailment, but pointed out that the supposed profitability of the existing set-up was illusory.

World War II may have saved Butterworths from a retrenchment which would have been disastrous in the light of its post-war growth. On the other hand, even without the war, no major change of policy would have taken place while Stanley Bond was in charge, for the simple reason that Bond did not want a change. It was his money, and if he chose to be the head of a world-wide organisation he was free to do so.

India was the only casualty. Canada, a blind spot, caught up with its publishing, belatedly, after the retirement and death of the faithful Owen Elliott. By the 1970s all four companies were flourishing, monuments to Bond's drive and vision, and to the men and women whom he dispatched, in military fashion and with missionary fervour, to serve the cause of Butterworths in far places.

Chapter 5

Stanley Bond
and his Managers

Butterworths excelled in managerial longevity even in those distant days when long service of senior executives was normal. Of the 'principal officials' at head office in 1928 (excluding the legal staff, which had a more rapid turnover) all but two were still employed in the same positions ten years later. The majority of them had already been working at Butterworths for fifteen years or more.

Before World War I the staff was young. Bond was thirty-seven at the outbreak of war. Owen Elliott, aged twenty-four, was interviewed for employment in 1911 by George Bellew, who had been appointed General Manager the previous year, at the same age. The interview lasted three hours. 'The only thing he did not use was a strong white light to shine in my eyes', Elliott recalled. A second grilling followed, and then an interview with the proprietor. The head of the department in which Elliott was to work played no part in the hiring process.

Dora Murray (now Mrs. Harper) was engaged in 1918 by Bellew for the typing pool.

> 'My interview with G.C.B. was gruelling. A shorthand and typing test and then the ORAL. Here I was really put through the hoop, rather cruelly I think, especially when he asked me if my shorthand was authentic and orthodox – two words which involved much popping of the tongue. I didn't know what they meant, and he knew I didn't.'

Perhaps his loyalty to Pitman, his former employers, was coming out.

When he started his new job, calling on contributors to *Halsbury's Laws*, Elliott was required to wear a morning coat, striped trousers and silk hat. One Saturday morning he wore a dark blue suit and bowler hat, and as a result was summoned to the General Manager's office. Bellew looked at him disapprovingly and said, 'Are you going to a cricket match that you are so attired?'

Most of the pre-World War I stalwarts – Burtt and Doe from the old Butterworths, Temple and Whelham from Shaws, Jerry

The BUTTERWORTH ORGANIZATION
THROUGHOUT THE EMPIRE
with names of the principal Officials

ENGLAND.

BUTTERWORTH & CO. (PUBLISHERS) LTD., 4, 5 & 6, Bell Yard, Temple Bar, London, W.C.2.

Annexe : 11 & 12, Bell Yard.

Telephone : Holborn 4471-6 (6 lines and Private Exchange).

Telegraphic and Cable Address : Butterwort, Estrand, London.

Chairman - - - -	Mr. S. S. BOND.
Managing Director -	Mr. G. C. BELLEW.
Secretary - - - -	Mr. F. W. S. EMERY, A.C.A.

Overseas Manager -	Mr. J. J. HOLME, assisted by Miss M. R. CLARK.	*London Sales Manager*	Mr. R. A. ALLEN.
		Representatives -	Mr. F. C. ASKHAM.
Advertising Manager	Mr. J. H. BUTLIN, M.A.		Mr. W. CLARK.
Correspondence Manager	Mr. W. P. HILL.		Mr. T. B. DALZIEL.
Counting House Manager	Mr. W. G. WHELHAM.		Mr. P. H. LIGHTFOOT.
Production Manager -	Mr. H. J. SINFIELD.		Mr. S. A. NEWMAN.
Publishing Editor -	Mr. J. W. WHITLOCK, M.A., LL.B.		Mr. R. H. STRATHMORE.
			Mr. R. W. WOOD.
Showroom Manager -	Mr. A. W. TEMPLE.		

Private Secretary to Mr. S. S. Bond - - - - - - Miss M. E. JENNINGS.

Private Secretary to Mr. G. C. Bellew - - - - - - Miss A. E. GARDINER.

EDITORIAL DEPARTMENT.

Chief Editor - - - - - - - - - - - Mr. R. H. HANDOO,
assisted by Mr. KERR CHALMERS and Mr. MOBERLEY BELL.

Sub-Editorial Staff.—Mr. JOHN SOUTHALL, B.A., Mr. R. HARRISON, B.A., Mr. REGINALD DODD, Mr. PHILIP R. THOMASON, B.A., LL.B., Mr. L. C. BELL-COX, B.A., Mr. A. C. GRAINGER, B.A., Mr. E. M. HOY, Mr. W. J. WILLIAMS, B.A., Mr. A. CARRERAS, LL.B., Mr. H. ALLEYN PALMER, M.A., Mr. H. PARRISH, LL.B., Mr. J. R. O. JONES, B.A., Mr. R. HENDRY WHITE, Mr. G. I. A. WATSON, Mr. S. G. G. EDGAR, M.A., Mr. W. H. FLAHERTY, M.A., Mr. M. R. ELLINGER, Mr. F. GRAHAM GLOVER, M.A., Mr. W. A. HAMMERTON, B.A., Mr. A. P. ARNOLD, Mr. R. D. H. OSBORNE, B.A., Mr. P. F. SKOTTOWE, LL.B., Mr. E. R. E. OLSSON, LL.B., Mr. HOWELL JONES, B.A., Barristers-at-Law ; Mr. I. GWYNNE JONES, B.A., Solicitor of the Supreme Court ; and Mr. J. H. FISHER EVANS, Mr. R. H. CODE HOLLAND, B.A., Mr. E. STOPFORD HOLLAND, and Mr. R. POWELL, B.A., B.C.L.

Administration Organizer - - - - - - - - - Miss W. SMALLWOOD,
assisted by Mr. F. JUDSON, Mrs. CASSEY, Miss TREADWAY and Miss BROWN.

New Conveyancing Bureau and Digest Research Bureau - - - Mr. JOHN BURKE and Staff.

JUSTICE OF THE PEACE LTD.

Secretary and Manager - - - - - - - - Mr. F. W. S. EMERY.

Advertisement Manager - - - - - - - - - Mr. J. CAMERON GUNN.

THE COKE PRESS LTD. (" THE LAW JOURNAL ").

Secretary and Manager - - - - - - - - - Mr. A. B. COOPER.

Advertising - - - - - - - - - - - Miss N. McADAM.

Representatives - - - - - - - - - - Mr. D. FRASER ; Mr. C. E. FISHER.

Holme, Owen Elliott and Martha Clark, to name a few – were alive when Bond died in 1943. Office boys engaged before World War I and still at work in the 1950s included Gus Calcutt, who became Despatch Manager, and Henry Shaw and Stan London, who became senior representatives.

Most constant of all were the lady supervisors of clerical staff – for example, in the editorial departments, Mrs. Cassey (1913–46), Miss Treadway (1914–47), Miss Gosden (1916–51) and Miss Rich (1918–56). Dora Harper, who was in the typing pool for about six years from 1918, describes Miss Treadway as being

> 'a very earnest and diligent woman, with a plaited mane of lovely corn-coloured hair, also a dyspeptic affliction, I would say, as she always seemed to be clutching at her diaphragm – especially so when she paid frequent visits to the telephone to make private calls.'

The telephone calls were probably to a bookmaker, for Miss Treadway would always oblige her colleagues by placing bets for them; and it may have been her 'book' rather than her diaphragm which she clutched. Close to indispensable, these ladies aspired to no higher posts, except possibly Miss Winifred Smallwood who became Administration Organiser of the *English and Empire Digest*. One of the barristers who was on the staff in the 1920s describes her as 'Winifred Smallwood, whom we all wanted to take out to dinner, but were afraid to ask'. Dora Murray recalls that she was 'elegant, very blonde, floated rather than walked, and exuded the most delicious perfume as she wafted by this junior who dutifully stood back to the wall whilst she passed'. Her career was curtailed; while on sick leave in 1929 she was told not to return.

During World War I the proprietor and his manager continued to keep the business going, with an ever decreasing staff. Whether Stanley Bond was exempted from military service on the grounds of age, or health, or for business reasons, is not recorded. The story that he and Bellew tossed as to which should enlist is merely the staff's way of explaining why in the end Bellew did go – first into the Navy and then into the Pay Corps. Owen Elliott wrote about these war years:

> 'Mr. Bond was intent on keeping me out of the service as I was married, with a family; he had the same intentions for Mr. Bellew. The London office were losing staff to the Armed Forces, and as frequently as I could get permission, he brought me to London, where I acted in conjunction with

Stanley Shaw Bond
c. 1920

Miss Clark in running India, Australia and New Zealand from London. I crossed the Atlantic eight times in under two years, each crossing being more hazardous than its predecessor. Finally I ran into trouble and on my arriving in London, I was picked up by the military authorities as a deserter, my father having returned an official envelope addressed to me with the words "Gone to Canada" on it. Mr. Bellew, with the assistance of the High Commissioner in London, arranged my release on the understanding that I would go back to Canada within ninety days. By this time, Mr. Bellew's position was getting precarious; he was unable to get any further extension, and finally came the day when he must report. Like all other things at Bell Yard in those days, it was left to the last minute of the last day, and I well remember Mr. Bond and Mr. Bellew rushing off in a taxi to meet the deadline.

Mr. Bellew was first put into the Navy as an enlisted man, and he used to come to Bell Yard, from the Crystal Palace where he was stationed, on as many evenings as possible. I used to let him in after the staff had gone and he certainly looked out of place in his office chair in an A.B.'s uniform. Later he got a commission, in the Pay Corps, somewhere off Chancery Lane, so that his visits became more frequent, but I only saw him as George Charles Bellew, A.B., and I know that he had a very miserable time during his early days in the Navy. On one occasion, I was commissioned by Mr. Bond to go down to the seamen's supply shops in the dock area and try to get a seaman's overcoat that would fit Mr. Bellew, who was a big man, until such time as he could have one made for him; I delivered the overcoat to Mr. Bellew at London Bridge Station.'

Stan London, who joined as an office boy in 1915, and who retired as Senior Representative in 1962, wrote of the 1914–18 years:

'During the period we were so short of male staff that it was necessary to arrive very early, and remain most nights till 9.0 o'clock or 9.30, and the Company's office began to be known facetiously as the "Lighthouse of Bell Yard". Towards the latter end of the War, we were troubled by Zeppelin raids and I remember one night being apart from one other member the only one there with the exception of the M. Director and his secretary. We had to take refuge in the Strongroom as bombs were falling in Lincoln's Inn (slightly damaging the Old Hall) and we shared the M.D.'s cake and coffee together.'

Two men who joined soon after World War I were J. W. Whitlock and F. W. S. Emery. They were to become a duumvirate, controlling the company as Joint Managing Directors in the 1950s.

John Whitlock came to Butterworths in 1923 to work on text-books. He had been articled to a solicitor before the war. After returning from active service he went up to Cambridge to take a short course in law for ex-service men. Only Part II of the Law Tripos had to be sat; at the end of the first paper he had not written a word. His mind had gone a complete blank. He obtained a doctor's certificate and, on the strength of this and of his work during the year, was given an *aegrotat*. This was the last year in which an LL.B. as well as a B.A. was awarded to those who attained (or were treated as having attained)

Opposite (reduced) is a page from the 'forcing book'. Mr Bond, Mr Bellew and Mr Whitlock (Publishing Editor) each had a copy of this loose-leaf book, in which sales and advertising costs were recorded monthly. The advertising 'forced' the sales.

PRINTING No. 1350
Reprint (Feb 1931) 1000
QUIRE PRICE £..10%/. 44/5

Ryde on Rating

6th EDITION 19 30   PRICE 60/-

{ Further Advertising Allowance granted by Board 23.6.31

ADVERTISING ALLOWANCE £ 150

No. to be sold to cover cost (including £ 691 for advertising)

Year		Jan.	Feb.	Mar.	April	May	June	July	August	Sept.	Oct.	Nov.	Dec.	Totals
1930	Sales											875	166	1041
	Advtg. Costs									53.1.4	58.0.5 / 91.2.0	73.13.6 / 165.0.6	1041	165.0.6
1931	Sales	86	31	59	16	12	5	63	19	11	6	40	24	362
	Advtg. Costs	1127	1158	1219 / 28.0.0 / 193.0.6	1233	1245	1250	1303 / 22.8.0 / 215.8.6	1322	1333	1339	1379 / 21.12.4 / 237.0.10	1403	
1932	Sales	12	15	15	12	26	4	6	4	10	6	7	12	129
	Advtg. Costs	1415	1430	1445	1457	1483	1487	1492	1496	1506	1512	1519	1531	
1933	Sales	11	6	8	6	7	8	5	4	5	15	9	11	95
	Advtg. Costs	1542	1548	1556	1562	1569	1577	1582	1586	1591	1606	1615	1626	
1934	Sales	9	8	13	8	5	8	6	2	3	8	15	6	91
	Advtg. Costs	1635	1643	1656	1664	1669	1677	1683	1685	1688	1696	1711	1717	

honours in Part II of the Law Tripos. J.W.'s luck became proverbial. He was an expert in being at the right place at the right time, and knowing the right people.

When he was interviewed, he passed muster, but Bond was concerned that he was living in Cambridge – it was too far to commute, he said. J.W. was told to come back when he had found somewhere to live. He went straight to an estate agent, where there was a queue of applicants. J.W. got into conversation with the person next to him in the queue, and found that she had come to put her flat into the agent's hands. J.W. said 'Come outside and we can fix something.' J.W. got his flat and the agent lost his commission. He returned to Stanley Bond, within hours, and got the job.

Whitlock was a great clubman. He belonged to a dozen Masonic Lodges. He was proud to have become a member of the Athenaeum, with Lord Macmillan, the editor of *Macmillan's Local Government*, as his proposer. J.W. was also a member of the Oxford and Cambridge Club. He became a member of the Gardeners' Company, and rose to be Master. He made the maximum use of these social contacts for the benefit of Butterworths.

J.W. loved practical jokes. There was always a danger of finding a couple of teaspoons in your pocket as you left a restaurant in his company. On a visit to Exeter to see James Whiteside (the editor of *Stone's Justices' Manual*), they met back-stage at the local theatre, where Whiteside was involved in a Gilbert and Sullivan production. As Whiteside approached, J.W. seized a crucial rope and gave it a hearty pull – the alarmed Whiteside did not observe that he was not gripping the rope, but sliding his hand down it.

Subsequent generations are grateful for the excellent relations which Whitlock built with the university law teachers. Within a year of joining the company he had arranged for Butterworths to become the publishers of the *Journal of the Society of Public Teachers of the Law*. A letter from the late Professor Arthur Goodhart after J.W.'s death recalls:

> 'I first met him many years ago at Cambridge when I was a young don. I was greatly impressed then by his enthusiasm and energy which convinced me that he was certain to make a success of his life. It was a tonic to meet him because his interest made one feel that life was exciting. . . I do not think that it was generally realised whan an outstanding contribution he made to legal literature in England by the encouragement that he gave to young authors.'

The second of the pair, F. W. S. Emery, had no nickname,

and comparatively few people used his Christian name, Sea-brook. A chartered accountant, he was reserved and correct. This is not to say he was disliked, although the curtness of his memoranda could well have had that effect. The description given so often of J.W. was that he was a 'lovable rogue'; Emery was the image of convention – but hard to love.

One year, when they were Joint Managing Directors, Whit-lock's expenses amounted to £1,800 and Emery's to £18. Of course accountants don't travel and need not entertain, but there was more to it than that.

Emery was Company Secretary, and Manager of the *Justice of the Peace*. Later he also had charge of Medical Sales. In these capacities he had ample opportunity to work closely with Stanley Bond, and he became a high-grade personal assistant to Bond. When S.S.B. was called for jury service at an inconvenient time, it was Emery who 'arranged the matter'. Emery was closer to Bond than Whitlock was; and Whitlock closer to the staff than was Emery.

A third recruit in the 1920s was the Advertising Manager, J. H. Butlin. (Wags said that his second initial stood for 'Halleluia'.) He apparently gave satisfaction, but he did not go as far as Emery and Whitlock. He joined the forces in November 1939. When he was demobilised he found that the Sales Director did not want to appoint him to his old job, and that his former colleagues, now directors, were unwilling to share their power with him, just as Bond had not included him in the top team in 1937. He went elsewhere.

In 1931 E. C. Leader* was appointed Joint Secretary and Chief Accountant. Bond thought that Emery, then sole Secre-tary, was coming too much into Bellew's camp. Furthermore he wanted someone to take complete charge of the accounts, which were not part of Emery's job. Bellew was against the appointment and took advantage of his influence with Bond's secretary to suppress the applications, but the agency wrote a personal letter to Stanley Bond, and Leader was engaged. Leader's appointment was seen as a demotion for Emery. He became 'Joint' instead of sole Company Secretary; he was moved physically to a back room at 12 Bell Yard.

Leader carried out successfully the commission he received from Stanley Bond to develop Butterworths from a private concern (whose counting house produced books of original entry, from which the proprietor's personal advisers produced confidential final accounts) to a business with a responsible

---

* There was some professional jealousy because Leader was not a chartered accountant, like Emery. He belonged to one of the bodies which now form the Certified Accountants.

Finance Department. He acquired in the process a great respect
for Bond, and he wrote in 1943 to a member of his staff in the
forces: 'Would to God S.S.B. were still with us. He was a tough
'un, but he knew his business and was ethical, by and large.'

George Bellew was the key man between the wars. General
Manager in 1910, he became the first Managing Director when
Bond's U.K. business was turned into a company in 1927. There
is a tendency to belittle his contribution to the development of
the company, for the reasons that he was overshadowed by
Stanley Bond; that he was feared rather than loved; and that
he was removed from office in 1938, at the comparatively young
age of fifty-one. Yet Bond relied on Bellew as his second-
in-command for nearly thirty years. Inspiration came from
Bond; his was the creative genius. Bellew was the administrator
and the salesman. The florid and self-important tone of the
advertising between the wars was attributable to him. He
recorded on gramophone records sales talks for the *English and
Empire Digest* and for *Halsbury's Statutes*; the representatives were

George Charles Bellew

expected to coach themselves from these. The opening words, in his rather high-pitched pompous voice, call up a familiar picture: 'I am George Charles Bellew, Managing Director of Messieurs [sic] Butterworth and Company (Publishers) Ltd, and I am taking this opportunity of having a talk with you with regard to one of our very important works, namely *Halsbury's Statutes*.'

It appears that he set out to make himself feared in his daily dealings with the staff, whereas Bond from his more Olympian height was able to afford benevolence. Such kindnesses on Bellew's part as are remembered seem to have been designed to modify a decision of Bond's. Bellew tended to talk in riddles, with the result that he did not get the best out of the staff.

It is imprinted on the memories of his contemporaries (but not recorded in the archives) that Bellew found a series of mistresses from among the female staff. Most of them continued afterwards with the office careers in which Bellew had started them. But this propensity certainly complicated office politics.

Those who delighted in intrigue had ample opportunity for playing Bond and Bellew off against each other, but the excellence of the product and the hard core of conscientious workers made Butterworths proof against the effects of this. It was rumoured that Bellew kept a revolver in his desk. Certainly he had on his desk, not only a switch to light the 'engaged' sign over the door, but a switch to lock the door, which could be a very frightening ploy. Bond was liked and respected; Bellew was disliked or feared. Bond used him as a watch-dog, but the watch-dog (through his secretary) also watched his master. A member of the staff who had been seen by Bond could expect to be questioned by Bellew's secretary.

Bellew was the target of an anonymous skit – undated, but probably in the early 1930s – which is revealing of the inter-personal attitudes of the period.

'The scene opens on a tessellated hall of a great business house. The time is 10.30. The normal activity of business is obvious. Some beautiful girls are seated in little glass hutches with typewriters; one is making up her accounts and another her face. One glass hutch is screened off so that we cannot see what goes on behind there in business hours. Two others are at a table in a corner playing Beggar-my-neighbour with reference cards.

In the centre is a man at a table pensively sucking the gum off a stamp and looking at two flies on the lofty ceiling. Some small boys are grouped around him eagerly awaiting orders.

In a smaller room adjoining the hall, a large three bladed

Not to be pressed
except by Mr Bellew
instructions 23/9/13

920

ACCOUNT NO. 1

NAME

ADDRESS

SHEET NO. 1

Date							Date		£	s	d
1912 Jan	20	Brought forward		3	11	11	1912 June 30	Balance c/d	11	8	5
May	21				15	=					
June	7	Carriage				2					
	15	Set of Framed Windsor Repairs	30/7	2	8	3					
July	1	Balance	b/d	11	8	5	£	11	8	5
Aug	6			1	1	6	1913 Jan 21	Cash	7	16
	21	Base Service		15	8	6	1914 April 30	By Balance c/d	13	14	11
1914 Jan	30	To Balance		15				By Cash	15	8	5
April	30			13	4	10	June 27	do	9	2	8
Feb	1				10	6	Dec	Balance	10	—	1
June	21				10	7			£14	6	=
			£	14	6	=					
Dec	6	To Balance		10	—	1	1917 Dec 31	By Amount Taken			
1917 Mar	14			10	8						
1918 Nov	11			10	7			3/9/14			

fan can be seen suspended from the ceiling. Its function is to keep cool the giant brain of the profound thinker who sits immediately below it with the weary air of Atlas on whose shoulders the whole statistical burden of the enterprise devolves.

Seen through a doorway is a large airy room, one side of which is lined with new books. In the centre, leaning nonchalantly against a pillar with an indescribable elegance, is a tall handsome figure engaged in thinking constructive, businesslike thoughts.

In a room the door of which is marked Counting House, young men and girls are seated on high stools before massive ledgers. They are all gazing at a glass door through which can be seen one of the firm's representatives making representations on the subject of commission to a solid, prosperous looking individual who replies at rare intervals in staccato monosyllables.

The scene changes to a narrow street or lane, bounded on one side by buildings and on the other tall, spiked, iron railings. Down this lane is approaching a figure in an overcoat and bowler hat, which as the lane grows narrower, looms larger and larger until it virtually fills the lane from side to side, giving an impression of tremendous power. This character is Big Business himself.

He halts and eyes the narrow door of the business house, then with an adroit sideways turn he effects an entrance.

The whole office springs to life. Typewriters rattle like machine guns; the small boys dive below like startled rabbits: the occupant of the desk places his stamp on an envelope and gives it a business-like thump; the flies stop crawling on the ceiling and turn and stare. The three bladed fan in the adjoining room buzzes like mad. The word goes in a flash from basement to roof, "He's here!"

Without a glance to right or left, Big Business pads swiftly up the stairs to the first floor. Here one boy jumps to attention, a second flings open the door of his room, and a third with an impressive ritualistic movement raises before him the sacred slate. One lady secretary curtseys, the other stands silently with downcast eyes. The door closes and an electric sign flashes the word "Engaged".

The scene changes back to the Hall and a stranger enters. He presents his card and says he has an appointment. He is given a seat on a comfortable settee and a card is put in his hand, which reads –

"If you think you have been waiting too long you are at liberty to do the other thing."

Opposite (reduced) is a page from Butterworths' loose-leaf Sales Ledger showing Bellew's credit instructions

The scene switches back to Big Business's office. This is an imposing room with three telephones. A noticeable feature on the wall is a device in the form of a barometer. This, in fact, registers Big Business's blood-pressure and visitors find it pays to watch it. Big Business is dictating, signing letters and holding a telephone receiver to each ear.'

Many remember the three-bladed fan, and the glimpse from the Central Hall into the showroom; the leather-upholstered sofa travelled to 88 Kingsway, and remained for many years in the entrance hall there. The 'sacred slate' really existed; it recorded the names of the people to be seen.

Bellew was a person to be taken seriously. The devices he used to keep the staff in their place seem ludicrous in retrospect (as do also the relaxations). At the time, they were grimly effective.

*　　*　　*　　*　　*

Stanley Bond's concern for his staff found expression in financial support for the Butterworth Society, which was founded by W. G. Whelham, the Counting House Manager, in 1907. Whelham recorded in 1944 that the Society was first known as

The High Table at the Butterworth Society's Dinner, 1930. Left to right: Mrs Cassey, Mr Whelham, Miss Jennings (secretary to Mr Bond), Mr Bond, Mr Bellew, Miss Clark, Mr Holme, Miss Gardiner, Mr Allen. In front Mr Judson and Miss Kitchener ('Official Stenographer' to the Butterworth Society)

the Thrift Society but assumed the name The Butterworth Society as its activities extended. He wrote:

'For a good number of years the employees enjoyed the support of Mr. Bond in Annual gatherings, which took the form of a Dinner and Dance, or Dinner and Cabaret, and although those attending had to pay a small sum (quite a nominal one in the case of junior members of the staff) Mr. Bond's contribution was very substantial.

The Society finally came to an end at the end of 1938. It had therefore existed for over thirty years, and could only have been made successful by the enthusiastic support of the staff and perhaps in a smaller degree by its officers.'

Stan London also thought highly of the Society:

'It was not all work [he wrote in 1944] as during the period our "Butterworth Society" was formed...Mr. Bond thus helped the staff to save, as the foundation was our original "Thrift Society", and our Patron paid out special interest rates, to encourage us to save, and I am sure many of us owe our start in homes of our own to this source. The social side, which was excellent, enabled the staff to get to know our

Chairman better, as many successful dinners, and dances –
Fancy dress and otherwise – were arranged, in which our
Chairman could be seen – as on one occasion impersonating
David Garrick, and dancing round during the Paul Jones
hand in hand with the youngest office boys disguised as
"Bags of McDougall's Flour".'

The Society's annual dinners from 1926 to 1930 were held
in the Connaught Rooms, the New Burlington Galleries and the
Northumberland Rooms. The 1930 dinner constituted the
twenty-first birthday celebrations of the Society. There was a
special dinner-dance in 1934 to welcome 'Stanley S. Bond, Esq.'
on his return from India. The Society's last function, on 1st
February 1937, was a Fancy Dress Coronation Dinner Dance
at Grosvenor House. The entertainment was invariably lavish.
Stanley Bond was both the guest of honour and the host.

At the December 1927 function, members of the staff put on
'A Legal Revue Entitled *So this is Butterworths*'. The music was
written by W. A. Hammerton and the lyrics by John Burke,
both on the editorial staff. The opening chorus ends with the
words:

'Butterworth! Butterworth!
We be books by Butterworth!
All the law of England stated,
Every case that's been decided,
Every precedent that's needed.
Who owns us is well provided.'

It seems fair to conclude that there was more hilarity than
humour on these occasions.

Stanley Bond was an entrepreneur, who owned people rather
than employed them. He made a considerable personal fortune
out of his forty-seven years of work and enterprise, in the days
before taxation became confiscatory. Generous and paternal in
his private life, he had a hard edge to his business mind. 'Did
you know Stanley Bond?', Bernard Elliott, the son of Owen,
asked a recent visitor to Canada. 'No, I didn't', confessed the
visitor. 'He was a hard man', said Bernard.

Bond kept himself secluded from the day-to-day hurly-burly.
This enabled him to be seen as the friendly cheerful employer,
with a smile for everyone. It may have been harder to achieve
this in the early days when he kept the business in his own hands.
But even during World War II, when the staff had been
evacuated to his country home, he was able to maintain this

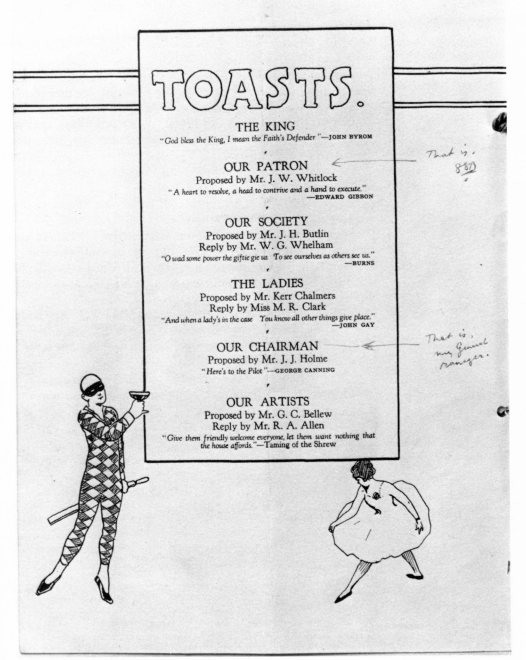

TOASTS.

THE KING
"God bless the King, I mean the Faith's Defender"—JOHN BYROM

OUR PATRON ←
Proposed by Mr. J. W. Whitlock
"A heart to resolve, a head to contrive and a hand to execute."
—EDWARD GIBBON

OUR SOCIETY
Proposed by Mr. J. H. Butlin
Reply by Mr. W. G. Whelham
"O wad some power the giftie gie us To see ourselves as others see us."
—BURNS

THE LADIES
Proposed by Mr. Kerr Chalmers
Reply by Miss M. R. Clark
"And when a lady's in the case You know all other things give place."
—JOHN GAY

OUR CHAIRMAN → ←
Proposed by Mr. J. J. Holme
"Here's to the Pilot"—GEORGE CANNING

OUR ARTISTS
Proposed by Mr. G. C. Bellew
Reply by Mr. R. A. Allen
*"Give them friendly welcome everyone, let them want nothing that
the house affords."*—Taming of the Shrew

That is.
8 8?)

That is,
my General
manager.

A page from Mr Bond's copy of the programme for the Butterworth Society's
Dinner, 1926, showing his pencil notes

separation of business and personal life, by dealing with business matters 'through proper channels'.

But when he emerged from his Olympian seclusion, he could be direct and rough. He wrote to one overseas executive:*

'Now I am writing this personal note to you couched in personal terms because I do not know you personally very well.

What is your outlook as regards your business life? Do you like a strenuous life, do you like the heat and burden of the day; are you ambitious? On the other hand, is your make-up more suitable for a good steady job? There is nothing against you if the latter is your point of view and fits more conveniently into your out-look.

Personally I revel in the heat and burden of the day, but we are not all alike...

Would you like to be considered for advancement in the organisation of my Companies?

There is nothing against you if you prefer to carry on [where you are] so do not let us have any misunderstanding.

There are a lot of people in this world who would like to have a progressive position, who would like to have as it were better positions but their make-up does not enable them to earn them; they have not the necessary ability or they have not the necessary mental drive to conquer difficulties.

Now from the view of my organisation I must have 200% men in their respective jobs.

I have tried to make things clear to you through the medium of this letter and I want you to write to me quite frankly...

It is obvious from the point of view of the organisation that there must be young managers coming along. Our particular business requires some years of experience before a Manager can really understand it.

Now take counsel with yourself and look frankly into your kind of make-up and write to me as clearly as I have written to you.'

The recipient of the following letter (written from Braemar) remained with the company till his death.

'...You have very easy work at the present time; you have

---

* The letter has all the marks of being dictated – the words pour out. 'Taking shorthand notes from S.S.B. was a traumatic experience,' writes Dora Harper; 'he mumbled (and I believe purposely) so that the initial shock of being in THE PRESENCE was exacerbated by the difficulty of catching the thread of the dictation.'

short office hours, and you have from late Friday afternoon to Monday morning off and if you cannot do office work except in the limited hours at Bell Yard your brain must have deteriorated most seriously.

From the point of view of the country and the war, keeping the business going is as important as guarding the shores. Keeping export business going is as important as making munitions. Patriotism demands that we all should work all out on whatever job we are at. If you have not sufficient patriotism to work at home then you should consider your wife and children.

I mention this for a very definite reason, at West Dean I was exceedingly dissatisfied with you.

Something had gone wrong with your morale, in my opinion.

If you have nerves you should cut out all forms of alcohol from beer upwards and should have the guts to do it absolutely. I am speaking quite plainly and do so with intent. I tried to assist you in various matters at West Dean but it was clear to me that something was wrong with you and that you were not being manly and pulling yourself together.

Butterworths is my own show in Company form. If it was a Public Company and I was Chairman I think it is very doubtful that I should consider I was justified in retaining your services. It is because of the point just mentioned and because you were efficient many years ago and because of your wife and children that I have been willing to be considerate but your inaptitude during the week or so that your Director was away as indicated in the early part of this letter, is beginning to make this attitude wear somewhat thin.'

Who today would stay around after receiving such a letter? Who today would write such a letter?

All his employees were, in a literal sense, Bond's men. Loyalty to the firm and to him personally had to be absolute. He was a combination of military commander and head of a biblical family. He was a leader, a despot and a father figure. Above all he was a great publisher, and his 'lengthened shadow', in Emerson's phrase, became the institution known as Butterworths.

Chapter 6

Bond's Last Decade

In the fifth and last decade of Stanley Bond's business life he remained in vigorous control. Further major works and the *All England Law Reports* were planned; the Board was expanded; new management styles were developed. And he got married on 24th November 1938,* an event of far-reaching significance for the future of the company.

One of his main efforts to strengthen the company was to extend the range of major works. *Halsbury's Laws*, *Halsbury's Statutes* and the *Encyclopaedia of Forms* had established that core of ongoing publications which is vital to the success of a publishing house. What new and similar ventures could he devise? Bond demonstrated that he had plenty of ideas and the energy to implement them by initiating three more major works:

> *Atkin's Court Forms in Civil Proceedings*, 1937–50
> *Macmillan's Local Government*, 1934–41
> *Words and Phrases Judicially Defined*, 1943–5

The first of these was a natural successor to the *Encyclopaedia of Forms and Precedents*. If it was less successful commercially than the earlier work, this could be attributed to the fact that, while all firms of solicitors do conveyancing work, many do not undertake litigation. The detailed planning of the work on this, and on the other two major works of that period, was organised by J. W. Whitlock. As with the earlier major works, Stanley Bond was able to engage an Editor-in-Chief of the first rank, Lord Atkin, a Lord of Appeal in Ordinary and one of the most distinguished common lawyers of his day. In retrospect, the work seems somewhat pedestrian, but it was hampered by difficulties in achieving continuity in the internal editorial team, especially during the war period.

---

* The bride, Violet Myrtle Fletcher, was the daughter of Lieutenant-Col. A. F. Fletcher and Lady Theresa Fletcher, sister of the 7th Earl Fitzwilliam. Bond was then, at the age of 61, Chairman of the Bachelors' Club. Two sons were born of the marriage – Ian in 1940, and Brian in 1942.

Stanley Shaw Bond, *c.* 1930

Macmillan's Local Government Law and Administration in England and Wales had a predecessor in seven volumes, the first of which was published in 1906. The new work in fourteen volumes was planned entirely afresh. The blue-print, issued in April 1933, was a printed document of 180 pages, giving for each title an indication of length and scope, together with exhaustive cross-references. Lord Macmillan was also a Lord of Appeal in Ordinary, but his special experience of local government, particularly in England and Wales, was tenuous. (It was brave to appoint a Scottish Law Lord as Editor-in-Chief.)

The Editorial Board and the Revising and Managing Editors were most carefully selected for their varied experience (and included men from Joshua Scholefield's chambers), but the actual task of preparing the blueprint was undertaken by G. E. Hart, a solicitor who had been involved in *Halsbury's Statutes* and on whom J. W. Whitlock placed great reliance. It caused a terrible shock when Hart was run over and killed in Parliament Square a few years later. *Macmillan* was probably the least successful of all the major works.

The first volume of *Words and Phrases Judicially Defined* was not published until after the death of Stanley Bond, but it was his concept. Owen Elliott noted how Bond, touring the United States in 1930, had collected ideas for such a work, and had in consequence turned down de Boo's proposals in 1931. The project seems to have remained in cold storage for some years, but in 1940–1 K.J. (the author of this history) was instructed to do some preliminary work. He prepared a specimen containing short extracts from judgments, those under each word or phrase being grouped by context and compared. Bond's idea was different – simply to use extensive quotations, and to let them speak for themselves. Once again his shewd discernment of the 'possible' was justified. Even if it was desirable it would have been very expensive at any time to engage workers of the calibre necessary to do the analysis which K.J. recommended – and in time of war such persons were just not available. Stanley Bond unerringly proceeded with a work which could be done by freelance workers, many of them of a fairly low calibre. Part of his genius was the ability to synthesise the work of others.

As well as the three new major works just described, this period saw the commencement of a third edition of the *Encyclopaedia of Forms and Precedents*. This caused Stanley Bond much anxiety. It was barely ten years since the second Edition, but some volumes (particularly Volumes 14 and 15, dealing with the 'Sale of Land') were in serious need of revision, and had been so heavily used as to be falling to pieces. The question whether to embark on a completely new edition, or whether to replace certain volumes only, was canvassed by Bond in a number of visits to solicitors throughout the country, usually accompanied by Whitlock or by one of the representatives.* As a result he decided upon the compromise of replacing the whole work, but doing it out of order – first the essential volumes, 14 and 15, and then a judicious mixture of crucial and less urgent volumes. This was the kind of judgment which Bond, who could then look back on over forty years of boldness rewarded and caution justified, could make.

His bravest and most successful venture of these last years was beyond question the *All England Law Reports*. Not since *Halsbury's Laws of England* had Stanley Bond devised a greater contribution to legal literature than what came to be called the All E.R.

Until that time there had been a number of privately owned general series of law reports, and the 'official' Law Reports, published by the Incorporated Council of Law Reporting. The word 'official' is deliberately put in inverted commas. It is not a government publication, but it is published by a charitable body of which the Attorney-General is an ex-officio member. It is a typical British compromise. None of these various series was published more frequently than monthly; none was particularly notable for its speed of reporting. There was also a number of specialised series.

Stanley Bond's scheme was to publish a weekly series of general reports (including such cases on specialised subjects as were of general interest), and to bring cases to the reader within one or at the most two months.

In view of the present world-wide circulation of over 14,500 it is difficult to appreciate the resistance of those early days. The judiciary of the time were particularly hostile – both to revising their judgments for the All E.R. and to receiving citations from any other report of a case to be found in *The Law Reports*. Once again Stanley Bond persevered and Butterworths reaped the harvest.

The first editor of the All E.R. was 'Polisher' Williams, one of the most remarkable all-rounders in the company's history. Starting on the *English and Empire Digest*, where he had acquired his nickname, he was transferred to the *Encyclopaedia of Forms and Precedents*, and became there one of the most knowledgeable

---

* These journeys with representatives were usually unpremeditated. S.S.B. found out where the rep. would be, sent him a telegram, and followed within hours. On one occasion he arrived at Machynlleth (which he had had to write down for the booking clerk at Paddington) before his telegram, and found the rep. at breakfast.

of all barristers on the 'New Conveyancing' – the fruits of the Birkenhead legislation. Polisher Williams was a walking encyclopaedia. Answering a telephone query, he would grunt comprehension of the long story of the enquirer, while reaching a volume of the *Encyclopaedia* down from the shelf behind him. By the time the story was finished he had identified the appropriate form (without the aid of an index) and was able to say 'You want form – – – on page – – – of Volume – – – . You'll have to modify clause – – – , and the – – –th recital is unnecessary. Etc. Etc.'

Polisher Williams established the *All England Law Reports* on lines upon which later editors could build, without themselves having been law reporters. Only one Editor of All E.R., G. F. L. Bridgman, had a life-time experience of law reporting before reaching the Editor's chair.

As a result of the commencement of the All E.R. the Lord Chancellor, early in 1939, set up the 'Law Reporting Committee' to consider the proliferation of law reports. It was unable to make any recommendations to curtail the number, and the activities of the All E.R. continued unabated, offering something quite new – speed. It was left to Butterworths to absorb, by commercial procedures, the two main 'unofficial' rivals, the *Law Journal Reports* and the *Law Times Reports*.

Meanwhile Bond was also launching a competely new side to his activities in England – medical publishing.

In 1936 the first volume of *British Encyclopaedia of Medical Practice* (B.E.M.P.) was published. Bond recalled that the inspiration 'Why don't I do for the doctors what I have done for the lawyers?' suddenly came to him when walking through the streets of an Indian city. Butterworths had already published quite an extensive medical list in India. The file set of Indian medical works (probably incomplete) contains forty-two books or new editions published between 1916 and 1940. Nearly all had a local slant, and varied from specialist monographs to standard text-books running to several editions.*

In designing B.E.M.P. Stanley Bond met some opposition to the alphabetical arrangement which he copied from his success-

---

* Examples of the former are Brahmachari's *Kala-Azar and its Treatment* (1920); Gunewardene's *Heart Disease in the Tropics* (1935); Webb-Johnson's *Painless Childbirth through Twilight Sleep in the East* (1918). The last named was still in the English catalogue twenty years later.
Standard text-books included Modi's *Elements of Hygiene and Public Health* (1918, 1920, 1928); Modi's *Text-book of Medical Jurisprudence and Toxicology* (1920, 1922, 1924, 1932, 1936, 1940); O'Meara's *Medical Guide for India and Book of Prescriptions* (1920, 1924, 1929, 1935); Chatterji's *Handbook of Operative Surgery* (1936).

ful legal publications. He was told that doctors preferred an arrangement by parts of the body, or by types of disease or condition. Bond persisted in the alphabetical arrangement, and all the early medical encyclopaedias followed this plan until *Operative Surgery* was published in 1956.

As with his legal encyclopaedias, Bond was successful in securing an Editor-in-Chief of the highest calibre and reputation, namely Sir Humphrey Rolleston,* and titles were contributed by eminent physicians and surgeons.

B.E.M.P. was well received, but its thirteen volumes were not completed until 1941, by which time World War II had prevented a broadly based entry into the medical market. But Stanley Bond's ideas were sustained. In 1947 the first volume of the companion *British Surgical Practice* was issued. Butterworths' future role as a diversified publisher had been initiated – by Stanley Bond by way of India.

*   *   *   *   *

Towards the end of 1936 the iron rule of George Bellew, Stanley Bond's right-hand man since 1910, was showing distinct signs of cracking. Arrangements for the publication in that year of the *Yearly County Court Practice* for 1937 were a near fiasco, and Bellew was largely to blame. As a result of an Order-in-Council dated 3rd July 1936, the new County Court procedure, enacted in the County Courts (Amendment) Act, 1934, and the County Courts Act, 1934, was to come into force on 1st January 1937; new Rules were made on 29th July containing the details. Whitlock got wind of this through a friend in the Lord Chancellor's office; Bellew and the editors of the *Yearly County Court Practice* seem not to have known about it. The 1937 *Practice* was prepared, and parts even passed for press, ignoring the impending changes. Whitlock, however, adroitly arranged to have the Rules speedily printed by Butterworths' own printers for official use (and of course for use by Butterworths) pending the publication of the Stationery Office print.

A serious gap in the editorial procedures was revealed. The encyclopaedias had their qualified editorial staff; text-books were supervised by Whitlock and his assistant; but the Annual Practices went straight from the outside editors to the production department, passing through no internal editorial sieve.

---

* Bart. (1924), G.C.V.O. (1929), K.C.B. (1918), C.B. (1916). Physician in Ordinary (1923–32) and Physician Extra-ordinary (1932–6) to King George V. Regius Professor of Physic, Cambridge (1925–32). President of the Royal College of Physicians (1922–6).

Whitlock was then asked by Bellew (or perhaps volunteered) to save the day, and built up two teams to reconstruct the *Practice* – writers outside, and copy editors within the office. The inside team (J. P. Gaudin, Arthur Harris and K.J.) worked seven days a week for three months, and the *New County Court Practice** was published in January 1937. The glory was Whitlock's.

J. W. Whitlock, *c.* 1937.
(Photograph by
Howard Coster)

Not long after, Whitlock decided to take up ski-ing and, not by chance, found himself in a neighbouring resort to that in which Bond was taking a holiday. There, unobserved, they discussed the future. In April 1937 Whitlock became a director.

Whitlock was not the only rising star to challenge Bellew. E. C. Leader, the Chief Accountant, who was one of Bond's 'blue-eyed boys', had been demonstrating that Bellew often misquoted or misinterpreted figures to a dangerous extent. Leader prepared the first draft of a new operational plan for the business.

---

* Not only was the name changed to the *New* County Court Practice, but the colour of the binding was changed – the 'Yellow Book' became the 'Green Book'.

On 18th November 1937 S.S.B. told the Board that:

'With the rapid growth both in size and importance of the Company he had for some had in mind the desirability of strengthening the Board of Directors. Indeed Mr. West had on several occasions during the past few years advised him seriously to consider the matter.

It was true in business as in everything else, that nothing can stand still but must either go forward or backward. For the moment, however, the Chairman gave it as his opinion that the policy to be followed was to consolidate and review everything connected with his Companies, and then go forward again, after an interval of a few months. Very considerable developments had taken place during recent years in the Company's business, particularly in the last two years, and notably the entry of the Company into the field of Medical Publishing. He would not be accused of an undue optimism when he said that this departure bade fair to prove to be an outstandingly successful one, and there was every sign that the name of Butterworths would stand as high in Medical Publishing as it did in Legal Publishing.

The Chairman then referred to the "Working Plan for the Organisation" a copy of which had been placed in the hands of each Director. It was designed to bring the organisation of the Company into line with modern practice. He said that the Company's business was a very specialised and technical one, and that the growth in size of the Company's operations demanded strong, and above all, clear-sighted direction.'

To implement this plan, four new directors had been added to the Board, which was now to consist of seven people:

Stanley Bond (Chairman and Governing Director)
George Charles Bellew (Managing Director with direct
  responsibility for Sales)
J. W. Whitlock (in charge of all legal publishing)
E. C. Leader (in charge of accounts and administration)
Kenneth E. A. Moore (a partner in Edward Moore & Sons,
  chartered accountants, who shortly afterwards became the
  company's auditors)
Gilbert West (a partner in the company's solicitors)
J. C. Denton Carlisle (usually called Major Carlisle; a
  neighbour of Stanley Bond's in Sussex, and a banker)

The last three were non-executive appointments.

Para. 3 of the Working Plan, which was formally adopted by the enlarged Board, stated that 'each Director [had] an equal responsibility to the Chairman'. Bond had become in fact, though not in name, his own managing director. Bellew's long reign as Bond's *alter ego* was clearly at an end.

A year later Bellew called the staff together and made this statement from the staircase in the Central Hall:

'My dear friends,

I believe this is quite a correct description of the vast majority of those present who have known me – many from my young manhood upwards.

As you know, considerable alterations in this organisation have taken place during the last eighteen months or so, and by the middle of this year the limit of my acceptance of the new conditions had been reached. As a sequel to this, the following announcement would have been placed on the Notice Board, either last night or this morning, in the ordinary course of things.

MEMORANDUM FROM THE MANAGING DIRECTOR'S ROOM
This is to notify all concerned that I have resigned my Managing Directorships of Butterworth & Co. (Publishers) Ltd., and all the Associated Companies as from the 31st of October last.

GEORGE CHARLES BELLEW

Instead of allowing this Notice to be placed up without explanation, I decided to take the opportunity of calling you all together in order to say farewell, and to thank those who have worked with me for the support that they have given during the long years in which I have held my high office of responsibility, first as General Manager, and since 1927 as Managing Director.

I am not in a position to judge, nor is it necessary for the purpose of this statement to know, what degree of surprise the announcement I have just read to you will cause. I am perfectly certain however, that a number who have known me very well will feel surprised and in all probability pained, that I have not made any personal or private reference to the event which is now an accomplished fact. I should like to explain to them, and to all, that it was my desire to spare them any embarrassment, particularly from the point of view of their business career, and to avoid increasing the position of delicacy, that has caused me to endeavour to act in the Office during the period that certain negotiations have been going on, just as though they were not taking place at all. In other words, for everyone's sake, I have maintained a position of normality as far as it has been possible. It is for the same reason that I am confining my observations within the limits of a written statement, and it is my wish that the customary farewell speeches, which in usual circumstances would be made on an occasion like this, should not be given. I hope I am correct in feeling that generally speaking your good wishes will go with me.

For my part I want to take this opportunity of expressing a hope for your own continued and progressive careers. I trust you will always be able to think of me as one who played a very great and important part in bringing the Company up to its present world-wide position; who, in dealing with matters of business and those working under him, always endeavoured to be fair, even at times when that was inconsistent with his personal interests; as one who, when he gave his friendship, always remained loyal to it; and who, when circumstances called him to face the greatest decision of his life so far – a very hard decision to make in any event – made it unflinchingly.

Having "said my piece" it now remains for me to say "Goodbye and good luck".'

Leader maintains that while the intention of the Working Plan was to clip Bellew's wings, the other directors had not intended his departure. But after the reorganisation Bellew had not enough to do; he drank more heavily and was unable to conceal it. Those who have been involved in such an episode know that when the departure becomes inevitable, it is not possible to say to what degree an exit is voluntary. But Bellew disappeared abruptly and totally.*

Bellew's resignation took effect from 31st October 1938. Major Carlisle was appointed Deputy Chairman and Managing Director, but remained part-time. On 1st November Bond wrote a seven-page letter to Lawrence Jones, Resident Director in Australia, asking him to return to England as a director of the home company and to take charge of Sales. The letter surveys the events of the past year, including much discussion of the supervision of the overseas companies. Lawrence Jones had in any case been expecting to return to England the following year, after six years overseas, although he had offered to stay in Australia for a further three-year term.

In this letter Bond describes his plans for future publishing, prefaced by the following self-revelation:

'To speak quite plainly, the driving power, whereby the business has progressed to its present size, from quite a small beginning, has emanated from me personally – the creative ideas have also come from me.

* One person at least remained faithful to Bellew. His secretary kept house for him until her death in 1954. He survived her by only a few months.

I have an endless number of ideas; they come to me out of the blue.'

The letter ends by considering where in England Lawrence Jones should live: 'it would not be wholly inconvenient to me if you decided to live in Sussex'. Lawrence Jones acknowledged the letter by cable dated 14th November: 'Very many thanks for your exceedingly kind letter greatly appreciated by my wife and myself will reply after a few days consideration'. He did not consider for long; his acceptance followed the next day.

His letter in confirmation, dated 16th November, refers delicately to Bellew's departure:

'I must admit that your decision to allow Mr. Bellew to retire upon a pension very much eases my mind. It would be ridiculous if I pretended to you that I have been blind to the friction which has existed in the London Office during the past twelve months. I hope you will appreciate the difficulty of my position. Whereas my loyalty to you is my only tie to Butterworths, Mr. Bellew in past years has been very kind to me when I was new to the business. I have kept myself firmly and definitely aloof from these troubles but I could never have felt happy working in the office in London had I had to do so, feeling that the team was not at one. Your assurance that I need have no doubt as to my welcome if I return to London has greatly reassured me. There is nothing I enjoy more than working in a team and the division of work as set out in your letter seems to me to be ideal.'

On 2nd November, the day after he wrote his seven-page offer, Bond realised he had failed to act in accordance with his new style of management and sent a postscript:

'In continuation of the letter of 1st Nov. 1938
(17) In order to conform with my general rule of consulting the full Board, the contents of this letter are subject to the Board.'

A covering letter starts:

'I add the enclosed, as although the whole show is mine, I always consult the Board, – and I should do this in due course.'

By the time the postscript had arrived, Lawrence Jones had not only accepted, but told his friends. He had to cable saying: 'Please explain other directors no discourtesy intended as could not know they were not aware of your offer'. Stanley Bond's reply to this is contained in a cable covering several assorted matters:

'Agree Orama stop this cable acknowledges your cables to Inhopetter stop have explained other directors everything satisfactory stop being married Thursday twenty-fourth stop will notify you day Nichols agreement mailed.'

Orama was a ship arriving in Toulon on 12th May. Inhopetter was the cable address of Stanley Bond's flat in Cleveland Row.

Lawrence Jones wound up affairs in Australia and New Zealand, handing over his responsibilities to Harry Henry in Sydney and Bill Nichols in Wellington. He travelled back to England via Canada, and on 8th June 1939 he took up his appointment as a director of Butterworth & Co. (Publishers) Ltd., Butterworth & Co. (Africa) Ltd., Butterworth & Co. Ltd, Coke Press Ltd. and Justice of the Peace Ltd. He was already a director of the Australian and Indian companies; directorship of the Canadian company followed later.

When this episode closed, no one could have known that Bond would be dead in less than four years. It was doubtless as well that the younger men – Whitlock, Leader, Lawrence Jones and Kenneth Moore – who were to run the company after his death, had these four years to work directly under Bond as a team, without being dominated by Bellew, who had been so long Bond's sole lieutenant. Bond's plans, as usual, worked out. But he continued to take the decisions – they had no practice at that.

*   *   *   *   *

By Monday morning, 4th September 1939 (the day after the outbreak of World War II), Butterworths were already established at Stanley Bond's country home, West Dean Park,* near Chichester. (It was not, for some, the first experience of evacuation – a year earlier, at the time of the Munich crisis, part of the staff went to nearby Graffham.)

Although a skeleton staff from Sales and Publishing was left in London, most of Bond's home was occupied, either for offices or staff sleeping quarters. One wing was reserved for Stanley Bond's private use. Even that was invaded when the servants' hall could no longer accommodate the staff for meals, and first the 'officers' moved to a separate 'mess' in the Chairman's library, and next the whole staff ate in the great dining hall, with the 'officers' sitting at the ends of the tables, like schoolmasters.

---

* This house he rented from the eccentric Edward James. After the war it was used by a girls' school. Now it is West Dean College, part of an educational trust set up by Mr. James, at which traditional crafts are taught both to professionals and to amateurs.

In London the Chairman's private flats in Cleveland Row
were pressed into use for offices. Bell Yard, however, came
through the war years practically undamaged.

London staff tackled the rigours of wartime commuting
resolutely. Unprompted, the *Law Journal* staff decided

'...to form, without delay, a Law Journal Cycling Club, and
all the staff who can ride bicycles must secure one at once,
and ride that bicycle in fair weather or foul through bombs,
if bombs there be, from their homes to the office, and must
be punctual on all occasions.'

It was thought unwise to allow girls to join the Club.

On 7th September 1939 Stanley Bond put pencilled annotations on Whitlock's list of forthcoming publications. The list
was classified under Books; Books to be postponed; Books to be
finished with (apart from those already decided); Queries; and
Books to be considered. Only four in the first group were ticked.
The commonest annotation is 'Hold up', with variants like
'Hold up 3 months', 'Hold up pro tem', and 'Try and get held
up'. In the list of 'Books to be finished with' the annotation 'Try
and cancel' is common. Not all the cancellations took place;
some of the books postponed were published later. But the
course was cleared for the mass of publishing necessitated by the
emergency war-time legislation.

Similar lists of staff are also annotated by Bond, right down
to the office boys, varying from those who should stay, through
those who were to be put on half-pay, to those who were to be
given notice (a month or two weeks). Both lists, publishing and

staff, are marked for reconsideration on 1st October. Another matter urgently considered was whether the representatives should be kept on the road. The details to be considered resulted in a six-page agenda of forty-six items for the Chairman's Departmental Conference held on 20th September. The agenda was based on two manuscript notes to Emery. The first, dated 'Friday evening' (i.e. 8th September) is on the Chairman's blue memo paper and is headed 'in a very uncomfortable shaky train'. The second, dated 9th September, was probably written after a break at Grantham, since it is partly on notepaper of the hotel there; it is headed 'In a better train'.

Meanwhile by 14th September Whitlock had prepared proposals to publish an *Emergency Legislation Service*. The Emergency Powers (Defence) Act, 1939, which was the ultimate authority for the bulk of the wartime and post-war controls, had been passed on 24th August. Further legislation followed fast: fifteen Acts on 1st September; six Acts on 3rd September; ten Acts on 5th September; and a further six on 7th September, making a total of thirty-eight Acts. Whitlock also listed seventy-nine emergency orders, regulations, circulars, etc. which should be published. Whitlock's plan was for a bound volume of Acts, and a loose-leaf service of orders. The Acts were to be annotated only lightly for the sake of speed.

By the middle of October Sammy Edgar (later of the Statutory Publications Office and a C.B.E.) and K.J. were in a hotel at Andover finalising the manuscript and passing proofs for press. They were joined by Alan Yonge, who was writing the index; for K.J.'s thirtieth birthday on 20th October, his wife (and also J. W. Whitlock) joined the indexing party. They found a double-bed a very convenient thing on which to sort index slips.

The Acts were classified, in the traditional Butterworth style, and this enabled the loose-leaf service of regulations to be conveniently organised, new pages being inserted at the end of each title. The original two binders increased by the end to seven. The fortnightly loose-leaf issues grew to about 500 pages. The basic plan survived for twelve years. The whole system was called *Butterworths Emergency Legislation Service*, abbreviated by the staff to Emers. Leg., or 'Emma's Legs', as it was mistyped on one occasion.

Emers. Leg. illustrated the ability of Butterworths to produce speedy publications by means of inspired improvisation and team work. It also introduced Butterworths to the problem of preparing, printing, assembling and despatching a large-scale loose-leaf publication.

Meanwhile the other publishing and selling activities went

on. Polisher Williams continued to produce not only the *All England Law Reports*, but also the third edition of *Encyclopaedia of Forms and Precedents*, of which nine volumes were produced during the years 1940–5. *Atkin's Court Forms* also continued under N. P. Shannon (later to become Chief Legal Editor); Whitlock had persuaded him to leave University College, Aberystwyth, and to join the Butterworth staff in 1941.

Stanley Bond spent part of his time at West Dean Park, where the bulk of the staff were; part at Dycheham Park, near Petersfield, which he had acquired as a refuge for his family, within easy reach of West Dean (though one department ended up at Dycheham); and part at Braemar. But he continued in absolute control. In April 1940 on the resignation of Major Carlisle due to his military duties, Bond finally designated himself Managing Director, which he had been in practice as 'Governing Director'.

In February 1943 Stanley Bond fell ill. He died of pneumonia on 14th February in his sixty-sixth year. The staff were stunned. Their leader was, in all their minds, a man still in his prime, though in truth his days were numbered, for he had leukaemia. But it was war-time; death was common: people 'carried on'.

Stanley Bond had tried to make sure that Butterworths were equipped and ready to carry on. Nevertheless he left the

Stanley Shaw Bond,
c. 1940, from a portrait
in oils by Oswald Birley
in the Butterworth
Board room.
(Photograph by Focus 4)

company vulnerable, and not only because of the problem of death duties. An experienced publisher, Ron Watson, has said in retrospect:

'Divide and rule was the technique of Bond's management. .. . He failed in building and organising a structure which could survive him and continue to expand and flourish after he had gone. He left a perfect take-over situation; a situation unable to withstand the "corporate" publishing concept which even then had appeared in the U.S.A. and within a few years was to cross the Atlantic and change the face of British publishing.'

Bond's success was that of an autocrat. As a bold innovator and the sole proprietor of the company, he neither wanted nor needed to devolve the decision-making process down the line. In this respect his successors tried to imitate Bond's methods without the strength of his personality and his unique position.

*   *   *   *   *

This is a history of Butterworths, not a biography of Stanley Shaw Bond. But some glimpses of the man illustrate how the company he built was so largely an extension of himself.*

Owen Elliott wrote of his journeys in the United States with Stanley Bond:

'. . . no matter where he was, Mr. Bond went to church on Sunday morning, if at all possible. Between trains in Chicago, we managed to squeeze in a service, and again in New York when every minute was precious as he was sailing the next day.'

The Rev. J. J. Clark said at Braemar Parish Church on the Sunday following his death:

'He was a man of sterling Christian character and the more I got to know him the greater was my esteem for him. During the past five years I got to know him well, and I can honestly say that in all our conversations the question of the Christian life cropped up sooner or later. He was never shy or ashamed to witness his faith in Christ. I could see that day by day he was growing in grace and in the knowledge of his Lord. Although not a member of the Church of Scotland he was a faithful attender at our services as often as he could.'

---

* The quotations which follow are mostly from correspondence and other documents sent to Mrs. Myrtle Bond after her husband's death, and kindly made available by her.

Bond's attachment to Braemar was significant. It was shooting country, and had royal connections. The *Aberdeen Press and Journal* noted that Bond 'rented part of the shootings and became more closely associated with the district as tenant of Braemar Castle from 1931 onwards.' The *Evening Express* (also of Aberdeen) mentions his large house parties at Braemar.

In West Dean Park, where he lived from June 1935 and where he died, he had a large and convenient house for entertaining, and could indulge his hobby of shooting, closer to his business activities than at Braemar. These were never out of his mind.

He was involved in many charitable causes: a governor of Queen Alexandra's Hospital Home for Soldiers; Hon. Treasurer of the Royal Association in aid of the Deaf and Dumb; Hon. Secretary of Beauchamp Lodge Home for Children. Even more important was his work for the Church of England, as Vice-Chairman of the Central Board of Finance, and as Chairman of the Financial Commission of the Church of England.

Lord Grey, Chairman of the Central Board of Finance of the Church of England, said at its meeting on 17th February 1943, three days after Stanley Bond's death:

> 'It is almost ten years since Canon Partridge* approached Sir Robert Kindersley and asked if he could put us in touch with somebody of first-class ability in the business world. This Board perhaps visualised Mr. Bond as chiefly sitting and listening and therefore it may not have realised what a wise head there was behind his listening attitude, or his complete readiness to answer any call for help at whatever sacrifice to himself. Those of us who had the opportunity of talking to him and getting his valuable advice learned more and more to rely on his judgment.'

An anonymous tribute from the same background says:

> 'I have been expecting an abler pen than mine to add a tribute to the notice of the death of my friend Stanley Bond. I only knew him as a friend – a valuable friend – for a short time and as Vice-Chairman of the Central Board of Finance. All who came across him will remember the gay button-hole which ever adorned his person, emblematical of the cheerful heart which was ever displaying itself in the quick smile and

---

* The resulting friendship between Canon (later Bishop) Partridge and Stanley Bond had a further consequence. After the sudden death of Bishop Partridge and his son Simon's discharge from military service on medical grounds, Stanley Bond invited Simon Partridge to join the staff of Butterworths in 1942. He is now Legal Publishing Director and Chairman of the Board of Butterworth (U.K.) Ltd.

happy phrase and hearty laugh. But beneath that gay and
joyful exterior was a man of inflexible rectitude and of a
devout and holy life. Many a time did he talk over the things
of the spirit with me, making much of his own shortcomings
and failures; for he regarded himself as a Steward of God and
all his financial success in the world of publishing as a sacred
trust to be used for the Glory of God and the assistance of
his fellow men. Few knew of his many acts of generosity, for
he never let the right hand know what the left hand did.

In his position at the Central Board of Finance he brought
to bear not only his vast experience as an organiser and
administrator to the business side of the Church Finance but
also those principles of inflexible rectitude which came first
in his life – first before the getting of money or the getting of
his own way. Intrigue was as foreign to him as black is to

white; and many a time did he in private deplore some cunning by-way which was being traversed to obtain some particular end, which though perhaps good in itself, had not the support of the Board as a whole...

Of his hospitality there can be no two opinions. Whether at West Dean Park or Scotland or his flat in town, visitors were assured of nothing spared to make their visit enjoyable and remembered.

The Church has lost a great Christian gentleman; the nation has lost a great business man; and all of us, who knew him, have lost a friend well nigh impossible to replace.'

Tributes came from members of the staff also. Owen Elliott was, as usual, eloquent and warm about the man who dispatched him to Winnipeg in 1912:

'Kindness, courtesy and an infinite consideration for others were second nature to him. Difficulties and troubles of the staff; sickness and death; all these received his earnest and kindly attention so soon as they were brought to his notice, and never did such incidents pass without some word of consolation or cheer from the chief.

Recognition of work well done was also never overlooked by him. On many occasions a short note has been received by the writer indicating that some matter or difficult situation had been coped with to the satisfaction of Mr. Bond...

He was the guest at a luncheon given by a group of well-known publishers in the U.S.A. and they had spent very considerable time in explaining to Mr. Bond that by the introduction of labour-saving devices, they had been able to dispense with a substantial number of employees. I could see that Mr. Bond was getting very fidgety, and in a moment or two he said – "Gentlemen, I think you should be ashamed to say that. Those employees whom you have dispensed with have helped to build the business and should receive the fullest consideration".'

Other members of the staff remembered kindnesses:

'After dealing with business matters, Mr. Bond would then go on to enquire about the Staff and their welfare, and lastly about my son, which naturally, being a mother, touched me most of all; I had never experienced such kindness and thoughtfulness from the Head of a Firm before and I shall never forget the interest Mr. Bond took in him.'

'One characteristic of Mr. Bond to which I should like to refer...was his ready sympathy in cases of serious illness. I

have in mind one colleague who had T. B. and was sent by
Mr. Bond to Switzerland for some months and another whose
wife died of cancer after a very short married life and to whom
Mr. Bond made a most generous offer of financial assistance.
In addition no bill for his nightly trunk calls to her (she was
nursed by relatives far from London) was ever charged to
him.'

But these recollections came from middle management (to use
today's description), and junior members of staff found him
aloof and frightening. One lady who was in the typing pool just
after World War I writes:

'[The telephone operator] was able to cope with SSB's idiosyncrasies, one of which was to demand a call, usually in a
monosyllable – no niceties, like please or thank you, nor any
apparent knowledge that the call would involve a number.
However, one fateful day I was deputed to operate the
switchboard during the lunch hour – a normally slack time;
the dreaded "eyelid" No. 1 on the board fell, and SSB
boomed "BOODLES". Frozen with terror I did nothing, and
not many minutes passed before a messenger was despatched
to the telephone room to see "what fool was operating the
board".'

Numerous affectionate anecdotes by 'Bond's men' record his
idiosyncrasies. Many of these come from those who were at one
time or another his 'landing boy'. For instance, he had the
habit, when going through his post, of holding out a letter to
the boy, saying 'In my hat, upside down'. It is obvious that he
would not fail to take home with him the cache of letters which
would fall from his hat when he put it on.
  One Bond ploy was to have a window partly open when a
visitor (presumably a member of the staff) arrived. Presently the
visitor was asked to close the window because of the noise
outside. Upon getting up to leave, the visitor was given a test
of observation and memory. He was asked to open the window
again. Very few opened the same window to the same distance.
  It was customary for the boys, on seeing Mr. Bond alight from
a taxi at the bottom of Bell Yard, either to raid the petty cash
or to take the cost of the taxi out of their own pockets since Bond
seldom carried enough cash. The boys used this as a convenient
way of saving, and put in a claim when they wanted to go on
a spree.
  Some said that Stanley Bond was mean. He certainly had the
reputation of underpaying both his authors and his staff. Once
a packing-case of books left the warehouse bearing the inscrip-

tion: 'The wages of sin is death, but the wages of Butterworths are worse'.

One barrister employee, having been refused an increase in salary, was stung to say to Bond: 'You know what they think of Butterworths in the Temple'. When S.S.B. replied 'No. But I should very much like to know', he got the answer 'Well, you shall. The name of Butterworths stinks over there'. It seems that Bond didn't care – at any rate he made no change. His reputation, and the consequent bad relations, had an important effect on the getting of contributors in post-war years, when the bar was more affluent. Whitlock tried to counter it by personal contacts and entertainment. The publishing staff pressed for and obtained improved terms. It was slow work, and took many years.

In Ron Watson's view, 'Stanley Bond was more autocratic than Gollancz, though without Victor's panache; more parsimonious than Unwin, he lacked Uncle Stanley's benevolence.' He was a benevolent dictator, who went to some pains to keep his benevolences secret.

But nobody had to work for Bond, and most people were proud to do so. He would have hated unions and the hatred would have been mutual. If you were not satisfied, you could always leave. But when you were in trouble, he responded generously to your need.

Bill Purser, Credit Manager under Stanley Bond, wrote:

'Very, very often, while working at his desk, he would sing softly to himself the nursery rhyme "Humpty Dumpty".

Now, I may be wrong, but it seems to me that this may have been a reflection of thought indicating that ambition must be tempered with caution. No sitting on the wall – cock-a-hoop – like Humpty Dumpty, or the fall would be bound to come and the damage irreparable. Or it may have meant that Mr. Bond disliked that attitude in others.

Another little personal thing that intrigued me was the lump of coal which rested on the lamp shade in Mr. Bond's office for many years. Spring cleanings had to be done, but the piece of coal must remain.

I have only recently learnt that Mr. Bond kicked the coal while out walking with his father, Mr. Charles Bond. A very vital and weighty problem of business was being discussed and a decision had just been arrived at when the incident occurred. Mr. Bond pocketed the piece of coal, and as the decision which had been made during that walk turned out to be most fruitful, the coal was kept as a sort of talisman.'

Let Martha Clark, the epitome of the loyalty and community spirit which S.S.B. inspired, have the last word:

'Mr. Bond and the then General Manager were in conference over some special instructions to go Overseas. For some unavoidable reason these were late in being done, with the result that we were all working against time in order to catch the mail. The pages as released from being typed were sent down to him but meanwhile the clock was creeping on and when at length the letters were finished there was less than 15 minutes to spare before the mail closed at 8 p.m. at the General Post Office in the City.

I had given instructions for a taxi to be held in readiness at the end of Bell Yard so that our messenger could get off promptly and seal up the packets while on his way but when I took the packets to the Central Hall there was no messenger and no taxi.

It was a cold dark night in February and snow was falling lightly which no doubt accounted for the scarcity of taxis. However, there was no time for thinking so I just rushed to Fleet Street and jumped into the first omnibus that came along. When the conductor came for the fare, I realised for the first time that I had no coat on, neither had I any money with which to pay my fare. A soldier on leave gave me a penny and then he gave me another for my return fare (the minimum fare was a penny in those days – February 1919). Thankfully I accepted, meanwhile hurriedly tying up my mail packets and affixing the stamps. I left the bus at St. Paul's and ran for my life through the passage-ways to the G.P.O. in King Edward Street and just had time to thrust the packets into the Post Box as the clock of St. Paul's struck 8 o'clock.

As I turned round to go back, I saw a car draw up and who should alight but Mr. Bond. He had come down from his room and on hearing that I and the mails had disappeared into the night, had come himself to find out what had happened. I was so glad to see him and he brought me back to Bell Yard; he was highly amused.

There were many other kindnesses shown to me by Mr. Bond. The loan of his Box at Covent Garden one night – tickets for Wimbledon and Ranelagh – and the grouse that used to be sent from Braemar...'

Chapter 7

The Quennell Period

The day after Stanley Bond's death the Board met, and after honouring his memory elected Kenneth Moore as Chairman. On the death of the Governing Director, Article 74 required a General Meeting at which all directors had to retire, being eligible for re-election. This meeting was held on 13th April 1943. The retiring directors (Moore, Lawrence Jones, Leader, West and Whitlock) were all re-elected. There were two new directors – Mrs. Violet Myrtle Bond,* and F. W. Seabrook Emery, the Secretary of the company. The latter appointment was in accordance with a request to the executors by Stanley Bond.

On 1st May the Board issued the following statement to the staff:

MEMORANDUM FROM THE CHAIRMAN TO ALL
BUTTERWORTH STAFFS

In accordance with the Will of the late Mr. Stanley Shaw Bond and the Articles of Association of Butterworth & Company (Publishers) Ltd. an Extraordinary General Meeting of the Company was held recently at which the following were appointed Directors:-

Mr. Kenneth A. E. Moore (Chairman)

Mrs. S. S. Bond	Mr. E. C. Leader
Mr F. W. S. Emery	Mr. G. L. West
Mr. E. L. Jones	Mr. J. W. Whitlock

Similar appointments have been or will be made in connection with the other Companies: Mr. W. H. Nichols will continue as a Director of Butterworth & Company (Australia) Ltd. and Mr. A. B. Cooper as a Director of Coke Press Ltd.

In his Will Mr. Bond expressed his strong desire that Butterworth & Company (Publishers) Ltd. and the other

---

* Mrs. Bond remained on the Board until 1949. In the summer of that year she married David Willis, a partner in Willis, Faber and Dumas, insurance brokers. Mr. Willis replaced his wife on the Board in October 1949, but resigned through pressure of work in May 1952.

Companies in the Group should be carried on after his death on the same lines as during his lifetime.

That will be the keynote of the policy of his Executors and of their colleagues on the Board.

Owing to the incidence of Death Duties the sale of some part of Mr. Bond's shareholdings in the Group is unavoidable. The introduction, in due course, of additional shareholders will facilitate the carrying on of the business on the established lines and contribute to its stability and prospects.

Mr. Bond not only wished his businesses to be carried on without loss of identity, but also that no loyal and efficient member of his staff need fear that any changes following his death would be to their disadvantage.

There is no reason why the Butterworth organization should not continue successfully to surmount war-time difficulties and afterwards go from strength to strength.

It is now up to all, whether Director, Manager, Senior or Junior, to give of their best to the Organization and in so doing each will contribute to the wellbeing of the whole.'

By the end of June Hambros Bank had agreed to purchase, on behalf of themselves and associates, 92,400 shares for a consideration of £231,000. The Bond executors retained 138,350 shares, and 3,900 shares were held by legatees – directors and senior executives. Hugh Quennell, a solicitor in the City who had acted for Hambros, was appointed a director and Deputy Chairman.

'The new money' is the title which J. W. Whitlock gave to Hugh Quennell in describing his first visit. He said that Quennell asked a lot of questions, and drank Kümmel.

Quennell was at this time on military service, which limited the part he could play in the management of the company. He did not start to attend Board meetings regularly until February 1945. But his influence was strongly felt.

Whitlock and Lawrence Jones provided Quennell with elaborate publishing and sales plans during this period. These deal exhaustively with the legal and medical programmes. Scientific publishing was not mentioned – this was to be Quennell's own contribution to Butterworths.

Quennell's letters of August and September 1943 refer to the purchase of the copyright of *Paterson's Licensing*; to new Articles of Association; to staff gradings; to additional publishing staff and accommodation; to the furnishing of the board room; and to pensions.

Lawrence Jones had proposed a pension plan to Bond before the war but was firmly told that such a thing was not appropriate to a company like Butterworths, since Bond looked after his retired employees. Leader had made similar proposals to Bond from time to time. The pension scheme, which started on 1st July 1946, is Quennell's best remembered contribution to the welfare of the staff. It was generous but selective.

There were now four full-time directors – Emery, Lawrence Jones, Leader and Whitlock. Leader, after a short experience of the new regime, decided that Butterworths was no longer right for him; he realised that there were many issues on which he differed from the 'new bosses'. Emery's influence increased when he became a director, and he worked very closely with Mrs. Bond. Leader's colleagues did not press him to stay. He left in December 1943 to undertake 'hush-hush' war work, and he later joined the National Coal Board, of which he rose to be an Assistant Director-General of Finance. Bond once wrote of Leader that he was the only full-time director of managing director calibre. There was not room for him and Quennell and Emery.

Leader was not replaced. Emery took over the Board responsibility for the Accounts Department and Phil Hogger, who had joined the firm in April 1942, was made Chief Accountant.

Within a few months of his appointment as Deputy Chairman it was clear to the other directors that Quennell intended to act as Managing Director in fact, if not in name. One justification of his role was the friction between Whitlock and Lawrence Jones. Emery tried to be the peacemaker. One appeal from Lawrence Jones to Emery for help, when Whitlock refused to listen to his criticism, referred specifically to the fact that it could not wait until Quennell's return.

For two years Quennell directed Butterworths from the distant excitement of his military service, while the other directors dealt with the daily round of business – varied by Home Guard or A.R.P. duties. (Whitlock used his Home Guard title of Major for many years after the war was over. There is a tradition that the rank was not operational, but given for help with a publicity film.)

In 1945 Quennell returned to civilian life and to practice as a solicitor.* About the same time the offices returned to London. Part of the daily round, in which Quennell was not involved, had been concerned with the inevitable high spirits (or even indiscipline) of staff in an isolated community. Disregard of coal

* He did not return to Slaughter and May, with whom he had been before the war. Instead he set up his own office in the City, where he established himself as a 'super-solicitor', advising on tactics while other firms did the legal work involved. He was probably the first person to succeed in doing this.

The staff at West Dean, 1945. The seated row includes (left to right, starting from fourth): 'Gus' Calcutt, Bill Purser (credit manager), W. G. Whelham, Miss H. M. Osborn, P. A. Hogger, F. W. S. Emery, J. W. Whitlock, N. P. Shannon, E. C. Featherstone, Mrs Cassey, Miss Treadway. Others mentioned in the book are: in the third row from the back, Barry Rose (fifth from left), Simon Partridge (seventh from left), Allan Cook (fourth from right); in the third row from the front, Miss Gosden (fourth from left)

rationing, rowdyism on buses, pillow fights in the billiards room, are but a few examples. Even VE day did not bring jubilation into official notices:

'If the announcement should be made during normal week-end absence... the Monday and Tuesday will be holiday and the Office will open at 9.15 on the Wednesday.

All staff are asked to see that their desks are cleared and their work put away before they leave to celebrate.'

By June 1946 the move back to London and the consequent restaffing were complete. The company was bigger after the war than before, and spread from Bell Yard across the street to 227 Strand, over the Temple Bar Restaurant.

The Chairman, Kenneth Moore, remained non-executive: Quennell on the other hand, although he had no office at Butterworths, contrived by personal visits, telephone calls and a constant flow of memoranda to make it clear that, if the three full-time directors ran the business, it was he who ran the directors. Nor did he hesitate to deal direct with the next level

of management: Harry Henry, who had been brought back
from Australia to become Sales Manager; Phil Hogger (Chief
Accountant); and K.J., who became Publishing Manager
during this period.

Quennell's memoranda were brief and biting. One addressed
to Lawrence Jones, the Sales Director, reads:

'(i)   It is true that the first two months Sales are up on last
       year.
(ii)   This is, in part, due to a terrific production drive in
       December which has reflected itself in these two months.
(iii) What do you think March will show?
(iv)   On the Daily Sales Sheets it is likely to be down.
(v)   If Sales do fall what cuts can you make in the Sales
       Department Costs?
(vi)   They must go down.'

Another, addressed to Emery, and enclosing a copy of a
request to Douglas Niekirk (a non-executive director)* reads as
follows:

'1. Copy of letter to Niekirk attached.
2. This is a golden opportunity for you to find out what
   Niekirk really does expect to do for his £500. Will you
   please do so?'

The matter to be investigated was more innocuous than the
memo suggested. The question was to what extent the director's
fee covered professional work done by Niekirk's firm.

Quennell had an eye for detail. At one period Harry Henry
was required to tabulate the 'Special Section Letters'† from
Toronto, and indicate suggested answers. Against each item
Quennell placed a tick or gave instructions for some different
approach. It was not long before Whitlock was saying that he
'needed Quennell's permission to spend a penny'.

Not without charm and humour, Quennell, like many tough
men, respected those who told him that they disagreed with
him, though accepting his decisions. But those who had to work
closest with him knew him as a man with a fierce temper. It
was probably Lawrence Jones and Henry who suffered most
from this, because they were less malleable than Emery and
Whitlock.

---

* Niekirk, a trustee of the Bond estate, and a partner in Bull and Bull, the
  company's solicitors, became a director on the death of Gilbert West.
† The letters from overseas companies were in three sections: General,
  Finance and Special. The first two were dealt with departmentally; the
  third, concerned with policy matters, was dealt with by top management.

Jack Edgerley, Chief Legal Editor, who knew Quennell better than most, writes:

'Quennell had flair, brilliance and could be good company: he was capable of considerable generosity and he wished those who worked for, in effect, him to have a full reward according to the standards of the day. He was prepared to fight for them, when he felt disposed to do so. There was the other side, too; he was a gambler by nature, he was prone to drink, business was money-making only to him, he wished to occupy a "super" position at all times – to take the highest place. His nature was one of extremes, including occasionally temper. But he could bring inspiration to people – the spark that helps one to continue with dull labour.'

His principal, perhaps his only, hobby was horse-racing, where his gambling propensities found full scope. The shared interest in horse-racing led to a personal relationship between him and Jim Marsden far beyond that to be expected between Deputy Chairman and Advertising Manager.

When Lawrence Jones was on a tour of Australia, Henry wrote him a personal letter commenting on a decision of the directors. He sent a copy of the letter to Quennell who promptly complained by cable to Lawrence Jones:

'It has come to my knowledge that certain private letters on companys business have been written to you by Henry which contain expressions which at least are capable of interpretation that he is not being loyal to his colleagues or the Board in London   stop   As arranged with you he has always been present at any executive meeting when any matter affecting sales has been discussed with full opportunity expressing point of view of sales department   stop   Notwithstanding this and without having expressed any different view to me at meeting or otherwise he writes to you personal letter expressing doubts   stop   Am sure you will be first to decry this and agree with my decision that private letters not circulated on matters affecting companys business should as they will cease forthwith.'

Lawrence Jones sprang to Henry's defence in a long letter, but unwisely did so from Melbourne when the offending letters were in Sydney. This gave Quennell a new opening and he detailed complaints in a letter.

'I am sorry that you did not re-read the correspondence sent you by Henry before writing your letter to me of the 19th March [1947]. I am, of course, delighted that you should seek to defend Henry when you think his defence is justified, for up to the time of these incidents he had my complete confidence and I also had a very high view of his ability...In the light of what I have written I am sure that you will be the first to agree with me in deprecating Henry's conduct.

I do not look back and I hope I do not carp. I have told Henry that the incident is now closed and that his future work and conduct will no doubt quickly rehabilitate my confidence in him.'

Lawrence Jones subsequently surrendered. A month later he wrote a manuscript letter from Cape Town:

'Now that I have had the opportunity of reading his letters again I appreciate fully what you felt and see that he made a serious mistake in writing as he did. He is very young [Henry was then 38!] and the strong action you took will have done him nothing but good.'

The offending letter is not on the file, but according to Henry's recollection he had not criticised the decision of the Board, but had made an injudicious remark about the line taken by the Editorial Department upon which that decision was based. He was forbidden to communicate further with his absent director: communication was at a low ebb.

But Henry survived this and other confrontations, including the one when for the first time, but not the last, Scientific Sales were taken from his jurisdiction, and entrusted to the manager of a separate Scientific Division.

Quennell could carp on lighter matters too, as this exchange with Whitlock illustrates:

H.Q. to J.W.W.   28th Jan. 1946. How is Williams getting on with his "Magna Opera?"

J.W.W. to H.Q.   29th Jan. 1946. Your note Williams and his Magna Opus...

H.Q. to J.W.W.   30th Jan. 1946. With reference to your letter of 29th January on the subject of Williams – is your Latin quite correct?

J.W.W. to H.Q.   But see your original note!!

Quennell marked this N.A. and filed it.

Emery would not have made such an error. On one occasion, when asked whether he wished to review a decision in the light of a change in circumstances, he replied, quoting Pontius Pilate: ὁ γέγραφα γέγραφα (rather than 'What I have written, I have written'). Even though he knew no Greek himself, he made sure that he quoted the words correctly by using a reference book.

Quennell's relations with senior management were poor: the staff as a whole felt that he had their interests at heart. There were few at any level who did not fear him. He introduced Christmas bonuses (aggregating 4% of payroll), which lasted for many years. His name is also associated with extra holiday entitlement for long-serving staff, and with subsidised lunches. One member of the staff, asked what his salary was, replied with his heart in his mouth; Quennell to his surprise told him he was 'grossly underpaid', and gave him forthwith an unprecedented rise. He could be impetuously generous, as well as rude and domineering.

Phil Hogger, the Chief Accountant, sums the period up:

'Our directors of those days were not a happy team, were they? Fortunately the second XI got on with the business without squabbles.'

In August 1948 Edward Lawrence Jones was injured in a car accident and died within hours. He was known to be in poor

P. A. Hogger in 1968.
(Photograph by
Derek Berwin)

health, and had been warned about the wisdom of driving. Late
one evening, as he drove alone out of London, his car ran off
the road and hit a tree.

He was a stronger personality than Emery and Whitlock, and
the progress of the company in the immediate post-war years
owed much to his drive on the sales side. E.L.J. was enthusiastic
and impetuous, a man of extremes, a maverick with all the
characteristics which that word implies. It was the constant
problem of the other directors, and particularly of Quennell,
to keep him within his terms of reference when he went overseas
to negotiate over major publications such as the *Ontario Digest*,
or the *Union Statutes of South Africa*.

The unsigned obituary in *The Times* was eulogistic:

'Mr Edward Lawrence Jones, whose death at the age of 57
as the result of a motoring accident was recorded in *The Times*
on August 16, was a son of the parsonage. Educated at Eton
and Balliol College, Oxford, he took up a business career.
After considerable and varied commercial experience on the
Continent and in India he joined the well-known publishing
firm of Butterworth and Co. as one of their oversea managers.
Shortly before the 1939–45 War he returned to London from
Australia to serve as a director. He brought with him into his
business activities many qualities which helped to make him
an outstanding figure in the publishing world – creative
imagination, integrity, courage, immense drive, and a complete loyalty both to his firm and to his own subordinates.
Especially on the legal side of his firm's work he made
contributions which are likely to be of enduring importance.

With a very keen appreciation of beauty and of the good
things of life – books, food, wine, talk – he combined a
fundamental simplicity and naturalness. The hours that he
spent working in his garden, roaming through the countryside
which he knew and loved so well, or discussing village politics
over a pint of beer, were perhaps the happiest that he knew.
His zest for life was inexhaustible, and the exuberance of his
personality made him a most delightful companion, even
though he could be a source of embarrassment at times to his
less uninhibited friends.'

The exuberance could indeed be embarrassing. For example he
liked his coffee *after*, and not with, his breakfast. Staying in New
Zealand one week, he asked day after day that his coffee should
be brought to his room quarter of an hour after his breakfast
tray. Day after day they came together. On the last morning
he flung up the window of his room at the front of the hotel,
and threw the lot into the courtyard.

Lawrence Jones was not replaced by another full-times sales director. His executive duties devolved on Harry Henry as Sales Manager, and Henry was made responsible to the Board through Emery. The interposition of Emery did not have any real meaning in day-to-day practice as far as Quennell was conerned. But then he never did worry much about correct channels of communication. Henry had to wait another fifteen years for a seat on the Board.

This was the second occasion on which a director had not been replaced – first Leader, then Lawrence Jones. But whether the reasons in each case had anything in common will remain a secret. In 1943 it would seem a reasonable economy to have a single director in charge of accounts, administration and the secretary's office. By 1948 Quennell was preparing to get all the power into his own hands; the strongest rival was removed by death. But it was competent second-line management and the strength of the product, rather than Quennell's abilities, which kept the company going.

It has been said of the directors in the post-war period that they 'lived high and kept themselves remote', a style – at least as far as remoteness was concerned – that tended to be imitated by senior managers. Whether or not they observed this trait in themselves, directors could recognize it in one another. Emery sent a note on one occasion to Quennell criticising Lawrence Jones's behaviour towards the Australian director: 'Nichols should be met as an equal – not as an office boy'.

It was under Quennell that Butterworths managed to get itself sued for libel by the *Daily Mirror*. The case* was *Lea* v. *Justice of the Peace Ltd. and R. J. Acford Ltd*, but the protagonists were the *Daily Mirror* (Lea's employers) and Butterworths, who owned the Justice of the Peace Ltd. Quennell prompted the solicitors at every turn. Counsel for Butterworths were Sir Valentine Holmes and Mr. Gerald Gardiner (subsequently Lord Chancellor).

The case arose from a Cecil family wedding reception held on 18th December 1945 at a private house in Arlington Street. Press photographers were not to be admitted. Lea, a *Daily Mirror* photographer, got into the house, and photographed the bride and bridegroom shaking hands with guests. The incensed bridegroom assaulted the photographer and smashed his camera.

The bridegroom, Captain Robert Cecil, was convicted of

---

* For further details see *Privacy and the Press*, edited by H. Montgomery Hyde, published by Butterworths.

assault at Marlborough Street Police Court and fined £10, with
£185 damages. A fortnight later the *Justice of the Peace* published
a 'Note of the Week', referring to the epithets 'ungentlemanly'
and 'cowardly' used by the magistrate about the bridegroom,
and commenting that those epithets 'exactly fit these intruders
[i.e. the press photographers], and are still more apt to the
newspaper proprietors by whom they are employed'. There was
more to the same effect. An action for libel was brought by the
photographer. The case was heard by Mr. Justice Hilbery on
12th to 14th March 1947. Butterworths fought the case inch by
inch, bringing an impressive list of witnesses who contradicted
the evidence given by the reporter in the magistrate's court.

Much play was made of a remark the plaintiff made to the
best man: 'I come from the paper of the times'. Hilbery, J.,
extracted from the plaintiff the admission that he used this
curious expression 'because I hoped that he would think it was
The Times, if he did not like the *Daily Mirror*'.

Butterworths' counsel and the judge tried to establish why
and in what way the behaviour of a reporter or press photographer could differ from that of a private citizen.

> 'Mr. Justice Hilbery: . . . What rights had you in the way of
> conduct, rights to conduct yourself in any way which was
> different from any other law abiding citizen? Because you
> were the Press you thought you had some different rights.
> What were they? – A. There are the rights of a free Press, the
> recording of everything, Courts, weddings, which are all for
> the general benefit of the country and accepted as such.
> Hilbery J.: Anything can be excused providing you say it
> is in the national interest; is that it? – A. Yes, my Lord.
> Hilbery J.: I thought we should get to it. Disabuse your mind
> of that. This country is still a country which is in theory living
> under a reign of law.'*

The judge found for the *Justice of the Peace*. He said: 'It is
criticism and it is strong criticism; but it is a salutary thing that
strong criticism should be levelled at conduct which is deserving
of criticism'. He also noted that although the article said some
very hard things about the proprietors of the *Daily Mirror*, that
paper had not felt sufficiently wounded to bring any action
about them. But it was the *Mirror* which caused the action to

---

* In his judgment Hilbery, J., used these words: 'I do not think it can be
too strongly emphasised that in this country the Press has no right to go
upon private property or into private places and to intrude upon
private people and into private rights, and that the standard of conduct
and manners demanded of them is as high a standard as should be
demanded of every citizen in a civilized community.'

be brought. Butterworths vigorously defended their contributor, and won the case.

By 1949 the unhappiness of Emery and Whitlock under Quennell's rule became increasingly obvious. The 'Old Butterworthians' for the most part, although unhappy with the atmosphere of those years, kept their heads down and stayed. Whitlock talked of buying a cottage in the country, and retiring to live on his savings. He was saved at the eleventh hour.

On Christmas Eve 1949 Quennell saw senior executives one by one, some in their own offices, some in the Board room. To K.J. he seemed tired and less aggressive than usual. To Harry Henry he gave a Christmas present better than any box of cigars. He said he intended to return Scientific Sales to Henry's command as from the beginning of 1950. That was Quennell's last appearance in Butterworths' offices.

The reason given for his departure was ill-health. To a few senior people, who were in the confidence of the directors, it was vaguely indicated that he had entered into a financial commitment, purporting to be binding on the company, without consulting his fellow directors, and without informing them afterwards. Surviving papers confirm this.

Maurits Dekker, co-founder of Interscience in New York and one of the leading American scientific publishers, writes:

'Hugh Quennell had my respect, because he showed me the breeziness the British lawyer, and judge, can demonstrate and not only on television (!), and he was the only man genuinely feared by Robert Maxwell.'

Some of Butterworths' rivals may have been glad to see him go.

After Quennell left, Emery and Whitlock became joint Managing Directors. The division of responsibility remained unchanged – Whitlock looked after publishing, and Emery did the rest. They said there was a mess to clear up, but they probably exaggerated. There were some expensive new projects and innovations from which they withdrew. But there was no noticeable change in the direction or policy of the company.

Henry again got the thinnest slice of the loaf. In spite of his 'Christmas present' he decided over Christmas to accept an appointment with another organisation in Australia. On the day after the holiday he saw Emery, and tendered his resignation. Emery, white-faced and shaken, told him Quennell was going, and begged him to stay and help. Henry, unwillingly, agreed to think it over for twenty-four hours. Senior colleagues persuaded him to change his mind. He stayed, but got no promotion.

Chapter 8

Science, Medicine – and America

Butterworths' entry into scientific publishing after World War II was well-timed, and executed with panache at a very high level. At the heart of it, as far as Butterworths were concerned, was the mercurial Hugh Quennell. The proposal came from the British Government, whose emissary was Count Vanden Heuvel,* a shadowy and influential person, described as 'the epitome of a diplomat with his imperial whiskers and black homburg'. Also involved were some of the best-known scientists of the day; and, at a later date, a young British Army Captain, of Czech origin, who had adopted the name of Maxwell. With these auspices it deserved to be more successful than it was.

It began with a meeting on 25th November 1946 at the Cabinet Offices in Great George Street, under the chairmanship of Sir John Anderson (afterwards Lord Waverley). The meeting was heavy with knighted academics – Sir Wallace Akers, Sir Charles Darwin, Sir Alfred Egerton, Sir Richard Gregory, Professor R. S. Hutton and Sir Edward Salisbury – none of whom would have lent their names without encouragement and blessing from high Government quarters.

Professor Hutton was appointed Hon. Secretary of this 'Scientific Advisory Board', a position which he held until it was wound up in 1962. Sir Alexander Fleming (discoverer of penicillin) joined the Board at its second meeting. Sir Edward Appleton joined in 1949. Sir Richard Gregory resigned in July 1947, due to his association with Macmillans. The other members remained on the Board for most of its fifteen years' life.

In attendance at the first meeting were Sir Charles Hambro (representing Hambros Bank); Hugh Quennell (representing Butterworths); Dr. P. Rosbaud, who had been appointed Editor of a proposed monthly journal; and Count Vanden Heuvel, on whom Quennell and Whitlock, both of them novices in the world of science, leaned for advice and support in those

---

* *Who was Who* records his death in 1963 at the age of 78. He is shown as a member of the diplomatic service in Switzerland during the war, and C.M.G. (1945). He was a Count of the Holy Roman Empire.

early days. John Whitlock used to refer to the Count as the cloak and dagger man. He was called by his friends Van, but those who had known him longer, and perhaps a little better, than Whitlock, referred to him as Fanny the Fixer.

The Scientific Advisory Board planned an advance on two fronts, both of which implemented the Government's purpose to develop British scientific publishing through the medium of Butterworths. The first aim was to establish Butterworths as scientific book publishers. This aim was assisted by the fact that German scientific publishers, and particularly Springer Verlag, which had in pre-war days been the leading German scientific and medical publishing concern, were at that time prohibited from selling books outside Germany. It was hoped to make use of Springer expertise.

The second aim was to publish a journal to publicise British scientific and technological expertise, with 'correspondents' abroad to report on scientific and technological developments. It was to be expected that the reports of these correspondents would be of interest to the British Government, as well as to the editor of *Research*. Rosbaud, the editor of the proposed journal, is described by Ron Watson* as being formerly the editor of a German metallurgical journal, a Springer protégé and previously involved in the destruction of the German heavy water programme.

Two companies were formed: Butterworth Scientific Publications Ltd., and Research and Development Ltd. The first, a wholly-owned subsidiary of Butterworths, was to publish on commission for the second company, the shares in which were held equally by Butterworths and by Hambros and its associates. Research and Development would receive the profits, if any. It was intended that 25% of these should be used for scientific research (a cogent argument, no doubt, in enlisting the services of the distinguished Board), the balance being distributed to the shareholders.

Book publishing was kept operationally separate from journal publishing, and the Advisory Board eventually concerned itself mainly with the journals. All the publishing was at this stage in the hands of Butterworth Scientific Publications Ltd.†

Springer Verlag seem to have been unwilling to commit themselves too deeply to Butterworths, and by 1948 it was clear that they had other ideas. They became associated with Robert

---

* Much information on early scientific publishing has been furnished by Ron Watson, who joined the company in 1950.

† The journal *Research* was *not* published by Research and Development Ltd.

Maxwell. The full story of the association is not part of Butterworth history, but the Springer-Maxwell relationship interwove with others that do concern this story: Maxwell and Quennell both served with the Allied Control Commission; Maxwell had dealings with Springer over the rationing of paper and the rehabilitation of their plant; Vanden Heuvel knew all the parties except Maxwell.*

Maxwell became a director of two U.K. companies, Springer Publishing Co. Ltd. and European Periodicals, Publicity and Advertising Co. Ltd. Hugh Quennell was more interested in Springer than in Maxwell, but all the London parties wanted to keep Springer in the British rather than the American camp. Rosbaud was at this time not on the Butterworth payroll, but working for them free-lance. His reports on visits to Springer tended to reach Quennell via Vanden Heuvel, who got to know Robert Maxwell through Whitlock. Rosbaud transferred his considerable editorial talents to Maxwell at a later stage.

Tortuous negotiations secured a three-cornered association of Butterworths, Springer and Maxwell, and in 1949 two new companies were formed: Butterworth-Springer Ltd. (incorporated on 21st April 1949) and Lange, Maxwell and Springer Ltd. (incorporated on 7th September 1949).

The last named company was an export/import bookselling business, in which Butterworths were not participants. (Lange was the manager of Springer Verlag during the war, after Ferdinand and Julius Springer had taken refuge in Switzerland.) The main purpose of this company was to act, with the approval of the Allied Control Commission, as the exclusive selling agent for Springer publications outside Germany. But the company also had a contract to sell the publications of Butterworth-Springer and of Butterworth Scientific Publications Ltd. in all territories except the U.S.A. and Canada. (From May 1950 the U.K., Australia, New Zealand and South Africa were also excluded.) The link between Maxwell and Butterworths was a marketing, not a publishing, link.

The other company, Butterworth-Springer Ltd., was a wholly-owned subsidiary of Butterworths. It was a publishing company, designed to make available the Springer name and the Springer experience. Dr. Rosbaud, who had been Editor of the journal *Research*, returned to work for Butterworth-Springer, which had an editorial staff of four, but in all other respects was

---

* It was hoped to take over Beilstein's *Handbuch der organischen Chemie* from Springer, and to prevent it from becoming an American publication. In the event Springer continued to publish 'Beilstein' themselves, and a pirated American edition of the first two volumes had to be withdrawn.

serviced by Butterworth Scientific Publications Ltd.

This tripartite partnership between Butterworths, Springer and Maxwell was short-lived.

In the summer of 1950, according to Ron Watson, 'it became clear that Butterworth-Springer worked more to the advantage of Springer than Butterworths'; he adds: 'Springer's long-term intention was obvious'. Watson, as Butterworths' Scientific Sales Manager, prepared a report 'as a result of which Henry and I went to Berlin to talk to Lange and Ferdinand Springer. Our reception was cool and on our return Henry recommended that Butterworth-Springer be dissolved.'

In December 1950 a further meeting was held between Dr. Springer and representatives of Butterworths 'to consider the principles which should govern the severance of Butterworth-Springer from Butterworths'. It was agreed in May 1951 that the Butterworth interest should be purchased by Robert Maxwell, and that the name of Butterworth-Springer Ltd. should be changed to Pergamon Press Ltd. Butterworths received a net payment of £13,000. They waived a debt of £23,547 owed by Butterworth-Springer to Butterworths. In effect, therefore, Butterworths wrote off £10,547 on its adventure with Maxwell and Springer.

The stock of titles published by Butterworth-Springer was handed over to Pergamon Press, and arrangements were made for the completion of books in progress. The books which thus formed the beginning of the Pergamon list were:

Progress in Biophysics
Progress in Nuclear Physics
Progress in Metal Physics (except Volumes I and II which
    remained with Butterworths)
Introductory Statistics
Metallurgical Thermochemistry

Pergamon also took over three journals:

*Spectrochimica Acta**
Journal of Atmospheric and Terrestrial Physics
Geochimica et Cosmochimica Acta

Rosbaud went with Butterworth-Springer, where he started the Pergamon list on Springer lines, publishing journals whose content overlapped, like tiles on a roof, and a series of post-graduate books. Eric Buckley, a Butterworth employee (now

---

* Count Vanden Heuvel acquired *Spectrochimica Acta* for Butterworths from
  the Vatican.

Printer to the University of Oxford), became Pergamon's Production Manager.

There was no break between Butterworths and Maxwell at this stage.* Lange, Maxwell and Springer continued to market the Butterworth list in certain overseas territories for some years. But the influence of the Count and his friends on the activities of Butterworths declined steadily from this period.

The scientific publishing done by Butterworths in the immediate post-war years consisted firstly of the journal *Research*, the policy of which was set out in Sir John Anderson's editorial in the first issue, published in October 1947. It was not to be a journal of pure research, nor was it to be 'a mere organ of applied research'; its aim was to reduce the time lag 'between initial research and practical development based upon it...by the creation of a greater awareness of possibilities on the part of all concerned'. This broad and high-flown approach was reflected in the articles in the first issue, e.g. 'Chemical Regulators for Plant Growth'; 'Metallic Creep'; 'Polarographic Cystine and Protein Tests'.

By the second meeting of the Advisory Board, in January 1947, Butterworths were also ready with a programme of books. Two were given priority – Dr. C. E. H. Bawn's book on *The Chemistry of the High Polymers*, and Dr. C. J. Smithells's *Metals Reference Book*. The former had been offered conditionally on publication by August 1947; it appeared in July 1948, and was the first scientific book to be published by Butterworths. It was a book of very high reputation, and the fact that it only just broke even confirms retrospective suspicion that prestige may have overshadowed profit-potential. Professor Bawn remained a good friend of Butterworths, and was later Chairman of the Editorial Board for the journal *Polymer*. Through Liverpool associations he introduced the enormously successful Wood and Holliday books – *Organic Chemistry*, *Inorganic Chemistry*, and *Physical Chemistry*, by C. W. Wood and A. K. Holliday – which became widely used in schools, technical colleges and universities in the 1960s, and are still leaders in their subjects.

The *Metals Reference Book* appeared in 1949. The first edition of this also made a loss. The second edition, such are the vicissitudes of the market, succeeded in spite (or perhaps because) of the doubling of the price. Two more successful editions followed. It has become a classic in its field, and still

---

* Butterworths had no connection (other than as a trade creditor) with Maxwell's unsuccessful attempt, at this period, to rebuild the Simpkin, Marshall wholesaling business. But it was Whitlock who suggested the venture to Maxwell, and introduced him to the Pitman brothers, from whose company he bought Simpkin, Marshall.

sells in substantial numbers. Dr. Smithells, who produced all four editions, was described in his obituary in *The Times* of 12th April 1977 as 'a giant in the metallurgical world for over half-a-century'.

Fourteen books were published between 1948 and 1950. By the end of 1955 these books showed a loss of £3,250 before write-off, and in addition stock to the value of £6,700 had been written off. That would not have been Stanley Bond's idea of successful publishing. The editorial concept was good; the financial management was poor. The scientific publishing staff numbered four at the beginning of 1947; by August 1948 it had grown to fifteen.

The publishing of scientific journals was no more successful. In the autumn of 1947 Butterworths bought the journal *Fuel*, owned and edited by Dr. Lessing. The price was less than £1000, the journal having made a loss of £19 in 1946. Dr. Lessing continued for a period as consulting editor. No doubt Butterworths hoped that by the means of their sales organisation, and after the appointment of a Fellow of the Royal Society, Sir Alfred Egerton, as Editor in October 1948, the journal would become profitable. Like *Research*, it certainly made Butterworths better known. But by 1955 there was a cumulative loss of £18,000 on *Research* and £2,500 on *Fuel*.

In the summer of 1950 two men who were to make their names in the world of scientific publishing joined Butterworths. Ron Watson started as Scientific Sales Manager on 1st June and Charles Hutt as Scientific Publishing Manager on 1st July.

The Watson/Hutt set up was unwieldy and well-nigh unworkable. With Quennell gone there was no single Chief Executive. Whitlock and Emery were Joint Managing Directors; neither had a background in scientific publishing. Hutt reported to John Whitlock (the director responsible for publishing); Watson to Harry Henry (the group Sales Manager) and through him to Seabrook Emery. Watson was with the company twelve months before even meeting Whitlock.

The discreet use of 'Copy to . . .' ensured that a note was seen by those whom the writer wished to inform. But it was not certain (or even necessarily intended) that the answer would be given by the person to whom the note was addressed, or that the answer would be addressed to the writer of the original note.

Watson's sales responsibilities did not include promotion, which continued in the hands of Jim Marsden, who reported direct to Henry. Watson describes his situation thus:

'I had only three books to sell in addition to the very recondite *Fuel* and the unsaleable *Research*. I was excluded from all promotion, except the provision of mailing lists, and from all financial information and direct participation in print orders or prices. I never knew what gross profit was expected or received, nor was I asked for any budget or forecast.'

One of Watson's first tasks was to try to improve Butterworths' relations with the book trade, and his insistence on higher trade discounts provided his first clash with the hierarchy. (The discount on legal practitioner works was then 10%, and on legal encyclopaedias nil.)

The scientific publishing and editorial functions, though organised separately from legal, had a specious resemblance. Hutt imitated the legal side in that he built up a large staff of sub-editors and draftsmen, reaching a total of thirty-five by 1956. Commercially the scientific list could not sustain a staff of that size. But there was a fundamental difference between that and the even larger legal staff. A high proportion of those on the legal side were qualified lawyers or law graduates who were engaged in writing (or at least re-writing) the big encyclopaedias and services. The medical and scientific staff consisted largely of sub-editors who had grown up as proof-readers.

Hutt had as his qualified advisers the Scientific Advisory Board, but he, like Watson after him, found the system unwieldy and the advice of little practical value. He relied to a large extent on Professor Tomkins of Imperial College, Secretary of the Faraday Society.

Watson kept colliding with Henry, and Hutt with Whitlock. An uneasy system of project evaluation was evolved. Ideas for new titles came from both the publishing and sales sides. John Whitlock, as Publishing Director, made the final decision. Nothing took place which could be described as serious market research. The Butterworth approach, which had succeeded in the precisely identifiable legal markets, was not transferable to the scientific market.

A consultation process was devised in 1955–56 by the establishment of a monthly meeting. The Managing Directors took the chair in turn, and members were instructed to 'arrange their appointments so as not to clash with these meetings'. But decisions continued to be taken outside the meetings. Only eight were held.

At one period Hutt was given a mandate to amalgamate the medical and scientific editorial departments. The Medical Editor (Dr. Hesketh) and Medical Publishing Manager (Jack Burgess) not unnaturally opposed this. Burgess was asked by

Whitlock to document the disadvantages of a merger, and to prepare detailed plans for the separate reorganisation of medical editorial. Burgess's plan was adopted, without discussion.

In August 1956 Charles Hutt left Butterworths to join Pergamon Press, from which he transferred not long afterwards to Academic Press of which he was to become U.K. Managing Director. Ron Watson took over responsibility for publishing as well as sales. A unified control was once more possible. Watson was responsible to both Emery and Whitlock, as appropriate, via Henry who by then had been made General Manager.

In spite of internal dissensions a substantial list was built up during the 1950s. It consisted mainly of single-volume, short-life monographs and text-books at all levels in chemistry, physics, biological sciences and engineering. It established a fine reputation in some subjects. For example when gas chromatography was in vogue Butterworths published several text-books and symposia with good results. They also became, and still are, successful in information science. A notable 'first' in this period was Booth and Booth's *Automatic Digital Calculators*, the first book to be published in the new field of computers.

Books in the post-graduate field, if well chosen, produce immediate turnover and profit, but seldom lead to a steady income from new editions (in this they differ from college texts). Continuity arises not so much from new editions, as from concentration on well-defined fields. But the Butterworth list never displayed a thought-out publishing policy; instead it appeared opportunist.

Sales in the United States were of growing importance to the scientific list. Harry Henry as General Manager was fully alert to this, as was Sheila Carey, his personal assistant, to whom he delegated this work. (Sheila joined Butterworths as Stanley Bond's assistant secretary in 1940, and became in due course Publishing Director of both medical and scientific lists.) But the effect which American needs should have on list-building and on content was for long underestimated in relation to scientific books.

The Butterworth tradition of major work publishing found expression in the scientific field with *Chemical Engineering Practice* in eleven volumes, published between 1956 and 1965. A company called Chemindex Ltd. was acquired, and continued to publish its multi-volume loose-leaf *Faraday Encyclopaedia of Hydrocarbon Compounds* under the Butterworth imprint. Butterworths also became publishers to the International Union of Pure and Applied Chemistry, producing their Journal and their Proceedings in bound volumes.

Another co-operative venture was *Documentation of Molecular*

Sheila Carey, 1979, at the launching party for Scott-Brown's *Diseases of the Ear, Nose and Throat*, 4th edn. With her the editors of the new edition, both consultants at the Royal Free Hospital: John Groves (left) and John Ballantyne (right). Also two of those responsible for the sub-editing: Glen Hughes (left) and Sue Deeley (right). (Photograph by Neil Wigley)

Spectroscopy published in conjunction with Verlag Chemie of Germany. This was an index of rim-punched cards giving information on some 25,000 chemical compounds (including the infra-red spectral diagram).

Facsmile reprints of out-of-print learned journals (e.g. the *Transactions of the Faraday Society*, and the *Journal of the Chemical Society*) were undertaken as joint ventures with the Johnson Reprint Corporation of New York, a subsidiary of Walter Johnson's Academic Press. As libraries gained funds to rebuild their war-damaged collections, this became a highly successful undertaking.

It was Butterworths' deliberate policy to produce the Proceedings of learned conferences, although these did not bring immediate profit. They gave introductions to potential authors, and were the quickest way to get the company known among scientists.

Butterworths produced (and still do) the *British Union Catalogue of Periodicals* and the *World List of Scientific Periodicals*, which share a common updating service produced from a computer print-out. The *World List* was responsible for the one profitable year (1952) in the first ten. A union catalogue of music (the first ever attempted) was out of context.

Exactly what was meant by profit was never clear. A memorandum on the 1953 accounts contains the warning: 'No charge is made by the parent company for the staff of the accounts, sales and advertising departments who spend a proportion of their time on the scientific business'. Even with this understatement of overheads, the accounts of Butterworth Scientific Publications Ltd showed a cumulative loss on scientific publishing amounting to £60,929 by 1955, and the amount owing to the parent company was then £158,716. Thereafter the loss was reduced and the business broke even in 1959. To the losses of the 1950s the journal *Research* contributed unfailingly. But it was not until 1962 that the directors decided to cut their losses and end the bold concept launched by Quennell and Vanden Heuvel in 1947.

*   *   *   *   *

Meanwhile medical publishing pursued its course independently of scientific, and much more closely linked with legal. It had been Stanley Bond's last major new development, and was so regarded by his successors. It was no post-war innovation and required no external stimulus. Scientific was new and separate. There was no 'scientific profession', the argument ran, parallel to the 'legal profession' and the 'medical profession'. Lawyers and doctors were both, in the main, practitioners in private practice. But the parallel was in fact illusory. The book buying and reading habits of the lawyer and the doctor are totally different. There are more doctors than lawyers, but there are also more medical than legal publishers.

In India Stanley Bond had published medical text-books since 1918. Encouraged by his experience there, he decided in the early thirties to start medical publishing in England but with a difference. Why not multi-volume reference works parallel to the great legal works on which Butterworths' name had been built?

Publishing of the first such work, the *British Encyclopaedia of Medical Practice* (B.E.M.P.), began in 1936, and Bond lived to see it completed in 1941. Planning of its successor, *British Surgical Practice*, continued during the war, with Sir Ernest Rock Carling and Sir James Paterson Ross as Editors-in-Chief. This work, in nine volumes, was published between 1947 and 1951.

A companion work, *Operative Surgery*, dealing with operative techniques, under the editorship of Charles Rob and Rodney Smith, was published in eight volumes between 1956 and 1958. Each chapter described one operation. Hand-drawn illustrations occupied more space than the text. The drawings illustrated each step from incision to closure and, since the contributors were all leading surgeons in their fields, there was no doubting the authority of the work. It became known as The Bible in some hospitals.

Operative Surgery was part of Bond's grand plan for a series of medical encyclopaedias. He probably had in his mind's eye Chatterji's *Handbook of Operative Surgery*, a one-volume work published by Butterworths in India in 1936; this used the same technique of relying more on the illustrations than the narrative. Whitlock, as Publishing Director, took up the challenge and was adept at enlisting Editors-in-Chief of the highest calibre, and at opening doors, while Jack Burgess,* Medical Publishing Manager from 1950 to 1960, used to good effect the doors opened for him. *Operative Surgery*, more than any other work, was his baby. It was he who saw and contracted authors and artists. He shaped it into what it was, and still is.

The second edition of *Operative Surgery* (1968–1971) was greatly enlarged, totalling fourteen volumes. Whereas the first edition was almost entirely written by authors from the United Kingdom, the second had far more contributors from the Commonwealth countries and from the U.S.A. This policy was urged by the sales staff, and was facilitated by the fact that Charles Rob was by then living in America, as Chairman of the Department of Surgery at the University of Rochester, N.Y. Butterworths thus belatedly recognised the importance of the American market in terms of list-building and content. Jack Burgess had pressed long and fruitlessly for this in the 1950s. The second edition of *Operative Surgery* was planned to facilitate sale of separate volumes as well as sets. A third edition commenced publication in 1976. There have been several imitators, but no real rivals.

Encyclopaedias remained the core of the medical list. *Clinical Surgery*, in sixteen volumes, also edited by Charles Rob and Rodney Smith, replaced Carling and Ross's *British Surgical Practice*. The *Encyclopaedia of General Practice*, edited by Abercrombie and McConaghey, in six volumes, was produced in consultation with the Royal College of General Practitioners. A six-volume work on all aspects of *Cancer*, edited by Ronald

* Much information on the development of the medical list, and on the American office, has been supplied by Jack Burgess, who joined Butterworths in 1947.

Raven, also appeared. A second edition of the *British Encyclopaedia of Medical Practice*, under the editorship of Lord Horder, was published between 1950 and 1953.

Increased specialisation gradually reduced the demand for encyclopaedias, and text-books assumed greater importance. Butterworths' first standard text-book was Willis's *Pathology of Tumours* (1948); new editions and other books by this eminent pathologist followed. Perhaps the most outstanding of these text-books is Jeffcoate's *Principles of Gynaecology*, first published in 1957, and now in its fifth edition. An early triumph was the publication of *Penicillin*, edited by Sir Alexander Fleming, in 1946.

During the 1950s the editorial contacts formed during the production of B.E.M.P. and *Operative Surgery* helped the establishment of the text-book list. Authors came to Butterworths, or if approached reacted favourably.

Two medical series were planned by Butterworths' staff and advisers. The volumes of the *Modern Trends Series*, each dealing with a particular speciality, contained articles by experts from many countries, particularly the U.S.A. The series was not however designed to provide a steady flow of reprints and new editions. The *Modern Practice Series*, pitched at a slightly lower level, was less successful. But out of one volume, Evans's *Modern Practice in Anaesthesia*, 1949, grew the authoritative *General Anaesthesia*, the fourth edition of which was published recently. Scott-Brown's *Diseases of the Ear, Nose and Throat*, now in four volumes, has a similar ancestry.

If quality were the sole criterion, Butterworths' medical list has been distinguished since the beginning of the 1950s by the innovation of the encyclopaedia idea, the eminence of the authors, and the high standard of the production of its leading text-books. Much of the credit for the high standard of production must go to the Production Manager, E. C. Featherstone (and to his successors Allan Cook and John Carruthers). In the legal field the problems of design and printing technique were few; in the medical field the expertise of the department was used to the full.

Medicine was still a very junior partner in Butterworths. Other medical publishers had the support of long-established imprints, specialist sales organisations and above all their back-lists. In 1960 negotiations were initiated which could have brought all these to Butterworths. On 10th February 1960 the then Chairman of Butterworths (the Earl of Rothes) reported to the Board that:

'conversations had taken place with E. & S. Livingstone

Limited in connection with the possible purchase by Butterworths of that business. He had informed Mr. Charles Macmillan (the Chairman of Livingstones) that he would be prepared to recommend to the Board of Butterworths that, subject to the fullest investigation, an offer of £180,000 be made for all the shares in Livingstones. Mr. Macmillan had returned to Edinburgh to consult his colleagues and had suggested that he himself would like a seat on the Board of Butterworths if the deal went through. The Chairman agreed that this might be possible in due course.'

At the next meeting the Board were informed that the negotiations had been called off 'as unforeseen difficulties had arisen on their [Livingstone's] side'. There was a gap of £20,000 between the price asked and the amount offered by Butterworths. It is hard to credit that this constituted an 'unforeseen difficulty' or that it would have been impossible to agree a figure. The real difficulty lay in Macmillan's request for a directorship. Macmillan was furious at the suggestion that he would have to 'see how he got on' as a senior executive first. It was then seventeen years since Butterworths had appointed a working executive to its Board.

The whole history of Butterworths' medical list would have been different if the two businesses had been amalgamated in 1960. Livingstones' pre-eminence in clinical pre-qualification text-books would have provided a back-list and regular new editions, to complement Butterworths' strength in practitioner text-books and encyclopaedias. Livingstones later joined forces with Churchills, and they are now part of the Longman Group.

The manning of the medical editorial department during the first twenty-five years of its existence shows a gradual movement away from the professional Doctor-Editor towards the professional publisher. The first three Chief Medical Editors were doctors – Newfield, Adam Clark, and Hay-Scott. They were also managers and reported directly to Bond or Whitlock. After the war first Dr. Garland and subsequently Dr. Hesketh had a Publishing Manager, Lloyd, to control the department and process manuscripts. When Lloyd left in 1950 he was succeeded as Medical Publishing Manager by Jack Burgess, who had been the senior sub-editor. Dr. Hesketh concentrated more and more on editorial matters, and from his departure in 1955 Jack Burgess was seen to be clearly in charge. Jack Burgess was the Publisher, reporting direct to Whitlock, the Joint Managing Director responsible for publishing. Harry Henry as General Manager was the buffer when administrative or financial matters involved Emery, the other Joint Managing Director.

*   *   *   *   *

The growing importance of medicine and science pointed inexorably to America. Medicine is international to a greater degree than law, and the habit of treating the medical market as parallel to the legal led to unwarranted reliance on home sales. But in that one particular area Butterworth executives were, during the 1950s, becoming increasingly aware of a serious gap in the publishing and selling programme. The United States was not significant to Butterworths so long as they were only legal publishers. Though the U.S. legal system is based on the common law, it has diverged so far that English legal books are needed only for research and for use by lawyers with international practices. But with the development of medical, scientific and technical lists, the exploitation of the United States market became indispensable.

For thirty years, from 1945 to 1975 – with an interval from 1960 to 1967 – Butterworths' books were sold in the U.S. by other publishers. Carswells (a partly owned associate of Sweet and Maxwell) had for many years a sole agency for legal books in the U.S. and thereafter shared the market with a number of U.S. firms. (It was not until 1972 that the Canadian company in Toronto began selling legal books direct into the U.S.). Some of the medical and scientific concessions were for the whole list, or for a defined portion of the list, while others related to particular books. Many American publishers were eager to market Butterworth publications, sometimes with their own name on the title page.

Among U.S. publishers who handled Butterworth books at one time or another were:

Academic Press
Appleton-Century-Croft
Archon Books
Matthew Bender
Crowell-Collier-Macmillan
Lippincott
Little, Brown
C. V. Mosby
Prentice-Hall
Van Nostrand
John Wiley (and Interscience Publishers)

Even so, sales to the United States took up much time of Butterworths' top management. Lawrence Jones visited the States in 1945, and John Whitlock the following year. Quennell was a regular transatlantic traveller. By 1952 it had almost become an annual event for either Whitlock or Henry or both. Between the two of them they must have made the acquaintance of nearly all the medical and many of the scientific publishing personalities of the day in the United States. John Whitlock also became interested in the prospects of legal publishing in America and, although this did not come to fruition, a number of contacts were made. Did those eager travellers have a genuinely international enterprise in view, or did they look upon the United States as an extension of the U.K. market?

During the mid-fifties it became the ambition of John Whitlock to publish a multi-volume medical encyclopaedia for American lawyers concerned with personal accident and medical negligence cases. He made lengthy attempts to interest American law publishers, particularly Matthew Bender, with one of whose executives, John Bender, he had a personal friendship. Ultimately a consortium was set up consisting of Butterworths, a small American publishing house called the Central Book Co., and Dr. Paul Cantor (one of the few people qualified in both medicine and law), who became Editor-in-Chief; the work duly appeared as *Traumatic Medicine and Surgery for the Attorney* (T.M.S.A.).

The leg-work was done by Jack Burgess, at that time Medical Publishing Manager in London. It involved, he recalls:

'first the gathering together of a team of the highest-ranking attorneys (plaintiff and defense), then the detailed analysis of their needs, then the creation of an equally powerful medical editorial board, and finally the recruitment of a large group of doctors and surgeons who would write or rewrite material according to a master plan. The majority of these groups had to be American, and it must be remembered U.S. doctors are very reluctant to write anything for a work which can be quoted in a malpractice suit. The task necessitated numerous visits to the U.S. between 1957 and 1960. I really lost count of them; it could have been ten or twelve or more. I do know that in those years I accumulated enough miles to qualify me as a member of the half-a-million mile club – quite an achievement in those days. I saw doctors and attorneys at their offices, at airports, in hotels, wherever, whenever.'

Burgess, having seen a legal editor, Ian Mail, sent to Toronto in 1956 to manage the Canadian office, determined to aim at an overseas managership. On Henry's advice he briefed himself in accounting and made his ambitions known. The close relations he built up with American doctors over T.M.S.A. attracted him to the American scene. He repeatedly included in his reports to Whitlock the question 'When will Butterworths publish American authors in America?'

As early as 1945 the Board had considered the possibility of selling the English medical encyclopaedias directly into the States. The idea came up again in 1956 in relation to the scientific list, and some research took place. The directors decided then that setting up a Butterworth organisation in the United States would involve 'unwarranted expense'.

In the following years there was a change of heart: Whitlock, Henry, Watson and Burgess all visited America, and the first three, like Burgess, commented on American opportunities. (Watson recalls that he recommended Boston, Pittsburgh or Philadelphia, in that order, as the place for a Butterworth office.) The upshot was that on 7th May 1959 the Chairman and the Joint Managing Directors submitted a memorandum to the Board in which they observed that Butterworths were the only major scientific publishers without both U.K. and U.S. offices and that this 'will soon begin to affect us adversely when approaching potential authors'. They concluded that 'an American venture is essential and that in 1960 we should set up our own selling and publishing organisation in the U.S. in a small way to commence with'. They recognised that 'the cost is likely to be very great and the prospects are by no means certain. The market is, of course, enormous, competition is intense, and the risk considerable'. They estimated a capital outlay of £100,000 spread over six years.

Jack Burgess was not involved in the discussion which followed. It came as a surprise to him and everyone not on the Board when he was invited to head the new undertaking. The secrecy was nearly as great as that which surrounded Elliott's emigration to Canada fifty years earlier. Jack never saw the background papers, nor was he told of the £100,000 estimate of initial costs.

On 8th June 1960 Emery was able to report to the Board that Butterworth Inc. had been incorporated, and that Jack Burgess was on the spot looking for offices. Despite other recommendations the spot selected was Washington, D.C., with the intention of being near Dr. Paul Cantor. The national capital was devoid of any pool of experienced publishing staff, and outside the mainstream of American publishing. The printing facilities were restricted, but at least, so it was thought, there would be little competition for those which existed. Washington was, moreover, convenient for shipments via Baltimore. Opinions differ as to whether the choice of location in the end affected the outcome.

More serious than the question of location was the question

of purpose. Was the new company to sell English books or publish American books or both? It is easy to say that the directors in London were more interested in the former, and Jack Burgess in the latter. What is certain is that the directors' plans were not clear; whatever plans they did have were equally certainly not made clear to Burgess.

Eighteen years later he wrote: 'So on 1st June 1960 I left for America. It is indicative of the lack of planning that when I left my American salary had not been settled; there was no blueprint for my activities; no estimate of costs; no decided location; no feasibility study. It was Whitlock playing the game by ear as far as I was concerned.' If there were a long-term plan it looks, in retrospect, as if it was to deal initially with medical and then with scientific books, and to be a publishing as well as a marketing outlet. Legal books could follow, for sales purposes, even if there was no local legal publishing.

The decision to appoint an editor rather than a salesman could be criticised only if the development of a local list was not intended. By now all the most successful overseas branches of British publishing houses were depending largely on local publishing.

Discussions took place between Sheila Carey and Jack Burgess as to selling arrangements, before Burgess left for America, and existing agencies were terminated. But stock began to arrive in Washington before he had a warehouse to put it in.

The brunt of the work on T.M.S.A. was intended to be borne by Dr. Cantor and the Central Book Co. However, Burgess, in view of his previous involvement, took a substantial part, and this was greatly increased when the Central Book Co. withdrew after the first two volumes. Butterworths now had but one partner in T.M.S.A. and Burgess had three hats to wear: he was building up an American list; he was selling the U.K. list in America; and he was Publishing Editor of a major work.

It may well be that, in spite of the labours of Dr. Cantor and his American associates, the work smacked too much of its English origin. It may be that the American lawyers are not so preoccupied with 'accident cases' as the media may suggest. Whatever the reason T.M.S.A., though it covered prime cost, did not make a profit commensurate with the amount of the management time and energy consumed, both in the U.K. and in America.

Meanwhile in London Jack Burgess's departure was the opportunity to revive the plan (which had been frustrated by Burgess in the days of Charles Hutt) to unite the scientific and medical departments. But whereas the earlier plan related only to the editorial aspect, the 1960 reorganisation applied also to production, to sales and advertising; and even to the order-processing and invoicing functions. Ron Watson was put in charge of the whole operation, thus reaching the summit of his influence at Butterworths.

Watson now reported directly to Emery or Whitlock (according to function), and no longer through Harry Henry. This was the second time that Scientific Sales had been taken out of Henry's control. In 1949 Hugh Quennell had established a Scientific Department under Rex Foy, complete with its own sales organisation; this arrangement only lasted a year. The 1960 reorganisation lasted slightly longer – until October 1963. On both occasions control subsequently passed back to Henry.

Henry was, however, responsible for the Washington office, just as he was for the other overseas offices. The close relation between Washington and the Scientific and Medical Division was not reflected in the chain of command. Sheila Carey now devoted her whole time to American Sales, being replaced as personal assistant to Harry Henry by David Perry, returned from South Africa. Sheila needed all her tact in dealing amicably with a Scientific and Medical Division which was not responsible to the General Manager, and a U.S. office which was.

This set-up could not be tolerable to Henry as General Manager of Butterworths and the natural successor to Whitlock and Emery, who were nearing retirement. He planned to regain control; Emery and Whitlock discussed the situation with each other, and each independently (and secretly) discussed it with Watson. One appointment at that time seemed to strengthen the independence of the Scientific and Medical Division; Lord Leslie, the son of the then Chairman, was made Sales Manager under Watson. (Leslie had joined Butterworths in 1952 at the age of twenty, and had recently been in charge of the legal representatives.) Watson found him able and likeable, and a potential successor to himself.

Watson was now feeling his own position to be uncertain. Whitlock was to retire at the end of 1961, and this could leave Watson vulnerable, if a new Publishing Director pressed for a different set-up. He sought assurances from Emery and Whitlock and discussed the possibility of a seat on the Board. He was told that Butterworths was essentially a legal publisher, and that the composition of the Board would always reflect the major interest. This does not confirm the optimism of a confidential memorandum which Emery drafted in March 1960 and which he planned to send to Henry and Watson, among others. This referred to:

'. . . the scientific and medical side for which there is enormous scope, especially overseas – such scope indeed that in ten years or less it may well equal in size and importance our legal business.'

Watson took his rebuff as the amber light, and left to become at first Editorial Director and later Managing Director of John Wiley & Sons' U.K. company. He was succeeded, as he expected, and indeed recommended, by Lord Leslie.

The Scientific and Medical Division lasted little over three years. Its dissolution forms part of the developments at Board level described in Chapter 12. In the winter of 1963–4 production, sales, order-processing and invoicing all came again under the same management as legal.

In one respect however the 1960 set-up left its mark. After its demise there continued to be a single Publishing Manager for the two lists. Ron Watson had been succeeded in 1962 by David Jollands, and he was followed in 1967 by Sheila Carey. Sheila had been involved with the medical programme for a long time as Harry Henry's assistant.

These Publishing Managers were supported by a series of Editors and Managers who supervised the work of the internal staff, and assisted in the commissioning of books. The division of labour was sometimes by functions, and sometimes by sections of the list. As one Editor was tempted away by another publisher, he was succeeded by the next in line, or a re-arrangement of duties covered the gap.

On the medical side the first Editor was Leslie Rayner, who had been Burgess's No. 2 (and is now Managing Director of Applied Science Publishers). But the position of Medical Editor was less senior than that of Jack Burgess who, as Medical Publishing Manager, reported directly to Whitlock, a member of the main Board.

Medical publishing was maintained during the next ten years or so on the foundations laid by Jack Burgess. He speaks in a recent letter of

'a period during which I travelled the U.K. extensively, knocking on doors, and finding out what was required and who should write it. A primary sort of market research resulted in close (and still existing) ties with the leading people in medicine.'

But there was little expansion after Burgess's departure.

The gap left by Burgess was not filled by the Doctor-Editor. And from 1962 Butterworths ceased to employ a doctor on their full-time staff.

The U.S.A. experiment lasted a little longer than the Scientific and Medical Division. But by 1964 the loss on Washington, as recorded in the books, was about £185,000 (more than the £100,000 initial costs anticipated before the venture was launched). Time-consuming demands from London for detailed statistics, and insistence on the reconciliation of London and Washington records, did not go to the root of the matter, and London did not identify the reasons for the continuing losses.

There are two ways in which an overseas company may be made profitable. One is to increase the 'mark-up' of local prices (Butterworths already converted at $4 to the £): the other is to increase the discount given by the parent company (which can often merely lead to a reduction in the parent's profits). Butterworths did neither. The financial problems of inter-company accounting, to which Leader had drawn attention in 1939, had still not been fully worked out.

In 1963 Richard Millett became Chairman of the parent company, and the U.S. company came increasingly under fire from him. During 1964 and 1965 the future of Washington was under continuous review, and Board resolutions only gave temporary reprieves. Jack Burgess visited London for 'consultations' – but London meant by this contingency plans for discontinuance, while he sought ways of resuscitation.

Burgess was embarrassed by postponed commitments to potential authors; 'several publishers', he writes, 'benefitted from the crop of books we had nurtured, but finally rejected'. He was isolated from London politics, and felt totally thwarted in his ambition to develop the local publishing programme (which he was convinced was the route to profitability); his search for pastures new was the natural result of this frustration. He found what he wanted (in Academic Press) in March 1966. His resignation reached Millett on 26th April. Burgess's departure was for Millett the opportunity he needed to close down and cut the company's losses.

David Kingham was lifted abruptly from commercial books, and appointed as caretaker 'Executive Vice-President'. His brief was to wind up the office, and make other arrangements for marketing. He was assisted by John Pope and David Jackson from the accounts department. Kingham produced plans for continuing a slimmed-down operation. But politically there was no going on – Richard Millett was cleaning up Butterworths, and loss-makers had to go. Harry Henry, the only director who had been prepared to fight for the continuance of the Washington venture, had resigned from the U.K. Board and gone to Australia in October 1965.

On 6th March 1967 it was announced that Butterworths were

amalgamating their two North American offices in Toronto. By
then American losses were approaching the quarter-million: it
is hard in a close-down operation to prevent further, and
sometimes faster, losses. David Kingham returned to London;
the Washington office was vacated in April 1967; David
Jackson went to Toronto for three months to help with the
transfer. Toronto took over the books published by Washington,
and distributed those London books which no U.S. publisher
wanted. All the best books were again entrusted to agents in the
U.S. This was irksome to the Canadian management. In 1970
when Dennis Beech, who was in charge there, complained about
having to sell 'all the dregs', he was urged to concentrate his
mind on the Canadian legal business.

Butterworths' return to the United States as a major publisher
had to wait until a new management was in power.

Although Butterworths, by the time of Watson's departure in
1961 and Burgess's transfer to America in the previous year,
were firmly established as scientific and medical publishers,
those programmes were a dinghy towed in the wake of the
company's legal flagship. In the 1960s Butterworths lost ground
as medical publishers; this can be attributed to insufficient
concentration of resources and attention – scientific at that time
looked so much more exciting. But both medical and scientific
publishing were at a disadvantage in comparison with competing imprints because of Butterworths' tradition that the
techniques and style of legal publishing were transferable to
wholly different fields. But above all it seems in retrospect that
what was lacking was a determined and experienced personality
at the top to drive and to lead – a Stanley Bond of science.

Chapter 9

Legal Publishing after 1943

For over thirty-five years after the death of Stanley Bond legal publishing was directed by three people, who were all Bond's own appointees – John Whitlock, K.J., and Simon Partridge. All three started as text-book editors. Whitlock retired at the end of 1961 and K.J. in 1974. Simon Partridge has been Legal Publishing Director since 1967.* Bred in the Bond tradition, they saw the maintenance of the major work cycle as their prime concern, with a supporting programme of practitioner and student text-books, and with controlled ventures into disciplines allied to law.†

In 1944 Whitlock summed up his policy in these words:

'The Company's success has been due to its Major Works conceived and carried through by the late Chairman and if we are to maintain not only that success but develop we must concentrate our main activities on Major Works and on the more expensive Text Books.'

Neither Hugh Quennell nor Richard Millett (who ran Butterworths from 1963 to 1967) did anything to change that priority. Individual publications were initiated by them, and they brought pressure where they thought it needed. But they wisely made no basic change in the recipe for Butterworths'

---

* Whitlock, while he was Joint Managing Director from 1950 to 1961, continued to be the director in charge of publishing. No new appointment was made on his retirement. K.J., having been Publishing Manager from 1946, was made Legal Publishing Director in 1964; after he became Deputy Managing Director in 1967, he shared the responsibility for legal publishing with Partridge until 1971.
  Imprecision in nomenclature never led to confusion over who had to do the work.
† Projects in mind in 1944, but not brought to fruition at that period, included: Encyclopaedia for Accountants, Encyclopaedia for Banking, Encyclopaedia for Industry, Butterworth Road Book, Major work on Military Strategy, Major work on Patents, McCurdy's Investments. A major work on patents, by Walton and Laddie, was published in 1978, and an encyclopaedia on banking is in preparation at the time of writing.

prosperity. In 1944 the major works, and the other subscription works (the *All England Law Reports* and the *Emergency Legislation Service*), provided 75% of the legal revenue, and an even higher proportion of the profits. The proportions are little different today.

Whether or not Stanley Bond consciously developed the idea of a 'cycle', he certainly achieved it. Legal encyclopaedias were published throughout his life in rotation and overlapping. But his successors rationalised the plan in the documents they prepared for Hugh Quennell in 1944 and 1945. From then onwards the idea of the 'major work cycle' was firmly implanted in the mind of the management.

The Sales Director, Lawrence Jones, addressed three memoranda to his colleagues in January 1944. The first was based on a survey of stocks, and indicated new editions and reprints needed during the year. The second described sales requirements in relation to major works (three volumes of *Encyclopaedia of Forms and Precedents*; two volumes of *Court Forms*; and three volumes of *Words and Phrases*); it also surveyed the prospects for new major works. The third recorded the accuracy of the sales forecast made in the previous March, which had been exceeded by 14%.

Whitlock reacted in May 1944 with a mammoth document covering the years 1944 to 1953; this discussed, in ninety-three pages of typescript devoted to law and sixty-six devoted to medicine, all the publications he was planning. It included views expressed by Stanley Bond, Lawrence Jones and others. It hoped for peace by the end of 1944 and envisaged a new edition of *Halsbury's Statutes* between 1946 and 1950, and of *Halsbury's Laws* starting at the end of 1951. These dates all proved to be about one year early.

This document formed the basis for discussion over the next twelve months. Quennell produced his comments on 13th February 1945. Lawrence Jones replied the next day. He followed it up by detailed sales forecasts extending to 1956, which were submitted to the Board on 23rd March 1945. In this report there appears the concept of the 'phoenix date', when 'each work, purged of any discovered weakness, arises like the Phoenix to a new life from the ashes of its earlier self'.

Whitlock's plan of May 1944 not only goes into considerable editorial detail, but contains financial information as to editorial and production costs, sometimes converted into a 'number to cover cost'. The Lawrence Jones document gives the sales forecast. Neither discuss overheads, nor do they give indications of gross or net profit. Even taken together they are not comparable to a modern business plan, but they were new to

Butterworths which had been built 'by guess and by God'.

The reliance on the major work cycle, and the extent of the planning and revision (and indeed original writing) done inside the house produced its own staffing structure. A series of small 'cells' each dealt with a particular publication or group of publications. Each was headed by a qualified legal practitioner (except for the department dealing with text-books). In the early Bond days these sectional heads had been responsible direct to Bellew as General Manager/Managing Director. In 1937 this overall control was given to Whitlock, who like Bellew was a business man rather than a legal practitioner. John Burke (the senior full-time professional lawyer and Assistant Managing Editor of *Halsbury's Laws of England*, 2nd Edn.) had not joined in the 'conspiracy' which resulted in Bellew's ultimate downfall, and he was passed over. He departed to Hamish Hamilton (Law Books), and moved to Sweet and Maxwell a few years later, eventually becoming Chairman of that company.

By 1945 Whitlock was clearly in need of a second-in-command. The lawyer Editors of individual publications were of a high calibre: W. J. Williams on the *All England Law Reports* and the *Encyclopaedia of Forms and Precedents*: N. P. Shannon on the *Emergency Legislation Service* and *Atkin's Court Forms*. But they had no responsibility outside their own publications. It was then decided to create a new post of Chief Legal Editor who would have a roving commission over all the company's publications, and would be concerned with administration as well as content. Shannon was given the post.

A high opinion of Shannon's editorial ability was generally held, but there were doubts as to his administrative qualities. This has been a recurring problem for Butterworths. When K.J. returned from agricultural work to law publishing in May 1946 the dissatisfaction of Quennell and Whitlock with Shannon's managerial capacity was clear. About a month later it was agreed to create a new office of Publishing Manager; K.J. was offered this for a trial period, and held it until he became an executive director in 1964. Shannon was persuaded by his colleagues not to oppose the division of his responsibilities. But the dividing line was never made clear. Shannon continued in the truncated post for nine months; he then emigrated to become a partner in a legal firm in East Africa, and died there not many years later.

Whitlock and K.J. both had law degrees. Other publishing executives on the legal side have had neither law degrees nor professional legal qualifications. The appointment of Shannon, an academic lawyer, as Whitlock's No. 2 was out of line. Editorial and commercial skills are seldom found in the same person. The practice of Butterworths has been to use the lawyer for editorial functions, but to use non-lawyers for top management, a practice not shared by other legal publishers. Butterworths were not very successful in finding good management, but their success in finding good editors ensured the continuing prosperity of the business.

Shannon was succeeded in 1947 by J. T. Edgerley, a Chancery barrister, known to Quennell from army days.* Edgerley was at that time employed in the Parliamentary Draftsman's Department, and was also, with their approval, free-lance Editor of the *Law Journal*. He was not a Quennell nomination. He had worked for Butterworths some ten years previously, both as one of the Editorial Board of *Atkin's Court Forms* and as a contributor of some of the earlier titles of that work. Whitlock wisely proposed a candidate he knew to be acceptable, not only for his superb encyclopaedic mind and memory, but because he was *persona grata* to Quennell.

Once again the division of the responsibilities between the Publishing Manager and the Chief Legal Editor was not spelt out – or rather the two were given conflicting accounts of their duties. Whitlock was all things to all men: he believed in 'divide and rule'. There were no service contracts in Butterworths then, but more significantly there were no job specifications. This omission suited the current style of management admirably.

Despite Whitlock's genuine desire that Butterworth publications should be good in all respects, including quality of content, he was first and foremost concerned with output and the maintaining of programmes. Furthermore he was not in any real sense a lawyer. These qualities in Whitlock produced a galling relationship with the Editor. According to Jack Edgerley 'he did not give one information that one should have been given, if the title of "Chief Legal Editor" was to be anything but a name'. K.J. felt more closely in Whitlock's confidence.

Nevertheless Edgerley and K.J. subsequently agreed (the words are Edgerley's) that:

'despite the seeds of conflict inherent in allocating responsibility for time to a publishing manager and responsibility for quality of content to a legal editor, the manager and editor continued peacefully in the business for over twenty years.'

When K.J. became Publishing Manager in 1946 he found

---

* Quennell frequently used Edgerley's army nick-name, 'Rollicking Jack', an unlikely name which Butterworth colleagues never adopted. It was originated, according to Jack himself, during a tedious time at Bulford Camp during World War II, by a commanding officer on watching a series of flukes which made a successful break at billiards.

already in existence an efficient 'cell' under Simon Partridge dealing with the practitioner and student text-books. When in 1967 Simon Partridge became a director he, like K.J. and like John Whitlock a generation earlier, enlarged his sphere to cover major works and ultimately the whole responsibility for legal publishing. The text-book department has since continued to be a training ground for top executives in legal publishing.

*   *   *   *   *

The first legal major work to be undertaken after the war (as envisaged in John Whitlock's 1944 report) was a second edition of *Halsbury's Statutes*. The Managing Editor was Ian Mail, who had been engaged on *Halsbury's Laws* and on the *Encyclopaedia of Forms and Precedents* before the war, and had been in charge of *Butterworths Emergency Legislation Service* since his return from military service. The work was completed in twenty-seven volumes between 1948 and 1951.

Quennell made one invaluable contribution to the production of the second edition of *Halsbury's Statutes*. Strict paper rationing still applied, and although Butterworths' quota was substantial, it could not have stood this large extra consumption. Adequate paper was available on the continent but could not be imported free of quota. Bound books however did not come within the paper quota. Quennell found a firm in Vienna with the necessary facilities. The text was typeset in England. The corrected type was printed with a special tacky ink on architect's tracing linen. The print was dusted with soot which adhered to the ink, and gave maximum opacity to the imprint of the type. With the loose soot carefully cleaned off, the sheets were flown to Vienna (for some time with Jack Pryke as escort) and used instead of a photographic negative, litho plates being prepared direct from the tracing linen pulls. Printing and binding followed in the usual way, and the bound books were imported to England.

The cycle was continued by the publication in 1968–72 of a third edition of *Halsbury's Statutes* in forty-one volumes and with improved typography. One of Ian Dickson's first tasks when he became General Manager in 1965 was to stimulate the production of this work, which had been talked about, but not put in hand. He recalls that the Board were not enthusiastic. Simon Partridge was given the overall responsibility for planning and publication, and this (his first major work) marked the beginning of his rapid transition from Text-book Manager to Legal Publishing Director. Alan Yonge, who had been in

charge of the Service to the previous edition, was appointed
Managing Editor of the new edition.

Many of the lawyers engaged on *Halsbury's Statutes* were transferred on its completion to a companion work, resembling it
in general approach and in typography. The original twenty-
six volumes of *Halsbury's Statutory Instruments* were published
between 1951 and 1954. It had long been the intention of
Butterworths to publish a companion work to *Halsbury's Statutes*,
dealing with subordinate legislation of all sorts. For nearly ten
years Mrs. Chappell (the mother of Sheila Carey) had been
systematically card-indexing all the orders and regulations from
original sources, with details of their authority, amendment
and, where relevant, revocation. The idea had probably been
Bond's, but it was post-war management which brought it to
fruition. Edgerley tried for some years to persuade Whitlock to
undertake publication, but it was Henry's advocacy of the
presentation described in the next paragraph which tipped the
balance. Mrs. Chappell's card index was used in the preparation
of the work, which was carried out by a team led by Freddie
Edwards, who had succeeded Ian Mail in charge of *Butterworths'
Emergency Legislation Service*. Indeed *Halsbury's Statutory Instruments*
was designed to supersede that work, for the Defence Regulations of the war days were temporary legislation, which was
being brought to an end. Practitioners needed a work which
dealt systematically with all subordinate legislation, and not
merely that which arose from war circumstances.

Halsbury's Statutory Instruments was notable for four things.
First, the bulk of the material made it uneconomic to include
the text of all instruments – full, annotated texts were given for
the most important instruments; many were summarised;
others, particularly those of a local nature, or following a
pattern, were tabulated. The editors' choice did not always
coincide with that of the purchaser. Secondly, just because not
all instruments were printed in full, an elaborate Enquiry
Bureau was offered with a system for supplying instruments not
printed. Thirdly, the supplement was planned to be loose-leaf,
and developed with a full supplement each year, and quarterly
advance information, all filed in the same binder. Fourthly, the
volumes were deliberately kept small, so that they could be
easily replaced.

Meanwhile a third edition of *Halsbury's Laws of England*, the chief
jewel in the Butterworth crown, was being planned. Whitlock's
aim in 1944 to produce the first volume in 1951 was nearly
fulfilled – it appeared in October 1952.

The appointment of the Editor-in-Chief again presented complications. Lord Jowett, who was Lord Chancellor in the Labour Governments of 1945–51, wanted the post, and actually made representations to that effect. He was told that the time had not yet come for Butterworths to appoint an Editor-in-Chief. In October 1951 Winston Churchill appointed Lord Simonds (a Chancery barrister, Gavin Simonds, who was then a Lord of Appeal in Ordinary) as Lord Chancellor (a non-political choice). Simonds was acceptable to Butterworths, and the Editorship more than acceptable to him.

Approaches were made to His Majesty King George VI, who consented to accept the dedication of the third edition, just as his father, King George V, had done for the second edition, and his grandfather, King Edward VII, for the first edition. Before the first volume of the new edition could be published the King died. Her Majesty Queen Elizabeth II expressed her wish that the dedication to her father should stand. She in due course accepted dedication of the fourth edition.

The editorial hierarchy of a major legal work is formidable. The Editor-in-Chief is a distinguished outsider, but the post is not purely honorific. Halsbury, Simonds and the two Hailshams have all played active parts in their respective editions. In the second and third editions there was the 'Editor', who had overall responsibility for the standard of the work, subject to the Editor-in-Chief, and the 'Managing Editor', who administered the editorial team.* In the fourth edition the duties have been redistributed between the 'Editor' and the 'Publisher'.

Sir Roland Burrows, a practising barrister of great skill, industry and experience, had been Editor of the second edition. He had been one of Birkenhead's 'ghosts', and became a worthy successor to Willes Chitty as Butterworths' regular common law consultant.

Burrows was once berated by an angry judge: 'You said you'd find a competent junior. This draft is appalling. The man's useless. He can't even write English. Look – there are three whiches in the first sentence.' Sir Roland was not at a loss. 'Well, what's wrong with that? – the greatest masterpiece in the English language opens with three witches.'

Sir Roland had been invited to be Editor of the third edition, but he died suddenly in the Spring of 1952. It was then proposed to Lord Simonds that Jack Edgerley should be made Editor. Simonds was familiar with Edgerley's work – they had both practised at the Chancery Bar – and he welcomed the proposal.

* The fact that in the second edition the 'Editor' was called 'Managing Editor', and the 'Managing Editor' was called 'Assistant Managing Editor', is confusing; but the functions were as described.

The appointment of a full-time member of Butterworths' staff as Editor meant a much deeper involvement than had been the case with Burrows.

Edgerley had already been involved, as Butterworths' Chief Legal Editor, in the preparation of the overall scheme for the work. As Editor of *Halsbury* he was able to implant his style, his precision and his strong sense of system upon the work, as the principal critic of the manuscripts.

After difficulties with the early titles, Edgerley repeated a proposal he had made earlier, namely that he should prepare a detailed scheme for each individual title. This time Whitlock agreed, and Edgerley assumed the mammoth task, involving at this late stage much burning of the midnight oil. These schemes not only produced uniformity and completeness of treatment, but assured contributors of Butterworths' determination to help them in their work. The same procedure was adopted from the start in the case of the fourth edition.

Ian Mail, who had had experience on the second edition before the war, and had just finished producing *Halsbury's Statutes*, was appointed Managing Editor. Edgerley was supported by Mail and his team of 'principal sub-editors', who in fact were employed as revising editors, concerned with the content, and not merely to style manuscript for the printer, as their title might imply. The senior of them, Leslie Jory, succeeded Mail as Managing Editor at the end of 1956, when the latter was sent to Canada to succeed the Canadian company's 1912 founder, Owen Elliott.

Several new features were subsequently introduced by Butterworths' General Manager, Harry Henry, including an Interim Index. This was followed by the addition of a Consolidated Table of Statutes. The most far-sighted of these features was the loose-leaf Current Service, designed for bi-monthly issue, bridging the gap between one Annual Cumulative Supplement and the next. This started publication in 1963, and was organised by the Editor of the Cumulative Supplement, Michael Walter, who ran it until his retirement in July 1978.

The Halsbury cycle is about twenty years – ten years to publish an edition, and ten years between editions. (The interval between completing one edition and starting work on the next is less!) The work of course gets longer and more complex as the corpus of legislation grows. Some day, no doubt, it will be a data bank. But in the early 1970s the management of Butterworths could discern no present or imminent demand for any format basically different from the existing one.

The long haul to publication of the fourth edition started in 1968, when Dickson, then Managing Director, persuaded Paul

Niekirk (a barrister who had worked for Butterworths for some years before joining Longmans) to return as Editor of the *All England Law Reports*, thus releasing Jack Edgerley to do the two-year stint of preparing the master plan, followed by the title schemes. (He continued with this work after his retirement, until resigning from it in 1978.)

The High Table at the staff luncheon to celebrate the publication of *Halsbury's Laws of England*, 3rd edn., Vol. 1. Left to right: Ernest Featherstone, Phil Hogger, Jack Edgerley, John Whitlock, Harry Henry, Ian Mail and Charles Venning (sometime Editor of *Laws Supplement*). (Photograph by Bishop and Stray)

Lord Hailsham of St. Marylebone, Lord Chancellor from 1970 to 1974 and from 1979 to date, and son of Viscount Hailsham, who edited the second edition, became Editor-in-Chief. The first volume of the new edition, which is expected to contain fifty-six volumes, was published in 1973. Publication is planned at a stately five volumes a year.

The third edition of the *Encyclopaedia of Forms and Precedents* was well on its way before the death of Stanley Bond, and its presentation was of his planning. Only wartime and post-war conditions prevented its completion before 1950. The fourth edition was planned in the early sixties, to follow the third edition of *Halsbury's Laws* and to employ a number of its editorial staff, including the Managing Editor, Leslie Jory. It was published in twenty-four volumes between 1964 and 1973.

The final months before the publication of Volume I coincided with the advent of Richard Millett as Chairman. From 1963 to 1967 the Chief Executive of Butterworths was a practising solicitor, and inevitably he made his mark. This was chiefly in the form of demands for excellence, rather than of publishing innovations. Millett knew exactly what he expected of a law book; the impression formed by the legal editors of the views

of other practising solicitors did not always agree. The *Encyclo-paedia* was particularly interesting to him, and he personally examined a number of titles, and provided precedents from the files of his practice. He involved himself in negotiations with contributors and potential contributors, and helped to chase late manuscripts. He was sure that the delays were due to bad planning, but no amount of planning can remove the difficulties of co-ordinating the work of a motley team of busy practising lawyers. Leslie Jory, though his burden was increased by Millett's criticisms and suggestions, was nevertheless sorry to lose them when the latter left Butterworths at the end of 1967.

The other encyclopaedia dealing with forms, *Atkin's Court Forms*, like the third edition of its companion, the *Encyclopaedia of Forms and Precedents*, was delayed by circumstances connected with the war, and like E.F. & P. was completed in 1950. It had suffered from its long period of gestation, and its uninspired typography.

The editor of the second edition was Peter Moore, the present Editor of *Halsbury's Laws*. He had been engaged from 1954 as a free-lance, and from 1956 as a salaried employee, to be John Whitlock's 'think-tank'. In that capacity he worked on forward plans for the *English and Empire Digest, Atkin's Court Forms, Canadian Oil and Gas*, and *Traumatic Medicine and Surgery for the Attorney*, and upon a bold project to publish *Butterworths Laws of New York* on the lines of *Halsbury*. This last (known to Whitlock and Moore as 'Bolony') never came to fruition.

Peter Moore, a keen typographer, gave *Court Forms* a new look.

The Procedural Tables, which are among its main features, had a prototype in the re-issue of the 'Companies' Volume in 1948, but Moore adapted and perfected these with enthusiasm. The first edition had included in most titles a preliminary narrative outlining the procedure to which the forms related. In the second edition where possible the procedure is set out in columnar form indicating the various steps to be taken, forms to be used, notices to be given, documents to be filed in court, etc. The steps are numbered; where alternative procedures exist, use is made of 'either...or...', and of 'now proceed to paragraph...'. Indeed the procedural tables are an application of the methods of the 'work flow chart' to legal business.

It is one of the great problems of the professional editor that much information can be obtained only in practice, and not from books. Contributors on the other hand are not always adept at presentation. Peter Moore and his staff prepared the tables for the title 'Divorce' by reference to the rules of court. The contributor, having re-written the tables, said that while

Opposite: Lord Hailsham of St Marylebone. (Photograph by Lotte Meitner-Graf, London)

Moore had obviously never practised in the Divorce Court, he (the contributor) could never have written the table at all without the benefit of Moore's draft. This sums up the essential relation between internal editor and practising contributor; they depend on each other.

After serious consideration had been given to a wholly loose-leaf form, the second edition of *Atkin's Court Forms* was spread over forty-two slim volumes (the first had been in sixteen) to constitute a permanent work, constantly renewed, and so requiring no new editions. The original forty-two volumes appeared between 1961 and 1973, and replacements are appearing regularly.

The *English and Empire Digest*, the third encyclopaedia to be evolved by Stanley Bond, was the subject of much discussion during the period immediately following his death. The original work with its supplements was unwieldy to use. But the opportunities for innovation were small. To quote from John Whitlock's 1944 report: '...Cases are far more static...There did not seem enough to change to warrant a whole new edition of a forty-nine volume work.' Four proposals were ventilated: the addition of editorial notes; the improvement of the typography; a new name (e.g. 'Halsbury's Cases of England'); pocket supplements. Lawrence Jones felt unable to sell a complete new edition, but intended to say in publicity that 'we proposed, in response to special requests, to replace certain of the volumes which most needed republishing'. A trial volume in 1945 was envisaged.

Whitlock's report contains the following terse comment: 'It ought to be said that Mr. Quennell in so far as I had explained the idea to him was much averse to it'. In the Sales Report of the following year the ground had shifted, and a new edition was proposed, subject to the proviso that Butterworths need not replace all volumes and that subscribers paid a higher price if they did not agree to take all volumes. Quennell agreed to this.

It was not however until 1950 that the management decided to proceed with the re-issue. It was not called Second Edition, but 'replacement volumes' (with a blue band on the spine) were offered. Only after several years was the intention to replace all the volumes formulated, and the name 'the Blue Band Edition' came into use. The fifty-four volumes were prepared by a small clerical team led by Philip Skottowe*, the only lawyer on the job. They took twenty years to complete. In 1971 the never-ending

* Skottowe joined the *Digest* staff in 1924, and died in 1979 at the age of 79.

programme of re-issue started again, this time with a Green Band and under a new editor.

Whitlock's 1944 report made it quite clear that the idea of a Service or 'mini-major-work' (to employ Butterworth jargon) on Income Tax was then already being considered. He referred to an earlier report he had prepared 'eleven years ago' (before ever he was a director, and when his association with major works had only just begun.) The 1944 report goes into greater detail on Income Tax than any other proposal, and a quite full synopsis is given, with proposed authors and page allocations.

About the same time as K.J. became Publishing Manager in 1946, Sir Roland Burrows delivered a new skeleton scheme. K.J. was entrusted with the task of providing the flesh and blood. Not only did he have to find Consulting Editors and contributors, but he had to learn sufficient about Income Tax to fill out the scheme, and to prepare instructions to contributors. Sir Roland (as General Editor) was requested to approach Viscount Simon to act as Editor-in-Chief, and his mission was successful.

By 1948 the first volumes were ready, and the work was completed the next year. It consisted of five volumes: three bound volumes of narrative text; one loose-leaf volume containing the text of Acts and regulations (annotated only with historical notes, definitions and cross-references); and one loose-leaf volume containing Tables and Index. Of these only the text volumes were written by outside contributors. The quality of the contributions varied enormously and it looks in retrospect as if the worst contributions ended up (after thorough revision by Butterworths) better than those which were approved without much alteration. The quality did not depend to any marked extent on the eminence or experience of the contributors.

The second edition was published in 1952–53, the inevitable result of the consolidating Income Tax Act, 1952. The sales resistance to a new edition so soon led Harry Henry to conceive in the early sixties the plan of re-issuing the bound volumes of *Simon* from time to time as part of the Service. Plans were complicated by the appearance of the Income Tax Management Act, 1964, consolidating and amending the procedural provisions, and then by the introduction of Capital Gains Tax and Corporation Tax by the Finance Act, 1965. The year 1965, producing the most fundamental changes in the tax law for two generations, was traumatic for all those concerned with books on taxation. By this time Richard Millett had become Chairman

of the Company, and his detailed interest in tax law and practice added to the strain.

In the event, the bound volumes of *Simon* were re-issued in 1965–66 under the heading '1964 Re-issue', incorporating the 1964 Act, but not the new taxes. The latter were put into a separate volume, and were fully incorporated five years later. This compromise did not appeal to Millett, and in retrospect it seems to have shirked the issue. But under the pressures of the time it was understandable.

The third edition, which appeared in nine volumes in 1970–71, was renamed *Simon's Taxes*, to recognise the new taxes, some of which were not 'income' tax. The work was thoroughly re-structured, in wholly loose-leaf form.

From 1950 to 1968 *Simon's Income Tax*, both the Service and the volumes, had been edited by Douglas Bruce-Jones, a Pickwick-like barrister, and a connoisseur of good food and wine. He had joined Butterworths from the department of the Solicitor of Inland Revenue, and used his contacts there to good purpose.

By 1965 Bruce-Jones was in failing health, and nearing retirement. K.J., by then Publishing Director, took the simple but unwise course of helping with the editorial work himself, rather than concentrating on finding an effective assistant and potential successor for Bruce-Jones. It took Ian Dickson, with all his accountancy contacts, a year to find that person, namely John Jeffrey-Cook, who was the chief architect of the third edition of *Simon's Taxes*.

Ian Dickson, then Managing Director, had for some time been considering the publication of tax reports, but without encouragement. When Simon Partridge returned from a visit to Chicago, fired to emulate the C.C.H. service, he received every support from Dickson. So, in 1972, *Simon's Weekly Tax Service* was launched, under the editorship of Jeffrey-Cook, containing reports and a weekly intelligence service.

Jeffrey-Cook attended conferences all over the world, he gave lectures, he examined, keeping Butterworths prominently on the tax map.

The frequency of the supplementation of the encyclopaedias has increased enormously in the past twenty-five years, facilitated by the introduction of loose-leaf formats. Until World War II annual bound volumes and annual cumulative supplements were considered an adequate form of service. The speed and

Opposite: Sir John Simon, K.C.V.O., K.C. (created Viscount Simon on becoming Lord Chancellor, 1940). From a cartoon in a series of ten by Edmund X. Kapp, published by the *Law Journal* in 1925

complexity of post-war changes in the law demanded something more flexible.

Halsbury Statutes, second edition, broke new ground by its loose-leaf Service of current statutes. The cumulative supplement continued to appear annually until 1970, after which an advance noter-up in loose-leaf form began to be issued in addition. The Services to *Halsbury's Statutory Instruments*, *Simon's Income Tax* and *Atkin's Court Forms* (second edition) were loose-leaf from the start, and were issued quarterly. A current loose-leaf Service to *Halsbury's Laws* (third edition) was issued every two months; this became monthly for the fourth edition. A similar Service to the *Encyclopaedia of Forms and Precedents* was introduced in 1965.

During the immediate post-war years an opportunity arose to purchase R. J. Acford, Ltd. of Chichester, printers of the *Law Journal*, the *All England Law Reports* and the *Justice of the Peace*. The purchase was designed to safeguard the production of these weekly publications.

At a party to celebrate the 150th anniversary of the *Law Journal*. Left to right: Ian Dickson, Roger Burke (new Editor of the *New Law Journal*), Tom Harper (retiring Editor) and Mr Justice Scarman (now Lord Scarman)

Had it been seen to have no other purpose the purchase might have been considered a success. But the use of Acfords for book printing led to friction, as is bound to happen when a publisher owns his own printing works. Moreover a printer's return on capital is far lower than that of a publisher, and this led to an inevitable reluctance to invest in new plant with consequent loss of efficiency. Nevertheless the association continued until 1974 when Acfords was absorbed into the I.P.C. printing division.

Negotiations took place in 1949 for a close link with the Incorporated Council of Law Reporting. It made sense for the monthly *Law Reports* and the weekly *All England Law Reports* to share services, whether editorial, printing or sales.

No agreement resulted, and in 1952 the Council went their own way, by publishing the *Weekly Law Reports* in rivalry to the *All England Law Reports*. Perhaps it is impossible for a commercial company and a public body to cooperate easily.

After the breakdown of negotiations and the publication of the *Weekly Law Reports*, competition between the *All England Law Reports* and the Incorporated Council's reports intensified. Successive editors of the *All England Law Reports* led the battle by insistence on the highest editorial standards, combined with prompt publication. From 1946 to 1954 G. F. L. Bridgman, a former Assistant Editor of the *Law Reports*, was editor of the All E.R. He was succeeded on his retirement by Jack Edgerley, who thus edited at the same time Butterworths' two most successful publications – *Halsbury's Laws* and the All E.R.

One of Butterworths' hopes in 1949 had been to reprint back volumes of the *Law Reports*. When this hope was frustrated, they planned to reprint selected cases before 1936, the year when the *All England Law Reports* started. The two main problems in planning were the source of the material (having regard to copyright) and the basis of selection. The purchase of the *Law Times* and the *Law Times Reports* in 1947 had solved the first; the judgments could be taken from the *Law Times Reports*; the headnotes were written to a uniform style, under the direction of (and largely by the work of) G. F. L. Bridgman, who became Editor of the *Reprint* on his retirement from the editorship of the current reports. The second problem was resolved by a mixture of mechanical and subjective criteria. The cases were classified according to the number of times they were referred to in *Halsbury's Laws* and in subsequent cases reported in the *All England Law Reports*. The editor reviewed the cases omitted on the mechanical selection, and restored leading cases within certain limitations of space. No selection of cases will suit all readers, but at the time the *Law Reports* were largely out of print, and second-hand copies rare and expensive, and thus the *Reprint* met a real need. It was originally intended that the work should be in thirty volumes, going back to 1843, the year in which the *Law Times Reports* (*Old Series*) started. In the end a further six volumes were added going back to 1558, the beginning of the reign of Elizabeth I – which would include the earliest case thrown up by the mechanical test. The whole project was completed between 1957 and 1968.

From 1947 till 1965 Butterworths published two weekly journals – the *Law Journal* and the *Law Times*. (The Coke Press Ltd., publishers of the *Law Journal*, was bought in 1924 by Stanley Bond from Herbert Bentwich, father of Norman Bentwich. The *Law Times* was purchased from the Field Press Ltd. in 1947.) These were different in style and readership, but there was a strong case for rationalisation. Largely at the urging of Richard Millett when he was Chairman, the two were amalgamated as the *New Law Journal*. Tom Harper, till then the editor of the *Law Society's Gazette*, agreed to become the first editor of the new journal. Today the *New Law Journal* is a more lively journal than its main competitor, the *Law Society's Gazette*, probing into the social consequence of current cases, and representing the place of the lawyer not only in the law but in society.

Legal text-books, whether for students or practitioners, are subordinate in Butterworths' programmes to the major works and subscription publications. Nevertheless there has been steady growth in the number of books published, in turnover and in gross profit from text-book publishing under Simon Partridge. In the ten years from 1957 to 1967 the turnover from text-books increased in real terms by 88%. The output of text-books, text-book supplements, etc., which had been forty-three in 1953, rose to sixty-nine in 1963, to eight-four in 1966 and to one hundred and five in 1968.

The 1968 figure was maintained for five years, and this can be attributed to a venture into lower priced and more elementary books, both for the practitioner market, and also (with more determination) in the technical college market. *Scott and Sim's A-level English Law* (1964) was followed by a series of 'Note-books', 'Questions and Answers' and elementary casebooks. Few of these proved profitable and most have disappeared from the list. But in spite of the abandonment of this programme the current output is more than double that of twenty-five years ago.

Some of the books dealt with new legislation; others were new editions of successful standard works – *Rayden on Divorce*, *Tristam and Coote's Probate Practice*, *Erskine May's Parliamentary Procedure*,

for example; many were new student's text-books at university level. To the latter development Mary Warrington, the College Representative, made a significant contribution, both by selling the books when they were published, and by bringing news of likely authors. Such was the confidence in which she was held in the law faculties that she seemed to conduct an unofficial recruitment agency.

The 'N.P.P.' (New Publishing Proposals Meeting) in progress. Reading clockwise from left front: David Perry, Jim Marsden, Ian Dickson, K.J. and Simon Partridge

Chapter 10

Australia, New Zealand, South Africa, Canada

Stanley Bond had given little authority to his overseas managers. John Whitlock and Seabrook Emery saw no reason to give more than their illustrious mentor, and in this at least they saw eye to eye with Quennell.

In February 1944 Lawrence Jones wrote to Emery:

'When I was in Australia one of the things I objected to most was that I was never consulted as to what accounts should or should not be considered bad debts, in fact, on one occasion when I ventured some suggestion of my own I was told to mind my own business as such things were too high for me. I wonder whether you will think I am speaking out of my turn if I suggest that as a gesture of confidence and goodwill to our overseas representatives you might initiate your reign by telling them you would welcome their considered recommendations at the end of this year in connection with this matter account by account. I do not think that to know the opinion of the man on the spot can ever do any of us any harm, and it certainly makes him feel that we are putting great reliance on his judgment, and is therefore to the good.'

Harry Henry (who had taken over from Lawrence Jones in Australia) had been saying the same sort of thing to Stanley Bond.

In October 1941, Henry had asked for explanations of certain overhead calculations applied to Sydney by London. He felt that without this information he would be unable 'to supervise the Australian organisation to the extent that I would like; in fact to the extent to which I consider I should be responsible as Manager in Australia'. S.S.B. replied that 'actual' overheads are known only *post facto*. He did not explain why the provisional figures were never adjusted in the light of experience. He went on to say that since the company's accounts covered New Zealand as well as Australia, they would not help Henry.

Bond suggested that Henry should concentrate on monitoring local expenditure and not concern himself with London's figures. Henry proved a good housekeeper in Bond's eyes. Bond's last letter to him, dated 13th January 1943, concludes:

'I would like to state generally and particularly that your administration and economy since you took control have been very good indeed.'

Ian Mail, who succeeded Elliott in 1957 as Canadian Manager, complained that he needed London's approval to buy a typewriter. Daily sales were being reported by Washington even in the 1960s. Every staff appointment, every salary increase was vetted by London. On matters of policy, however, London was over-reticent, and on the development of new ventures contributed little.

In 1961 the first-ever meeting of all overseas managers was held in London. Designed as 'joint briefing', the conference afforded incidentally the first opportunity for the managers to compare notes. The experiment was not repeated until 1972. Since then gatherings of this nature, at all levels, have become such a regular feature of Butterworth life that it is difficult to appreciate the excitement the 1961 meeting caused. Most of the post-war story overseas has to be seen in the context of a tight rein in London, and for the success or failure in the five countries in which branches had been established in 1910, 1912, 1914, 1934 and 1960, London management is largely responsible.

Australia

In 1945 Harry Henry was brought back from Australia to become Sales Manager at Head Office. He was succeeded in Sydney by Bill Nichols. Bill was already a manager of proven effectiveness with seventeen years' managerial service in New Zealand, and nearly thirty years with the company. He remained the Resident Director for Australia and New Zealand until his retirement in 1965, when Harry Henry returned to the antipodes, to succeed his successor of twenty years earlier.

At the end of the war, the Sydney office had on sale twenty-one locally produced text-books and nine local periodical publications. There was thus the basis for vigorous local publishing after the war. Nichols, in spite of the entrenched position of the Law Book Company of Australasia, and although Sydney was still thought of mainly as an outlet for English publications, embarked on the task of building up the list over the next ten years.

Dick Venn Brown, who joined Butterworths in 1936 and retired as Sales Director in Australia in 1978, dates the serious attempt to penetrate the text-book market at about 1950. But, as we have seen, a start had been made as early as 1937 when the first edition of *Baldwin and Gunn's Income Tax* appeared. This has developed into a loose-leaf encyclopaedia known as *Australian Income Tax Law and Practice*. *Australian Company Law* also began in 1937, and this too has expanded into an encyclopaedia. A third work of a similar stature, *Butterworths' Industrial Laws*, is derived from *Nolan and Cohan's Commonwealth and New South Wales Industrial Laws*, one of Nichols's first Australian productions.

The vision of an Australian equivalent to the *All England Law Reports* was raised again by Nichols in 1946. The existing reports were mainly series publishing cases from a particular state (such as the *Victorian Law Reports*, published by Butterworths for the Council of Law Reporting in Victoria). The *Commonwealth Law Reports* (published by the Law Book Company of Australasia, a partly-owned associate of Sweet and Maxwell) were limited to cases from the High Court of Australia. The *Argus Law Reports*, a privately owned Victorian series and part of a Melbourne newspaper group, published both Victorian and High Court cases. The Board saw acquisition of the Argus series as a means to achieve the objective and Lawrence Jones was sent out to negotiate. He was recalled and sent to South Africa before a decision could be reached. It was not until 1960, after the group which owned the series had twice changed hands, that the *Argus Law Reports* were purchased.

Butterworths then proceeded to remove the Victorian cases, and rename the series the *Australian Argus Law Reports* with a sale throughout the Commonwealth. Unfortunately, the series was never able to overcome the predominance of the *Commonwealth Law Reports* as the 'official' series, and the association of the name 'Argus' with Victoria back to 1895 limited its appeal to lawyers outside that state, who were used to C.L.R. The relaunching of the series cannot be regarded as a success and it was not until the publication of the *Australian Law Reports* in 1973 that Butterworths made a sustained and determined attempt to get into the areas of Federal jurisdiction.

The outstanding publishing venture of the 1950s was the *Australian Forms and Precedents*, an Australian major work, as opposed to the Pilots and companion volumes published to support the English originals in earlier days. However, the English *Encyclopaedia of Forms* remained firmly as the base for the Australian work. Differences in the law of the individual states necessitated the circulation of the original draft, prepared by contributors and the Editor-in-Chief, L. A. Harris, to State Editors for the noting of local variants. Harris was initially reluctant to accept the task, as he intended to spend his

Celebrating the fifth anniversary of the *Australian Law Reports*. Left to right: Wayne Hayden (reporter for A.L.R. and consultant for *Industrial Law Service*), Howard Ednie (co-author of *Australian Company Law*), Robert Hayes (Editor of A.L.R.) and Kingsley Siebel. (Photograph by Identity Studio Pty. Ltd.)

retirement playing bowls, but after six months of bowls he was ready to take it on.

By November 1952 Harris was down to 'Companies', and the State Editors had nearly finished revising the first volume. It was then planned to pass the first volume for press about mid-1953 and to publish it early in 1954. Publication finally started in 1955 and the work was completed in eighteen volumes in 1962. Twelve volumes of a second edition have by now appeared.

Nichols pays a just tribute to the work of Frank Judson in developing the programme, and particularly the *Forms*:

'A great deal of credit for the successful publication of the *Australian Forms and Precedents* must go to Frank Judson, who joined the firm in London as a boy. In 1928 he was one of the assistants to Miss Smallwood, the Administration Manager of the *English and Empire Digest* in London. During the early 1930s he went to India as a manager, but returned to London about 1935, and was then sent to Australia as a general assistant in the Sales and Editorial Departments. He served in the Australian forces during World War II, and on his return to civilian life he was again in charge of sales in

Sydney. Later he was made Sydney Manager, and when the *Australian Forms and Precedents* started, he was placed in charge of production. Frank not only received the MS, but in many cases made revisions or made suggestions to the Editor-in-Chief, who called at O'Connell Street at least twice a week.

While I made all the arrangements for publications, Frank looked after the production of them, and after my retirement he was the one who took charge of arranging for publications.'

Many academics visiting England spoke more of Judson than of Nichols and his successors. Judson, who retired in 1972, was made a director of the Australian company in July 1965, a few months before Nichols's retirement, by which time it was clear that Judson was not to succeed him.

The reprint of the *Victorian Law Reports, 1875–1957* developed out of a project to produce a Victorian Digest. It illustrates in dramatic form the tensions between London and Nichols. The local management recognised all too well that if the company was to match its competitor, the Law Book Company, which had a very strong local list, it must put a large proportion of its resources into local products. London, although agreeing in principle, were deeply concerned about Sydney's effectiveness as agent for the parent company. In addition London was not completely confident in Nichols's judgment, and in some quarters his projects were thought ill-conceived or over-ambitious; there was a tendency to judge overseas projects according to how a similar project would be received in the English market.

This is how Nichols recollects it:

'The story behind this reprint was that in 1958 the management in London and I could not agree on the new volumes of the *New Zealand Annotations*, and a *Victorian Digest*. Finally I said "Tell me what to do and I will do it" or words to that effect. The result was a cable calling me to London. On the first day it was agreed to follow my recommendations in regard to the *New Zealand Annotations*, and the *Victorian Digest* was to be discussed the following day. But Harry Henry had mentioned to me the arrangement he had made for the reprinting of *Cox's Criminal Cases*; this gave me the idea of a V.L.R. reprint.'

Nichols thus resurrected a concept of Venn Brown's that had been put forward at least twelve months previously. It had, however, been rejected out of hand at that time due to the magnitude of the task and the feeling that the market was insufficient. This time the idea was accepted and the reprint was a major revenue earner in the 1960s, leading to a further reprint in the early 1970s.

Another successful reprint was the *Western Australia Law Reports, 1898–1959,* for which Fred Dennis of Buffalo arranged the printing and acted as American publisher.

The 1960s also saw the publication in Australia of the *All England Law Reports Reprint Supplementary Volumes.* The U.K. reprint omitted cases on obsolete law, e.g. the pre-1925 property legislation. Many of these cases remained valid in Australia. Supplementary volumes were expected to encourage the sale of the English work, and to constitute a worthwhile Australian product. The project finally saw the light of day in 1968 as the *All E.R. Extension Volumes* and comprised seventeen volumes. The potential sales were, however, markedly overestimated* and the series lost considerable sums for the company. So too did a new series of Law Reports started in 1960, to cover the State of New South Wales in competition with the Law Book Company, which ran until 1970.

The problem which these publications were to cause were, however, only on the horizon at the time of Nichols's retirement in 1965.† On the surface the company had never been stronger. In 1963 and 1964 trading profits were at a peak and local publications accounted for 53 % of the business with a list of local publications either in print or production of nearly ninety titles. These books, unlike those of most Butterworth companies, spread over both law and accountancy.

Underneath, the legacy Nichols bequeathed his successors was not entirely favourable. He had exercised an extremely firm grip on those aspects of the business he had not delegated to Judson as Editor. No middle management was encouraged or even allowed to develop, so that his departure left a major void. Nichols's success in building up a relatively small company in the forties and fifties by concentrating everything around him was no longer appropriate to a company of the size it had become in the early 1960s. At the same time sales achieved by sending and billing books on approval, whether wanted or not, were rapidly alienating Butterworths' goodwill in the legal

---

* In particular lack of enthusiasm among salesmen in London and the other overseas companies was discounted.
† Nichols, who had substantial private means, intended to retire in 1964 at the age of sixty. He was persuaded to delay his retirement by one year until 1965, while a suitable successor was found. The following year the Chairman, Richard Millett, failed to enlist him in a consultative capacity.

profession. The result was to be very heavy write-offs of unsaleable stocks and uncollectable debts.

It was in October 1965 that Harry Henry was again transferred from London to Australia.* During his second period of office in Sydney his health was not good, leading to his early retirement four years later at the age of sixty. The stress and strain of a business in decline plus faction fighting within that business cannot have helped. London, absorbed in its own problems, gave little support. Indeed Henry was glad when in 1968 John Patience, an Australian lawyer, was appointed to the Australian Board by I.P.C. (which had by then acquired Butterworths); Patience's advice was immediately available.

A report to the U.K. Board on the 1966 results illustrates Henry's difficulties. Gross profit margins were substantially reduced due to stock write-downs and costs of maintaining the *New South Wales Reports*; sales of U.K. books were depressed by the completion of the third edition of *Halsbury's Laws*. Major reconstruction of new premises in 20 Loftus Street had been found necessary due to white ant infestation† and claims were outstanding against the surveyors. Proceedings were also pending relating to former staff – for alleged breach of contract by the Company in one case, and for alleged defalcation by the employee in the other. The only positive feature was the growth in local publications, which kept the business alive. By 1967 local product had jumped to 62 % of the total, pointing to the wisdom of Nichols and his predecessors in emphasising the need for the business to have a strong involvement in Australian publishing.

Henry was succeeded in 1969 by David Kingham, whose experience in Washington has already been described. On his arrival Kingham was confronted with the need to write off considerable quantities of obsolete stock and uncollectable debts, and to scrap a computer system developed during 1968–9, which involved heavy development and staff costs and was totally unproductive. To compound his problems, a fire in the warehouse destroyed much of the stock. The operating losses incurred in that year plus the need to replace stock put tremendous financial strain on the Australian company. Without the support of the U.K. parent it would have been insolvent.

* Henry, having left Sydney in 1945 to become Sales Manager in London, was appointed General Manager there in 1951. His promotion to Managing Director and subsequent transfer back to Sydney are dealt with in Chapter 12.

† Certain beams, thought to be steel joists, turned out to be timber.

The financial separation of Butterworth Australia from the parent company in London from 1972 to 1978, and its association with Reed Consolidated Industries in Australia, was a matter of major importance at group level and was disturbing for local directors, but it did not alter the publishing and sales direction of the company.

In the area of sales and administration Kingham was helped by David Jackson until the latter's return to the U.K. in 1973. Their first concern was to keep the business going on a day-to-day basis, and then in 1971 to negotiate its move to Chatswood, a suburb of Sydney, as a base for future expansion.

When David Kingham's initial contract came up for renewal in 1973 he opted to return to London, where he became International Marketing Director. He was replaced in Australia by Peter Cheeseman, a barrister, who had been on the personal staff of Don Ryder, the then Chairman of Reed International. Peter Cheeseman in his turn came back to England and to head office in 1979, when David Jackson returned to Australia to succeed him as Managing Director.

Shortly before Kingham's departure Ted Impey had been

The Butterworth offices at Chatswood, Sydney. This drawing like those on pp. 185, 189 and 255 is by John L. Baker.

appointed Business Manager with a prime assignment to develop an effective computer system. This was successfully accomplished in 1976. At the same time, the tightening of financial and administrative controls instituted under Kingham continued at a quicker pace. In the sales area, Dick Venn Brown received his just award for years of service by being appointed Sales Director in 1974 (Impey and Siebel, the Chief Editor, also became directors at this period). Dick had come to Sydney unwillingly after being 'Mr. Butterworth' in Melbourne for many years. One of Butterworths' great salesmen, he retired in 1978.

Meanwhile the development of local publishing had been the responsibility of Kingsley Siebel, who was recruited in 1971 as Chief Editor on Judson's retirement. Siebel, a burgher from Ceylon, had gone to work for the Law Book Company some years earlier when his written application to Butterworths was rejected. A compulsive worker and editorial virtuoso, he undertook the most comprehensive revamping of the Australian publishing list in its history (probably more comprehensive than that of any Butterworth company to date).

By 1977 every publication in the existing list had been revised or scrapped; a major investment had been successfully made for the first time in the student market; and a range of new, mainly loose-leaf, updating Services was launched to give Butterworths an equal share with its competitors in the legal market and a significant representation in publishing for accountants and commercial lawyers.

In 1973 Butterworths launched the *Australian Law Reports*. This series with its unrivalled speed of reporting and coverage of all Federal Courts constitutes a serious attempt to emulate the success of the *All England Law Reports* in an Australian context.

The *Australian Commentary*, published in connection with the fourth edition of *Halsbury's Laws*, is more ambitious than the old *Australian Pilots* to the second and third edition, although it has to be used alongside the English work, whose sale in Australia continues. Only the future will show whether it is succeeded in years to come by an Australian *Halsbury*, complete in itself, like the *Law of South Africa* (which started publication in 1976) or the Canadian work now being planned.

The Australian company is the second largest company in the Butterworth Group and an important force in professional publishing in Australia. Undoubtedly its main thrust lies in its own publications. The current list now totals some 180 titles and in 1978 accounted for 68% of total revenue.

New Zealand

In 1945 Bill Nichols had been transferred from Wellington to
Sydney, and became 'Resident Director in Australia and New
Zealand'. C. A. (Ted) Allen was appointed Branch Manager
for the Wellington office. Allen had worked for Butterworths as
a representative for a couple of years from 1919, and again from
1931 onwards, mainly in Australia and New Zealand, where he
was very popular with the legal profession.

At this period it was difficult to recruit good staff locally, and
London were asked to send out a young man as a general
assistant. They sent out D. R. (Bob) Christie in 1946. Bob had
worked for four months as a clerk in the Dominions Department
(dealing with accounts in Ireland, Cyprus and India) before
being invited to go to New Zealand as 'Assistant to the
Managing Director' (in fact Ted Allen was never a director);
he found the job to be, in spite of its grand title, that of office
dogsbody. He made progress, however, and was appointed
Accountant in March 1948, and Assistant Manager five years
later. Ted Allen was due to retire in the autumn of 1955, but
died of cancer on 10th April of that year. The succession had
not then been settled. Bob Christie was confirmed as New
Zealand Manager in August 1955 as result of pressure from
Nichols.

The New Zealand office is a small one, and the Manager (or
Director) in charge must deal personally with every aspect –
publishing, sales and accounts. Christie was able to use his
experience to instal first the 'Booking Machine', then the
punched-card system and finally a small computer, with practically no upset to the day-to-day running of the business.

The post-war history of the company has been one of
consolidation. New Zealand has been described by Nichols as
the law publisher's paradise. There is no rigid distinction
between barrister and solicitor; there is no division of powers
between Dominion and State (or Provincial) Legislature; there
is no admixture of a legal system other than the English common
law. All the other overseas offices have to cope with one or more
of those problems. The New Zealand company used its
advantages to the full, and continued to hold a virtual monopoly.
It covers virtually the whole of the legal textbook market,
through books by local authors and adaptations of English
standard works.

Competition was almost eliminated in 1953 with the purchase
of the *Gazette Law Reports* and the *Magistrates Court Reports*
from the Estate of T. G. Russell. Nichols, who spent four weeks
in New Zealand to carry out the negotiations, was successful in

obtaining a lower price than had been offered to and refused
by Mr. Russell in 1928. Nichols thought he should have had
wider powers to negotiate, and London was irritated because
they thought he was irritated. Fortunately for all, he managed
to conclude the bargain at the top figure laid down by London.
This purchase and the resulting amalgamation of the *Gazette
Law Reports* with the *New Zealand Law Reports* formed part of a
package deal with the Council for Law Reporting, with whom
Nichols was able to arrange a twenty-year contract for publishing the *New Zealand Law Reports*. The Council also permitted
their headnotes to be used for Butterworths' new digest of cases,
the *New Zealand Abridgement*. The *Magistrates Court Reports* were
amalgamated with *Magistrates Court Decisions*.

The New Zealand Company have produced, as need arose,
reports to cover all the courts and tribunals of the country. In
1970–2 Butterworths reprinted, in ninety-three volumes, not
only the *New Zealand Law Reports*, but also earlier series,
covering in all 1861–1961.

The preparation of the *New Zealand Abridgement* turned out
to be a long and arduous task. It was not lauched until 1963,
when the first of sixteen volumes appeared. In the same year
publication of *New Zealand Forms and Precedents* in sixteen
volumes started.

In 1956 however there was a setback. Ever since the war
Nichols had been canvassing the Government to permit a new
edition of the *New Zealand Statutes*, published by Butterworths
in 1932. Details were under discussion with the Attorney-
General in 1955, such as the respective merits of chronological
and subject arrangement, and the fullness of annotations.
Butterworths favoured something approaching the *Halsbury's
Statutes* style. But in the event the Government decided to adopt
a chronological arrangement; to have no annotations
whatsoever; and to entrust publication to the Government
Printer, the editorial work being done in the Parliamentary
Law Draftsman's Office. Butterworths had to be content with
publishing revised annotations, in two volumes, as a companion
to the Government text.

In 1960 a separate New Zealand company was formed, of
which Bill Nichols became an original director. Christie was
made a director two years later. During the period from 1946
to 1962 (when he had his first home leave) Christie only once
saw a director from England. He did not attend the conference
of overseas managers in 1961, and when he went on leave in
1962 he called only once at the London office where he saw
nobody except Henry. New Zealand remained an Australian
fief.

During the 1970s New Zealand continued its unspectacular development, without the fluctuations in prosperity experienced by Australia; there was no need to rebuild the list. One experience which New Zealand shared with Australia was a fire. On 8th July 1977 the editorial department's offices were gutted. The department was operational in new premises ten days latter. Good came of evil, for the new premises (thought to be temporary) were able to house the whole staff permanently under one roof.

The major development of recent years was the production by the New Zealand company of its own *Halsbury Commentary*, separate from that of Australia, under the vigorous and distinguished editorship of Sir Alexander Turner, who is a Butterworth U.K. author and one of New Zealand's most distinguished jurists. The need for a complete national restatement of the law depends on the development of a legal system substantially different from English law. This is happening progressively in New Zealand (just as in Australia and Canada), but it will be many years yet before 'Halsbury-with-Commentary' is inadequate in New Zealand. The decision, when it comes, will be in the hands of a new generation of managers.

In the autumn of 1978 the New Zealand management was widened. Bob Christie, who had been in charge there since 1955, became Financial and Administrative Director, responsible first to David Jackson and then, from May 1979, to Derek Day, who was transferred from being Financial Director in Durban to become Managing Director in New Zealand.

South Africa

'Butterworth & Co. (Africa) Ltd. was formed in 1934 with the primary object of selling and distributing the works of Butterworth & Co. (Publishers) in South Africa...Whilst recently [it] has undertaken local publications and is continuing to do so, this has been a secondary object and has not been allowed to overshadow the main object of selling and distributing our main works abroad.'

So states a 1946 report. Fortunately for the future of the company, Lawrence Jones and Kenneth Sheppard, the local manager, did develop local publishing. By 1950, 47% of the gross profit came from South African publications.

The year 1947 saw two major successes and a failure. One success was Butterworths' first text-book in Afrikaans, *de Wet's*

Kontraktereg: the other an agreement with the Government for the production of the *Statutes of South Africa* from 1910 to 1947. J. C. de Wet is now one of the elder statesmen of the academic world in South Africa, and was a director of Butterworth & Co. (S.A.) (Pty) Ltd. until 1978.

The *Statutes of South Africa*, in thirteen volumes, were produced bilingually, with English and Afrikaans on facing pages.* Butterworths prepared the annotations at their cost; the Government Printer did the printing. Butterworths had the sole selling rights (other than to Government departments), and obtained a certain number of copies free, and others at varying discounts. The first volume appeared in 1949, and the work was completed in 1953, followed by a Service of bound annual volumes. The *Statutes* put Butterworths on the map as local publishers, and contributed greatly to financial stability.

The third 1947 project was a South African equivalent to the *All England Law Reports*. But the Government favoured a rival series started at the same time by Juta of Cape Town. After long and complicated negotiations, Butterworths withdrew their series. For nearly thirty years Butterworths' name was given, as co-publishers, on the title page of Juta's series, the *South African Reports*, Juta retaining editorial and production control. The agreement effectively precludes Butterworths from publishing current law reports in South Africa.

In 1948 Hugh Quennell sent Harry Henry, then London Sales Manager, on a visit to Durban. Quennell wrote to Lawrence Jones:

'The principles which should guide Mr. Henry are:
(i)   There is something wrong – I must find out.
(ii) What is to be done to put it right.
(ii) How is Shepherd [sic]?
(iv) Have we taken on too much?
(v)   South African Law Reports.
(vi) No *new* business.'

No irrevocable cut-back took place, but by July it was clear that Kenneth Sheppard was unable, for personal reasons, to sustain any longer the responsibility of the business.

After a short period, during which Derek Priestley (the Assistant Sales Manager in London) was seconded temporarily to Durban, E. A. (Barney) Barns was appointed Manager. He

---

* The index was so printed that the reader held it the opposite way up according to which language he wanted. The lettering on the spine corresponded, and the book could be placed on the shelf with the favoured language the right way up, and the unfavoured upside down.

Three directors of Butterworth & Co (South Africa) (Pty) Ltd in 1975. Left to right: J. C. de Wet, Barney Barns, Willem Joubert

became a director of the African company in 1952. Barney had joined the accounts department of the London company in 1935, and was responsible, under E. C. Leader, for the establishment of new accounting systems in the late 1930s. In that capacity he had had good opportunities to become familiar with the financial workings of the group as a whole. He soon exhibited a flair for finding the books that were wanted, and for making himself known and accepted in Government and professional circles.

He was joined in 1951 by Andrew McAdam, who was his second-in-command for twenty-four years (with a seat on the Board from 1970).

The build-up of text-books, both English and Afrikaans, continued steadily under Barney and Mac. They also branched out successfully from law into commerce and accountancy, medicine, science and technology, and even the social sciences. A scholarly triumph was the publication (starting in 1955) of the six-volume *Selective Voet*. Johannes Voet, who lived from 1647 to 1713, was the author of the standard text on Roman-Dutch law, his *Commentary on the Pandects*. The Hon. Percival Gane, retired from the Supreme Court of South Africa, used his retirement and his scholarship to produce an English translation; the work was 'selective' in that obsolete and otiose portions were omitted. The actual production of the work was undertaken in England, as Durban had insufficient editorial staff. This was equally true of England. Simon Partridge, who was detailed for the task, did most of it at home or in the train.

The first attempt to produce a 'Laws of South Africa', comparable to *Halsbury*, was researched between 1954 and 1956. Professor Tom Price of Cape Town University even approached suitable members for an Editorial Board. London, however, turned down the proposition on financial grounds. Even at that date Emery commented that the political prospect of the next ten years was uncertain. The capital involved was certainly substantial. But a lack of confidence in Tom Price's health and his ability to see the work through was also a factor. Emery wrote to Barns: 'I am convinced that under Price, this job would never be completed...he is still unable to appreciate the magnitude of this task and the time that is necessary to devote to it. What is worse, as was evident when he was here, he is not prepared to learn from others.'

Approval was given in 1965 to a scheme for an encyclopaedic *South African Forms and Precedents*; this produced difficult editorial problems, due largely to its production in both languages. Fourteen volumes were published by 1978, with three still to appear.

Also in 1965 Barns tendered successfully to edit, print and publish the *Statutes of South Africa* in loose-leaf form. While the whole copyright is vested in the Government, the cost and organisation fell upon Butterworths, and the Government Printer acted as the purchasing agent to acquire a guaranteed number for government use. The contract included the provision of a Service from 1967 to 1983, involving the replacement of some 5000 pages a year. While the price structure is determined by the Government, this enterprise affords a not unreasonable return. The securing of this contract, in the face of stiff local opposition, was a great boost to morale. The twenty-one volumes of about 1000 pages each were published within two calendar years, 1967 and 1968.

The Durban company, like the other overseas offices, started life in rented accomodation in the centre of the town. When they moved in 1954 to Beach Grove they occupied premises 'reconstructed at the owner's expense, which would provide not only the necessary office accommodation for many years to come, but also adequate and accesssible storage space'. The Board minute refers to 'the hoped-for expansion of the business in the next twenty years'. Twenty years proved to be about right, for it was in 1971 that new purpose-built accommodation was occupied in Gale Street, about two miles from the city centre.

The company, originally named Butterworth & Co. (Africa)

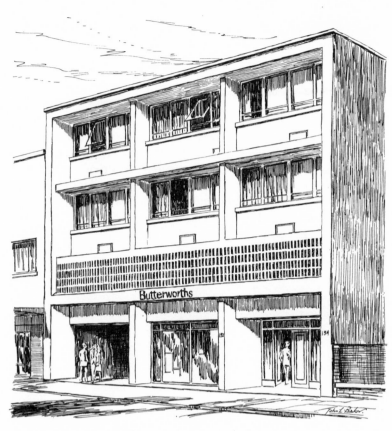

The Butterworth offices
at Gale Street, Durban

Ltd, at first traded in East Africa as well as Rhodesia. The
Eastern Africa Law Reports were started in Durban. In 1963 the
East African business* was transferred under political pressure
to London, and the company name changed to Butterworth &
Co. (South Africa) Ltd. In 1970 the business was transferred
to a company registered in South Africa, Butterworth & Co.
(South Africa) (Pty) Ltd.

The post-war vitality and success of the South African
Company were due in large measure to the work of Barney
Barns. He retired in 1976 and is now living in England. He was
succeeded by Andrew McAdam.

Before Barney left Durban he was able to set up the first
entirely local restatement to be published by any Butterworth
overseas company. In 1972 a Managing Editor was found in
Willem Joubert, Professor of Law at the University of South
Africa, who combined academic, administrative and business
qualities to a remarkable degree and was already a member of
the Butterworth Board in South Africa. The U.K. Board gave

* Subsequently Malawi and Zambia were also transferred to London.

the go-ahead and, under Joubert, the first volume was issued in 1976, under the title of *Law of South Africa*. This twenty-eight volume work is scheduled for completion in 1987.

During the same period the academic programme has extended so as to necessitate the opening of its own separate publishing office in Pretoria.

The South African company is unique in several ways. It is the only Butterworth company publishing for a system of law basically different from that of England. It is the only company publishing in two languages. It is the only company, other than the parent, to develop an extensive academic programme in subjects as diverse as biology and religion, for the colleges of the country. It depends less on the parent for its products than any other overseas company.

Canada

Canada was the slowest off the mark into local publishing. In sales of English major works their record had been excellent. Emery wrote to Owen Elliott in June 1951:

> 'As you know before the war the view which Mr. Bond took, when these proposals were first considered, was that the publication in Canada of books of Canadian law would reduce the sale of our English law books and might easily be an expensive project with very little return. After the war we did try to get going with the Ontario Digest, but Chitty let us down.* Mr. Nichols was in favour of trying again and his figures showed a gross profit of about £11,700 with most of the detail work being done in the office. Knowing cost of rents in Toronto and salaries generally we were not in favour of this "in the office" scheme.'

This letter was sent on behalf of the Board, in reply to one sent by Elliott to the Chairman, suggesting a revival of Elliott's pre-war publishing plans. Emery commented to the Chairman as follows:

> 'Without blaming Elliott unduly for this breakdown it convinced the management that Elliott was not the man to run a major work. The breakdown was in 1948 and in 1949 we sent Mr. Nichols to investigate the position in Canada.

---

* This failure was a traumatic experience for Elliott. Chitty did not produce the promised material. The letter of termination was one of Hugh Quennell's rudest. He dictated it to Owen Elliott and then ordered him to sign it.

Broadly his view was that our pre-war policy had resulted in our "missing the boat" and that Elliott, now over 60 years of age, still follows the rules laid down by London 25 years ago.'

This comes nearer to criticism of Stanley Bond than anything else of this period. Its truth is even more apparent today when the publishing history of Canada is compared with that of other overseas companies.

As in the pre-war days, so in Elliott's latter years, it was one of the representatives who was the most forceful character in the Canadian set-up. Indeed it seemed to some that it was Aicheson rather than Elliott who was in charge. Aicheson preferred to continue selling *Halsbury's Laws*, which he did with consummate success, rather than having to sell unknown works by unknown authors. His influence contributed to the slowness in the growth of local publishing.

A cautious beginning in local publishing was however authorised as a result of Elliott's approach in 1951. By the time he retired in 1957 six Canadian publications had appeared. Three

Owen Elliott at the launching of the *Canadian Converter to Halsbury's Laws of England*. He is holding a volume from the set of *Halsbury* in the Royal Library at Windsor Castle, which had been loaned for exhibition.

more appeared by the end of 1959. John Whitlock paid a number of visits from England. He considered he actually signed these books up, even if Elliott gave him some pointers. Probably the most famous book (as well as the most profitable) published by the Canadian office in this period was Dean Wright's *Cases on the Law of Torts* which had an international reputation and sale, and was one of the pioneer books for the case-book system of teaching, then spreading from the law schools of the U.S.A. Two loose-leaf publications sponsored by Whitlock also made important Butterworth history, namely *Canadian Income Tax* and *Canadian Oil and Gas*.

But the revival of the Ontario Digest was a disaster. It was not adequately reappraised after Chitty left the scene; the backing of the Law Society of Upper Canada had been personal to him, and was not renegotiated. Editorial problems recurred again and again, and the demand for a purely *Ontario Digest* (in competition with the Dominion-wide *Canadian Abridgement*) proved negligible in the first edition, although a second edition in loose-leaf form has been more successful. At the end of the second year of publication, the Chief Accountant, Phil Hogger, pointed out not only that the write-off had produced a gross loss of over £10,000 to date on a sale of £24,000, but that 'on these figures, this publication cannot earn a profit even if every copy is sold'. John Whitlock knew this before publication, but had not the courage to abandon a work on which so much had been spent. The overall result of eight years' work was a gross profit of £11,500, a fraction of the relevant overheads.

In addition to purely local publications the Canadian office marketed, starting in 1953, the *Canadian Converter*, to assist the Canadian users of the third edition of *Halsbury's Laws*. It cited Canadian cases and gave fairly general references to comparable Canadian statute law. It was a successor to the 'pink pages' in the Supplement to the second edition of *Halsbury's Laws*, which had contained citations of current Canadian cases.

From 1960 onwards the Canadian company continued to publish text-books, but this was not sufficient to give the company a dominant position against strong competition from companies which had started earlier. *Butterworths Ontario Digest* was the only Canadian major work.

The Canadian business occupied a series of different offices in downtown Toronto until 1940 when it was moved to a surburban area, Danforth Avenue, where part of a block of flats was occupied. Over the next twenty years further flats were occupied, until the place was a rabbit-warren of inconvenient offices. When eventually the Danforth Avenue block became intolerable the company moved even further out of town, first

The Butterworth offices
at Scarborough,
Toronto

in 1967 to Curity Avenue, and later to Scarborough, where they occupy a modern office-cum-warehouse block.

At the end of April 1957, Owen Elliott retired, after nearly forty-five years in charge of the Canadian office. Several potential successors had been considered, and in at least one case a probationary period had been served in the Toronto office. In April 1956 Elliott had been informed that Ian Mail had been appointed as his successor. Mail, a barrister who worked on *Halsbury's Laws* before the War, had subsequently been Managing Editor of the second edition of *Halsbury's Statutes* and the third edition of *Halsbury's Laws*. He was taken round Canada by Whitlock in May 1956, and then returned to England to complete the hand-over to his successor on *Halsbury*. He moved to Canada at the end of the year, and assumed full charge on Owen Elliott's retirement. Elliott, however, remained as a non-exective director. Mail did not become a director until 1962.

Succeeding someone with very long service, who had been allowed to grow old in office, Mail had no easy task. He was unfamiliar with sales and finance. His publishing experience had been on major works, where there is a large editorial staff writing and revising and co-ordinating to a high standard. For a text-book publisher every production is different, and it is necessary to rely to a much greater extent on the work of the authors themselves. He had to research markets and projects – something he had never done before. He had to learn the hard way. In the event he managed the Canadian office for nearly twelve years. His successor, Dennis Beech, took over in November 1968, and he was succeeded by Ernest Hunter in 1975.

The legal text-book list continued to grow under Mail, Beech and Hunter, at an ever quickening pace, but it was left to Hunter to initiate a new major publishing project – the *Laws of Canada*. Research started in 1978, under Prof. Alan Sinclair, and is planned to result in the publication of the first volume in 1980.

Progress has also been made geographically: a branch was opened in 1978 in Vancouver to develop legal publishing for British Columbia and Alberta. In Canada as in the other overseas offices local publications have overtaken imports from London, and by 1979 these accounted for 65 % of Butterworths' business in Canada.

But during Dennis Beech's terms of office the major questions were what should be done with medical and scientific publishing and what should be done about the United States. Canada is for any British publisher a territory which cannot be considered independently of its great neighbour to the south. Difficult questions are posed by the proximity of the United States, against the background of an expanding medical and scientific list: should Butterworths' operations in the American continent be divided geographically or by product? must every selling operation have a base in local publications? are there opportunities in Canada for legal publishing only, but not for medical, scientific and technical publishing? is the reverse true of the United States?

The two men who should have asked and answered these questions in the 1950s had other things on their mind. They left it to their successors to wrestle with them for well over a decade. Only after Gordon Graham took command at head office in 1975 was a firm answer given.

Chapter 11

Whitlock and Emery

Quennell's exit at the end of 1949 left John Whitlock and Seabrook Emery in joint command. They were the only full-time executive directors, and they remained Joint Managing Directors until Whitlock's retirement at the end of 1961. It was a decade of quiescence.

Kenneth Moore was still non-executive Chairman in 1950. Other non-executive directors were Douglas Niekirk and David Willis.

Moore was anxious to be relieved of the chairmanship. Neither of the other two non-executive directors was a candidate. The Earl of Rothes, an experienced company director and 'City' figure, was appointed to the Board in February 1950 to replace Quennell. He became Deputy Chairman later in the year, and succeeded Moore as Chairman in September 1951.

Early in 1950 Moore had recommended the appointment of Philip Mason as Whitlock's 'adjutant'. Mason was an ex-Indian Civil Servant (C.I.E., O.B.E.) without publishing experience. He left after about a year, becoming Director of Studies in Race Relations at Chatham House in 1952, and Director of the Institute of Race Relations in 1958. On his resignation from the staff he was appointed to the Board, and remained a director until April 1964.

Peter Smithers, M.P., completed the tally of non-executive directors, replacing Kenneth Moore.* David Willis resigned from the Board in May 1952, but he and Mrs. Willis (who was of course Stanley Bond's widow before her second marriage) kept in touch with management through personal contacts, and with the staff through the Old Butterworthians Society. This organisation for staff and pensioners with long service, founded in 1951, was the brain-child of Gus Calcutt. Myrtle Willis, as President, chaired annual dinners and gave lavish hospitality to members at her Hampshire home.

Mrs. Willis and Kenneth Moore were still trustees of the Bond estate and in that capacity had contact with the two trustee

---

* Smithers, like Moore, was a trustee of the Bond estate.

A dinner of the Old Butterworthians' Society, 1952

directors (Niekirk and Smithers). Mrs. Willis was informed by Stanley Bond's old City friends, and particularly by Sir Patrick Ashley-Cooper (a Governor of the Bank of England), that Butterworths' progress was not all that it should be. In 1954 she and Kenneth Moore resigned as trustees and were replaced by a company, B.V.W. Investments Ltd., of which the directors were Sir Patrick Ashley-Cooper, Brigadier Sir Henry Holdsworth (another old friend) and Richard Millett. The last named, who was to play a crucial part in the history of Butterworths, was recommended by David Willis; he was solicitor to Willis's family and to Willis, Faber and Dumas, Lloyds' brokers. Mr. Willis knew him to be highly regarded by Sir Patrick Ashley-Cooper and other prominent City personalities.

The resignation of David Willis left the Board of Butterworths as it would be for a decade:

The Earl of Rothes, *Chairman*
F. W. S. Emery and J. W. Whitlock, *Managing Directors*
Philip Mason
P. D. Niekirk
Peter Smithers

Emery and Whitlock were, in their different ways, dedicated

1 Mr Emery	11 Miss Crockett	21 Mr 'Polisher' Williams	31 Mr Whitlock
2 Mr 'Sam' Wood	12 Mr 'Buster' Brown	22 Miss Gosden	32 Mr Wilkes
3 Mr Thomas	13 Mr Penn	23 Mr Simmonds	33 Miss Chalmers
4 'Sergeant' Webb	14 Miss Robinson	24 Miss Dalton	34 Mr Piggott
5 Mrs Hurcombe	15 Mr 'Henry' Shaw	25 Miss Andrews	35 Miss Gwen Smith
6 Mr Frank Harris	16 Mr Mail	26 Mr 'Doug' Davies	36 Mr Holmes
7 Miss Russell	17 Miss Crabb	27 Mr 'Chick' Fowler	37 Mr Barton
8 Mr Purser	18 Miss Treadway	28 Miss Kidman	38 Miss Clark
8 Mr London	19 Mr 'Gus' Calcutt	29 Mr Kay Jones	39 Mr Skottowe
10 Mr Venning	20 Mrs Willis	30 Miss Rich	

to Butterworths and to their respective jobs. They worked together for many years in outward amity, and to the Board they made an admirable team. However, to many of those on the staff who worked under them, they seemed not to be happy with each other. Whitlock was the publisher; Emery the moneyman. They could have counterbalanced, but instead they pulled against each other. Under their duumvirate the company did not move forward. The fifties were in any case a time of relative complacency in British publishing; Butterworths had more than its share, it being hard for anyone publishing *Halsbury's Laws* not to feel some degree of euphoria.

Harry Henry was fated to be the buffer, and sometimes the shuttle, between Whitlock and Emery. His request to be given the title of General Manager, at the time of Quennell's departure, was not then granted. After Whitlock and Emery had held office as Joint Managing Directors for a year, Henry raised the matter again. After much discussion, Emery and his fellow directors agreed to give Henry the title. But he still did not get a seat on the Board. At the end of 1949 he would have been justified in expecting that Quennell's restoration to him of full responsibility for sales would have marked the end of his 'probation' and be the occasion for his appointment as Sales Director. But the directors did not want Henry on the Board, nor those others on the staff whose claims would have followed.

Increases in salary were given reluctantly at this time, and no one suffered more from this than Harry Henry, who found that getting a salary commensurate with his view of his responsibilities was like getting blood out of a stone.

Henry recalled that his decision to stay on with Butterworths did not bring him any reward. Unless of course the loyalty of his staff was its own reward. The accounts and editorial staff had few direct dealings with him, but even after he became General Manager (with a Sales Manager under him) the sales staff were peculiarly his. Indeed they loved him. Very little happened without his knowledge, for the 'grape-vine' ran right up to him.

Early in 1962 the Board proposed to turn Butterworth & Co. (Publishers) Ltd. into a holding company, the U.K. business being carried on by Butterworth & Co. Ltd. (legal) and Butterworth Technical Books Ltd. (scientific and medical). In preparation for this change Harry Henry, Jack Edgerley (Chief Legal Editor, and Editor of *Halsbury's Laws*) and K.J. were appointed to the Board of the legal company, and Lord Leslie (Manager of the Scientific and Medical Division, and son of the Chairman), to that of the technical company. But

John Wilson Whitlock.
(Photograph by
Lafayette Ltd.)

the reorganisation never took place, and the long-awaited staff
directorships related only to dormant companies.

The period during which Emery and Whitlock were Joint
Managing Directors seemed at the time to be happy and
prosperous years, but Harry Henry in retrospect called them the
'dull years'. The legal business (unlike the scientific and
medical) prospered, and the team of departmental managers
remained virtually unchanged throughout the period. Many of
these had been recruited soon after the war, and most were in
the prime of life.

The company's profit before tax increased year by year, though only marginally in 1949 pounds:

	£000	£000 (in 1949 pounds)
1949	149	149
1950	160	156
1951	186	165
1952	182	152
1953	200	165
1954	228	185
1955	214	160
1956	260	195
1957	309	223
1958	386	275
1959	358	251
1960	396	277
1961	356	240
1962	392	255

The question whether the legal business would have done better without the scientific and medical ventures was frequently debated – and most urgently below the level of the Board, which tended towards over-optimism.

Although 1958 was the first year in which the joint turnover of legal and medical was higher in real terms than that of 1949, the fact is not reflected in the self-congratulatory minutes of the monthly Board meetings, usually recording turnover in excess of the previous year. There was no budget or target, though occasionally an 'estimate' for the year is mentioned. One minute naively records 'The estimated rise in overheads of about £50,000 in 1956 would be taken care of by this increase in turnover – £63,000'.

Emery treated the figures supplied to him by Phil Hogger, the Chief Accountant, with a discretion which amounted to secrecy; they were seen neither by non-executive directors nor by senior executives not on the Board. Even Henry, as General Manager, was not officially shown the detailed year-end accounts. He and Hogger were both professional accountants; they were both equally frustrated by the lack of interest from above, and they discussed the figures together regularly.

The Board meanwhile were given only a few of the figures available in the Accounts Department; they considered monthly reports on turnover (but not profit), on cash in the bank (but not on collections), and on paper stocks with which they were curiously obsessed. The cash was stated at a given date, but the Board did not ask for 'highest and lowest' figures, an omission which shocked Millett when he joined the Board late in 1962.

Publishing policy, pricing, selling methods, and control of overheads played little part in the Board's deliberations. It was said unkindly (but not perhaps untruthfully) that the non-executive directors appeared not to know the difference between gross and net profit.

Hogger wrote to Emery in May 1960:

'Assuming that overhead expenses will increase by much the same amount in 1960, say by £35,000, we need in 1960, if we are to equal the 1959 group net profit, (subject to instalment and other adjustments remaining at the same total as in 1959) –

(a) an increase in the group rate of gross profit from the 1959 rate of 41.2% to a rate of 42.8%. This increase of 1.6% on the 1959 sales total £2,225,000 would give an increase in gross profit of £35,600.

or

(b) an increase in sales of £85,000 on which at the 1959 rate of gross profit of 41.2% there would be an increase in gross profit of £35,020.

It will be seen that a difference of only 1% in the rate of gross profit (on the sales of over £2,000,000) has a material effect on the results.'

In the event the turnover went up by 10%, and so did the net profit. A modest enough growth, but all Hogger had been asked was how to equal the previous year.

In the late 1950s Butterworths' share values and dividends also went up in current, but only marginally in real, terms. They had a bad patch before that. When the company went public in 1947 the share price was 36s. 6d. By 1950 it had dropped to 23s. 4d, reaching a new low of 16s. 6d in 1952. By 1962 the corresponding figure* had risen to 77s. 2d (45s. 7d in 1947 pounds). The yield to the shareholders on the current market price attained a heady 10% in 1957, but averaged close to 5%.

Dividends increased even more slowly than net profit owing to the amount ploughed back into the business. The cost of

* I.e. the market value of one voting and two non-voting shares (the equivalent of one pre-1955 share), adjusted for the rights issue in 1949. As to the share structure generally, see Appendix I.

keeping the business self-financing was considerable as stocks
and debtors increased. Despite the consequent increase in
capital employed, the return on capital showed an upward
trend during the Whitlock/Emery period – not that the concept
was then used as a criterion of performance. During the years
from 1963 to 1967 it was much in evidence, but the return did
not improve any further.

Furthermore, in common with the rest of British publishing,
Butterworths were timid in setting their prices – the price-graph
of Butterworths' books lagged far behind cost-of-living trends.
Had prices been increased progressively, the company would
have been more successful financially, and the stiff price
increases which eventually became inevitable would have been
less of a shock to customers. Sales resistance to elaborate
Services was feared, and publishing plans were tailored to fit
the price thought to be readily acceptable.

This was where Whitlock could have made more contribution
to the company's welfare had he and Emery been in rapport.
But his energies were mainly directed to the expansion of
medical and scientific publishing, and to the American market.
It has been suggested that Whitlock's weaknesses were a lack
of original ideas, and an unwillingness to take risks. The
question what risks are worth taking is a subjective one, but he
certainly was not a gambler like Quennell (although he took
avidly to betting on horses while Quennell was around). He was
successful in bringing together and bringing to fruition ideas
culled from others over a wide range, whether inside or outside
the company. But in relation to pricing he was content to accept
the line of caution.

He received detailed weekly reports on all aspects of his
departments, and he didn't miss much. His personal assistant,
Jack Pryke, acted as his eyes and ears. Whitlock stepped in
whenever he felt that pressure or encouragement were needed.
He always gave the impression of working from morn till eve.
He was an early riser, and his social activities kept him up late.
His office hours, unlike those of his colleague, were completely
erratic. Butterworths was seldom out of his mind.

Neither Whitlock nor Emery were men of extremes. They
were completely different from the mercurial, generous and
hot-tempered Quennell. As a result their reign was much more
comfortable than the previous one. But comfort is not really
what a business needs if it is to prosper. In business (as opposed
to private) life they were both parsimonious; but Emery gave
the impression of being even tighter than he really was, while
Whitlock skilfully covered this trait with a cloak of bonhomie.

Emery's office day was different from that of Whitlock. He

Whitlock at Guildhall. Left to right: Simon Partridge, James Whiteside (host at this dinner of the Justices' Clerks' Society), Mrs Whitlock, K.J., John Whitlock, Mrs Whiteside, Miss Whiteside

continued to live at West Dean or Chichester from the beginning of World War II until his death. Like most senior City men travelling up from Sussex, he caught the 7.55 train which got him to the office about 10 o'clock. He then went into committee with Miss Osborn, the Company Secretary, over coffee. The rest of his working day was available for other conferences. There were two 'stockbroker' trains back to Chichester, the 4.18 and the 5.30. Emery caught the latter in the immediate post-war days, but in the late 1940s he began to have bad attacks of asthma (possibly due to the strain of working under Quennell). These attacks continued for the rest of his life, and he was never entirely fit again. Increasingly he caught the 4.18 from Victoria.

He did not mix office and leisure more than he could help. His hobbies, which were many, and his local interests in Sussex, were not related to business as was Whitlock's club life. He was a much more disciplined person than Whitlock. His frugality with the written word saved time (just as J.W.'s verbosity used it up) – though it could also cause misunderstanding or ill-feeling.

Harry Henry's role as General Manager bridged the Whitlock/Emery gap, though he involved himself less with legal publishing than with medical and scientific, and less with accounts than with sales. Each of the Joint Managing Directors found Henry's involvement a useful way of learning about the activities of the other. In view of his Australian experience, Henry was the normal channel of communication with the overseas offices.

This picture of the 1950s can well be rounded off by the account given recently by Ron Watson of what it was like when he was Scientific Sales Manager:

'There existed a love-hate relationship between departments which fused into an idolatrous worship of Bond. At the top was the 16th Earl of Rothes, a somewhat nebulous figure. The executive function was exercised by Emery on the financial and administrative side and Whitlock on the editorial and production...Whitlock was by far the stronger of the two. A "very likeable rogue" with a Walter Mitty mentality and a great sense of theatre: machismo personified. First introduced to me as Major Whitlock, he belonged to no less than eleven masonic lodges and once received me in his office dressed in the full regalia of a Knight Templar, cloaked in velvet, crowned with a plumed bonnet, a drawn sword in his hand. I liked him and got on well with him...Emery and Whitlock, each the antithesis of the other, disliked each other intensely. Emery would tell me of the misdeeds of Whitlock and Whitlock would tell me of Emery's machinations. Life was not easy when I reported to both. In addition, Emery conducted a running battle with Henry. Since I also reported to Henry I received the sitreps of this battle. I was obliged to step like Agag, delicately and tripartite.'

Emery often referred to 'my side of the business'. Whitlock was responsible for all that happened up to the delivery of the books to the warehouse. Then Emery took over. Marketing, distribution, invoicing, sales ledger and collections, the preparation of the annual and half-yearly accounts and management accounts, and the Secretary's office, personnel and house management – all these were 'my side of the business'.

Emery's departments were conscientiously run, with a minimum of change. Resignations, retirements and deaths were normally made good by promotions. The Chief Accountant, Phil Hogger, had a qualified second-in-command, but was unable to keep first-class ambitious men, since there was no prospect of promotion.

Under Emery the whole order-handling function up to invoicing and packing was in the hands of the Sales Department, who were thus often drawn into service rather than sales. The Publishing Department was also affected by service problems: the publisher, having overcome delays by author and printer, wanted his book to reach the customer at once; but accumulation of work for the invoice typists, or of posting slips waiting for attention by ledger clerks, caused new delays.

F. W. Seabrook Emery.
(Photograph by Godfrey
Argent Ltd.)

Turnover figures depended on the completion of the cycle.
Warehouse and sales ledger had to agree the timing.

To the outside world a publishing house is judged by the
books it produces. But to those inside, the production and
publication of a book is only part of the story. It is no use
producing books if there is no one to sell them, and no use selling
them if there is no one to collect the money. Only the staff in
a publishing house know the delicate balance between editors,
salesmen and accountants.

Creative sales, the activities which produce the orders, are in
the case of Butterworths unusual. While the general publisher
relies for his sales upon press advertising and upon getting his
books stocked and displayed by booksellers, Butterworths has

traditionally used specialist representatives calling upon lawyers, and direct mail advertising. Representatives and mailings
support each other, and both are supported by correspondence
clerks. It is as usual for a representative to make a sale for which
a mailing has prepared the ground, as it is for a postal sale to
result from seed sown by a representative. Some publicity is
addressed to firms, and some to individuals by name – much
of it may end up in a clerk's waste-paper basket. But the
representatives have to make sure they see the principals.

Such a system has proved unbeatable for Butterworths' legal
publications; as has been noted, it worked less well with many
medical books, and it did not work at all with scientific books.
For these increasingly important areas of its publishing,
Butterworths had painfully to learn that booksellers and press
advertising were key factors.

The period from 1950 to 1954, when Jim Marsden was in
charge of an Advertising Department separately housed in
Breams Buildings, was the period of the maximum growth in
the department. It was also the period when Ron Watson was
working to get scientific publicity into his own hands; the
separation of publicity from other sales functions was something
Watson could not understand.

Butterworths had for many years maintained their own
mailing lists. Before the war these were handled by Dawsons,
to whom corrections and deletions were sent. Marsden developed an internal addressograph system which resulted in
greater flexibility and up-to-dateness. Not only were general
lists of the legal profession and of special interest buyers
maintained, but purchasers of encyclopaedias were separately
plated. Butterworths did not rely on the published mailing lists
which existed in the legal field.

The first decade after the war also saw the development of
staffs of skilled copy-writers and artists and designers, reducing
the reliance on the facilities of printers. In pre-war days most
'puffs' were printed by the Abbey Press of Westminster, whose
proprietor was Stanley Bond's brother Frank. By 1950 priority
was being given to Acfords.

Marsden was Advertising Manager from 1945 to 1954;
previously he had been with the Coke Press (publishers of the
Law Journal and the *All England Law Reports*). He had been
considered for the post of Sales Manager in 1945, but the
decision made then was to bring Henry back from Australia.
Marsden as Advertising Manager often dealt in practice directly
with the Sales Director, Lawrence Jones, until the latter's death.
Thereafter he reported to Henry, even though there was a Sales

Manager, Alistair Kerr, for legal and medical books from 1951 to 1954.

On the departure of Kerr some consideration was given to recruiting outside the company, but it was decided to promote Jim Marsden. Promotion from within was Butterworths' traditional preference. Experience of Butterworth ways was seen as outweighing the personal qualities of any recruit from outside. No new Advertising Manager was appointed. Advertising was divided into three parts, each still responsible to Marsden; advertising of Butterworth books, advertisements in Butterworth periodicals, and the maintenance of mailing lists.

Emery's 'side of the business', in brief, reached into every aspect except the actual writing and editing. He wrote at the end of 1961, on the eve of Whitlock's retirement:

'Consideration of this title ['Weights and Measures' in *Halsbury's Laws*] affords me the opportunity of emphasising to you and to three other very senior members of our Organisation my determination to let nothing prevent us from pulling up the publishing programme. The business has grown so large – and complicated – that unless we do this we are in for real trouble. There are several facets of this, not the least being the financing of the Organisation. Two years ago, our debtors (i.e. the amounts owing by our customers) represented four months sales; at present this is 6 months. Experience shows that customers pay much more regularly if their annual levy by Butterworths is more or less evenly spread over the year. If our publishing programme were more evenly spread and our publication dates kept, the desired result would be achieved.'

The accountant, in other words, was calling the tune to the publisher.

The other limb of Emery's responsibility was the Secretary's office. Helen Osborn, an influential figure, strict in etiquette, dealt not only with statutory requirements, Board minutes, etc., but also with personnel and house management. She had been personal secretary to Stanley Bond since 1938; after his death, she worked at first in the Editorial Department, but when Emery's responsibilities were enlarged on the departure of Leader, she became Assistant Secretary; in 1945 she was put in charge of Personnel. Helen Osborn had thus become Emery's No. 2 as far as his administrative and secretarial duties were concerned. In 1949 her position was recognised by her formal appointment as Company Secretary.

Even at that distant date inflation and differentials were

causing problems. A memorandum from Helen Osborn to Emery in 1953 said:

> 'We recruit people with a legal training for sub-editorial work at £450/500 p.a. with the prospect of an eventual ceiling of £800.
>
> When we returned to London in 1946, we recruited at £400/450 p.a. without tying ourselves to a ceiling, and in those days we compared quite reasonably with the Civil Service. About three years ago the Civil Service revised their salary grading for Legal Assistants and I attach a note of these as they now stand.
>
> From this you will see that the basic salary, plus pay additions, at age 26 is £655, rising after about 12 years to £1146. The higher grades are at the £1600 level. They work 5½ hours a week more than we do but on the other hand they have longer holidays.
>
> The question of ceiling payments has been raised particularly in the case of – – – – – –, a Barrister who came to us in 1946, aged 30, at a salary of £500 p.a. Now, aged 37, he earns his ceiling of £800, and is – – – – – –'s best man on – – – – – –. He has been put forward for a rise of at least £50 this Christmas. If this is agreed, the present ceiling will have to be raised. Perhaps it might be advisable to leave it undetermined without at the same time giving the impression that "the sky is the limit". If anything definite were laid down as a ceiling in the region of £1000, it would make it very difficult to define the position and prospects of, say, – – – – – now at £1100, and even – – – – – at £900.
>
> There has been mentioned to me the point that a man like – – – – – –, earning £800 a year now, does not really get out of it any more than he did when he was earning £600 in 1947. This is rather dangerous ground and I am not suggesting that we should adjust the salaries of one section of the staff strictly in accordance with the rise in the cost of living. In the lower grades, however, we are forced to recruit at salaries which have steadily increased with the cost of living so that it may not be unreasonable to bear this in mind when considering the higher grades.'

By 1956 it was not only salary rates that were causing problems. Butterworths was overstaffed. A comparison was made with 1947, though this comparison is made with reservations: 'We had not then fully settled down into our post-war organisation and the Quennell regime was apt to be a little lavish.' Helen Osborn then points out that 'partial amalgamation of the Tables Department and E. & E. Digest...has already shown how savings in staff can be made', and suggests a 'general overhaul of the organisation'. No serious attention was given to this proposal which would, if pursued, have pin-pointed the major increase (by forty-four) in the scientific department. Legal editorial, which rises and falls with the major work cycle, had gone down by fifteen. But Emery's 'side' had gone up by sixteen. Not all of this was due to increased business, and in some areas the remedy when work fell behind was to engage more staff.

Miss Osborn dealt also with matters of high and delicate diplomacy, e.g. cars for senior executives. There were only three company cars in 1954. This is her instruction to the Accounts Department:

'I have seen both the Managing Directors and the following has been agreed in connection with car expenses.

Mr. Emery: Pays licence, insurance and all other expenses.

Mr. Whitlock: Pays licence and insurance. He is arranging to deal himself with all other expenses as from 1st December, but such expenses incurred up to that date should be charged to Butterworths.

Mr. Henry: To pay for only the oil and petrol he consumes when driving the car for his own use. This decision applies for 1954 and is subject to review.'

Whitlock was apparently being brought into line with Emery. Henry had the best car deal, but salaries were not mentioned.

Whitlock reached the age of sixty-five in April 1960, but was asked to delay his retirement until the end of 1961. Since the ignominious exit of Quennell, Whitlock and Emery had reigned with undisputed supremacy (subject only to the presidency of Lord Rothes), over a company they did not own. Emery no doubt felt that he would continue as a plenipotentiary until his retirement (due in 1965). But Stanley Bond's sons were approaching their majority, and someone had been doing a lot of thinking and advising about Butterworths' future. That someone was Richard Millett.

Chapter 12

The Millett Intervention

On 19th September 1962 Butterworth notice boards carried this announcement:

> 'Mr. Peter Smithers has resigned his Directorship of the Company on his appointment to a post in the Government. Mr. R. Millett has been appointed a Director.'

Peter Smithers was a trustee of the Bond estate. A second trustee, Douglas Niekirk, remained on the Board. The third trustee was B.V.W. Investments Ltd., of which Richard Millett was a director.

After David Willis had proposed that Millett should join the Board, a flurry of correspondence and meetings ensued between the directors, with regard not to Millett's suitability, but to the question of who was responsible for the appointment. Were the Board as a whole? Were they obliged to accept a nominee of the trustees? Must the trustees be unanimous? Was it the trustees or the family who were making the proposal?

One director thought that Millett aimed to succeed Rothes as Chairman. Millett however wrote in 1978: 'I never expected to become Chairman of Butterworths, still less that I would have to perform any executive function. Indeed if I had, I would never have agreed to go on the Board.' But his qualifications made him a candidate. He had experience of company directorship; he was a solicitor, likely to understand the needs of Butterworths' principal customers; he specialised in commercial and tax work.

The Board accepted Willis's proposal. The argument took place in secret. A veil hid from the staff and shareholders the dissensions among the trustees of the Bond estate over how well or how badly the company was doing. Smithers and Niekirk, the trustee directors, were still satisfied; Millett and Mr. & Mrs. Willis, whom he represented, were not. Millett was now in a position to find out. His findings led Butterworths into a period of ferment, catalysis and re-formation.

Millett marked his arrival on the Board by peppering Emery, who was by then the sole Managing Director, with questions. The questions raised were basic and pertinent, but did not endear Millett to his new colleagues.

Millett found that Board meetings were planned to last about an hour. They started at 11.30, and were followed by lunch, at which there were usually outside guests. The papers available for discussion were exiguous.

After his first Board meeting on 10th October 1962 Millett wrote two letters. The first asked for:

'Names, ages, salaries, pension benefits and functions of all employees in any of the companies, whose combined salaries and emoluments other than pension contributions, amount to over £2,000 per annum.*

If the answer to the above can be accompanied by a tree showing the chain of command – where the executive's title is not self-explanatory – it would be helpful.'

The second reveals Millett's anxiety to induce the Board to take a greater interest in the type of legal work which the company ought to be publishing, e.g. tax books using *Simon's Income Tax* as a spring-board.

'You will remember that at the conclusion of the last Board meeting I expressed the view that Butterworths had missed a golden opportunity by not publishing a book on the Capital Gains Tax.

To the best of my recollection, no Director supported that view, but on the contrary a number of reasons were advanced why such a book should not be published. I was far from convinced and you will remember that I expressed the view that such book would be a success provided it was not a Sophian-type book, and should be written preferably by both a lawyer and an accountant.

It was therefore with somewhat mixed feelings that I saw an advertisement for Butterworths' new Capital Gains Tax Book written by Sophian in this week's issue of the *Investors Chronicle*. My first thought was that the seed which I had sown had not fallen wholly on stony ground and that someone had moved with great speed and produced an expanded rehash of the Capital Gains Tax pages from the Simon's Supplement. I thought, however, that it was as well to obtain a copy, but on making enquiries I was unable to purchase a copy, while the Law Notes Lending Library flatly stated they had never heard anything about it.

---

* Say £9,000 today.

The advertisement on page 381 of the *Investors Chronicle* of 2nd November indicates that the book is immediately available, and as my Secretary had to be near Butterworths this morning, I asked her to call on Mr. Kay Jones and borrow or buy a copy, preferably the former! She formed the strong impression that Mr. Kay Jones was unaware that the advertisement had appeared, and she was given to understand that the book would not be available before the end of the month.

I of course approve of the *Investors Chronicle* as a medium for a book of this nature, but I would suggest that the advertisement indicating that it is immediately available is likely to do harm rather than good. Furthermore, I would be intrigued who in Butterworths has the authority to publish a book without apparently any of the Directors being aware of what has happened. In view of my own remarks regarding the publication of the book I cannot but admire the initiative, and I also shall be delighted if my forebodings in regard to the contents are proved to be wrong.

May I suggest that there should be tabled at the next Board Meeting a list of what is intended to be published during the next six months, together with the following figures:

(1) An estimate of the total copies which will have to be sold in order to break even.

(2) An estimate of the period over which it is intended to sell these copies.

(3) An estimate of the total copies which it is thought will be sold, over say, the next three years.

Please do not trouble to answer this letter, but no doubt while certain faces may be red and the incident points a moral, it has its humorous side. I remember reading years ago a book called *The Bassoon Factory* – or some such title – not published by Butterworths. If I had not promised to amputate my horns and tail, I would bring a copy to the next Board Meeting.'

Whitlock had been present at the Board meeting, but in his retirement did not know that a book on Capital Gains Tax was in the pipe-line. There was no publishing executive on the Board. Emery was the only full-time director. It was, to say the least, rash of the directors to argue that a work on Capital Gains Tax was not needed.

The elaborate reports to be tabled were never produced in their fullness but not much later each Publishing Manager had to produce a loose-leaf book with a separate page for each month, listing the titles accepted during that month. As each title was published it was marked off with the date of publication. It is doubtful whether the directors ever looked at it, and after a few years it was quietly discontinued.

Millett probed during the next three months into losses on scientific publishing, capital employed and calculation of overheads. The last was connected with the first, because Millett believed that the method employed favoured scientific and medical publishing to the detriment of legal. He maintained that the medical and scientific losses for 1962 would be about £30,000. Emery replied that they were £6,500 in the first half-year, and that in 1961 the second half-year had done better than the first. But Emery had been working on a notional 20% for overheads; the accounts departments were allocating *pro-rata* to sales; Millett advocated *pro-rata* to *cost* of sales. The eventual net losses on medical and scientific for the year 1962 on these three bases were £14,000, £20,000 and £55,000 respectively.

By April 1963 Millett was ready to fire his big guns. A four-page letter to Emery began:

'The more I see of the figures relating to activities of the Butterworth Group, the unhappier I become. From what you have shown me, it would appear that some half or more of the assets are either employed unremuneratively or at a substantial loss, and that the position of Medical and Scientific goes from bad to worse.'

Millett's letter continues by expressing fears that the improvement in the results for 1962 (as compared with 1961) might cause some to think his views alarmist, but he remained convinced that the trustees and the non-executive directors did not fully understand the accounts. Having surveyed the position in detail, he proposed the employment of management consultants.

'I know [he wrote] I shall be told that the publishing business is unique and that of the publishers, Butterworths' business is unique. In my experience, nearly every client thinks his business and problems are unique. I shall also, no doubt, be told that if business consultants were brought into Butterworths there would be an uproar and people would walk out. The answer to that is I think that if the Board can be persuaded that this is the right approach then you should have no difficulty in selling the idea to the staff – that the consultants are being brought in to help them.'

The Board adopted his suggestion. Years later Millett recalled:

'I was told subsequently by Emery that one strong influence with the Board was that they were confident that they'd get a clean bill of health from Deloittes and that I'd be so ashamed of my criticisms that I would resign.'

Deloitte, Plender, Robson and Morrow were Millett's recommendation as consultants. After less than two months they reported that they could help. Emery told Heads of Departments:

'The Board have decided to review the organisation of the Butterworth Group of Companies with a view to greater efficiency and more modern methods of working. Similar steps have been taken by go-ahead companies during the past few years with advantage not only to the companies concerned but also to the staffs of all grades who work therein.

At my suggestion two months ago Messrs. Deloitte, Plender, Robson, Morrow & Co., who have great experience in these matters, were invited to undertake this task. After preliminary talks with senior people at Kingsway and Bell Yard, they are convinced that they can help us, and they are starting forthwith...

I look to all members of the staff to give [Deloittes] every assistance during their time here. They will approach heads of department whose help they require and these heads will introduce appropriate members of their staffs according to the circumstances.'

Throughout the summer Deloittes probed and prodded. Their first report was ready on 24th October 1963. In their preliminary proposal of 31st May they recommended that policy and operations should be examined under the following heads:

(a) Profitability of activities – United Kingdom and abroad;
(b) Inter-relationship of activities and basis of inter-company transactions;
(c) Development prospects;
(d) Financial resources and employment thereof;
(e) Budgetting;
(f) Group control structure and functional organisation – including the functions of the Board and of the chief executives;
(g) The Bond family interests.

Deloittes would have preferred to deal with matters in that order, but later realised that the most urgent problem was to find a successor to Emery as Managing Director, for which a prerequisite was to define and agree the specification for that appointment.

In 1959, when John Whitlock had been asked to continue for another two years, a Board minute recorded:

'Mr. Emery was due to retire at the end of 1964. . . . There were therefore only five years in which to build the Management team which would function when both the present Managing Directors had retired.'

That task had not been carried out.

Deloittes reported in October:

' 1. It is evident that the present organisation structure of the company is the result of development over many years. The most important relationship is the link between the Board and the executive management. This is achieved at present through the Managing Director.

2. The Board consists of a Managing Director and a number of part-time directors. The routine information supplied to the Board is sparse and inadequate by normal standards. No system of budgetary control is in operation.* This restricts the Board's function relating to the formulation of policy and the effective control of its application.

3. In these circumstances responsibility for both vests in the Managing Director, who, we understood, maintains close contact with the Chairman. All routine statistical and accounting information is prepared for his personal use and not for the Board.

4. We consider that the development and growth of the company has reached the point where too much responsibility is imposed on the Managing Director alone.

5. We recommend that a fundamental change should be introduced.

6. Control of the activities of the business should be exercised through executives responsible for the main functions, and each should be responsible for the control of his function throughout the business as a whole. They should also be members of the Board and play their part in the formulation of policy. One consequence would be that the present Medical and Scientific Department would cease to be an autonomous department and would be merged with the Legal department. The operational structure of

---

* Phil Hogger recommended the installation of budgetary control in a memorandum dated 29th November 1946. His recommendation was ignored. Perhaps he should have pressed harder, but it would probably have been of no avail.

this department would not be greatly changed but the post of chief executive of the department would become redundant.

7. We recommend that the Board of Directors should comprise:

Part-time directors:
  Chairman
  Advisory Directors

Full-time executive directors:
  Managing Director
  Publishing Director
  Marketing Director
  Financial and Administrative Director

Their responsibilities would be as follows:

Chairman:
  His activities would be restricted to acting as Chairman of the Board. In our opinion there is no place for him otherwise as part of the functional organisation structure. This is no criticism of special duties performed in the past which no doubt have been valuable.

The Board:
  The responsibilities of the Board may be summed up as the formulation of policy and the overall control of the organisation.

Managing Director:
  He holds a dual office as do other executive directors. As members of the Board they each would share the corporate responsibility of the other directors.
  The second responsibility is as principal executive director charged with the day-to-day management of the company in carrying out the Board's policies and co-ordinating the efforts of the executive directors.

Publishing Director:
  Responsible for directing and managing all Publishing, Editing, and Production.

Marketing Director:
  Responsible for directing and managing all Sales, Advertising, Promotion, Despatch, Book stores.

Financial and Administrative Director:
  Responsible for directing and managing all Accounting, Secretarial, and Administration activities of the company.'

The Board met on 31st October to consider Deloitte's recommendations. The Earl of Rothes had already decided to resign forthwith. The Board accepted his resignation, and Emery took the chair. The Board then agreed to the abolition of the autonomous Scientific and Medical Department (headed by Lord Leslie, Rothes's son). They also appointed Harry Henry as a member of the Board. They then dispersed without appointing a new Chairman.

A night's thought apparently revealed no alternative to Richard Millett. Harry Henry, who felt the need for a new broom, favoured his appointment. Millett feared for his practice, but was ready to accept the task.

The appointment was made on Friday 1st November, without announcement. On Monday morning the staff arrived to find Millett literally in office. A group was accustomed to meet at about 9 a.m. in the library (then situated on the executive floor) for an informal 'brew up' organised by the librarian, Harris. Leaving the library to refill the kettle, Harris met a stranger in the corridor. 'Can I help you?' he enquired courteously. 'I'm your new Chairman', came the reply. 'Tell me, what time does this floor come alive? And why are you carrying that kettle?' One of the group hastily snatched up a pile of periodicals and walked boldly out with them just as Millett appeared to investigate the reason for the kettle. He passed the new broom in the corridor with a polite 'good-morning' and so made his escape. Millett's meticulously-kept diary records that he arrived at 8.50; a typist at 9.05; and the librarian at 9.12. He met Henry in the Central Hall at 9.17. He found little to please him in his first hour as Chairman.

Deloittes had found some difficulty during their investigation in 'understanding the definitions and relationships of the functions and titles in the present organisation'. They had been told, for instance, 'Henry...on retirement of [Whitlock] succeeded him functionally as publisher of the Legal department...He has clearly succeeded to Mr. Whitlock's function already without being given the same title.' Deloittes' recommendation that, during a transitional period, Henry should be given the title of Publishing Director was overtaken by their further recommendation 'that provided the principles of our recommendations for reorganisation of the management structure are accepted, [Henry] should be regarded as the Managing Director-elect. In reaching final decisions on reorganisation matters his views would be pertinent.'

Although Deloittes' report says guardedly 'If and when Mr. Henry succeeds Mr. Emery', it assumes that he was likely to do so, with the proviso that he should not be so appointed 'until suitable persons have been installed as Publishing Director and Finance Director respectively'. Harry Henry certainly expected to be Managing Director and told everyone so.

For several months Millett, Henry and Deloittes argued over how Butterworths should be reorganised. Their principal differences were over the selection of the other directors, and the timing of appointments. Millett wanted people from outside, and to have them on the Board in a matter of months, over the heads of Hogger, Marsden and K.J. An unsigned pencil note (possibly written by one of the Deloitte team and intended for Millett) says 'the quality of the present staff. Good enough for a time – not good enough for the Board.' Henry wanted his old colleagues on the Board for the remaining five to ten years of their service, on the ground that this would give time to train their successors in Butterworth traditions and methods.

By February 1964 a way out of the dilemma was put forward by Deloittes, with Henry's support. This was the creation of a new class of director, to be called 'Executive Director', without a seat on the Board. This required an amendment to the Articles of Association of the company, which it was decided to place before the shareholders in June. This was a real break with the past, and a first step towards having full-time executives on the main Board, as envisaged by Deloittes.

Five senior executives were summoned to meet Emery and Henry on 26th February 1964: they were Phil Hogger (Accounts); Jim Marsden (Sales); David Jollands (Medical and Scientific Editorial); and Jack Edgerley and K.J. (Legal Editorial). They were told that, if the shareholders agreed to the amendments, they would be appointed the first Executive Directors. Emery was to be Deputy Chairman, and Harry Henry Managing Director.

The Executive Directors were given letters in which they were asked to 'play a greater part than heretofore in recommending policy and assisting the Board and the Managing Director to agree upon and formulate policy'. Their views would normally 'be channelled to the main Board through the Managing Director and *vice versa*, but where policy matters in spheres over which they have direct responsibility are to be discussed at meetings of the main Board, they will be invited to attend'. They were reminded that 'the office of Executive Director will not attract any remuneration as such'.

Harry Henry, as Managing Director-elect, started to hold formal meetings of his Executive Directors-elect. At their first meeting they had before them Henry's 'Review of Financial Position of Butterworth Group over past five years', dated 6th March 1964. A memorandum on capital employed, from Phil

Hogger, dated 31st March, was produced in response to a question asked at the Executive Directors' meeting on 13th March. The accounts were off the secret list at last. None of the new Executive Directors (apart from Hogger, the accountant) had seen such figures before.

Millett resented the fact that the Executive Board, under Henry, did not wish Millett or a representative of Deloittes to join its meetings, and preferred to minute decisions only, not arguments or underlying reasons. Occasionally Millett would burst unheralded through the communicating door between his office and the Board room to speak to one of the Executive Directors, thus interrupting their meeting. All in all the Executive Board's methods, and its recommendations, were a great disappointment to Millett, for whom they were a poor substitute for the dynamic newcomers he had envisaged.

Henry was not Millett's idea of what a managing director should be. The staff, on the other hand, believed that they could go forward under Henry's leadership. Millett and Deloittes were the interlopers; Henry had been with the company for thirty years, and had been General Manager for twelve. Henry felt initially that Millett's intervention was badly needed, but he and Millett could not work together. Millett involved himself in detail, and was in a hurry. Henry wanted the authority that Whitlock and Emery had enjoyed.

Their first collision came in December 1963 over staff salaries. Millett was known to be against any increases, because of his low opinion of the Butterworth staff. Henry recommended rises for most of the staff. He told Emery that if the two of them stood firm, Millett would not be able to turn down the combined recommendation of both executive directors on the Board. Emery went alone to Millett's City office to go through the list. Every recommendation was turned down. Henry told Millett that evening that he was 'shocked'; he knew now where the power lay.

Millett was in a dilemma. It would have been easy for him to court favour by generous increases; but he had been assured by Deloittes that no one of worth had left for higher paid work, from which it was deduced that Butterworths' salaries were in line. On the other hand, commenting recently on the fact that he received no payment for precedents he produced for use in Butterworth publications, he added 'I could hardly pay myself more when the salary list of Butterworths was so low'.

On 20th January 1964 Millett recorded in his diary a 'long and amicable discussion' with Henry, in which he said that there appeared to be three choices open:

'(1) To make him Managing Director with a completely free hand, and call off the pressure from Deloittes in strengthening the management in any direction at the present time.

(2) To sell the business (leaving it to Henry to make his terms with the purchaser or go to Australia), which the Bonds certainly would not want.

(3) To build up a team as recommended by Deloittes but at perhaps a slower pace than they envisaged in their second report.'

The second choice was not a real one. At that stage it would have been totally unacceptable to the Bond family. Henry obviously preferred the first choice, but Millett, having been responsible for introducing Deloittes, would have felt diffident about advising the Bond family to ignore their recommendations. Millett 'formed the impression that Henry felt that Deloittes had served their purpose by getting rid of Lord Rothes and his son, and that apart from help on the accountancy side, there was nothing for them to do at the present time'.

Millett appeared to favour the third choice, which took account of Henry's misgivings about the effect on staff morale of bringing in new senior executives from outside. They parted, according to Millett's diary, 'on the basis that each recognised that he had completely failed to convince the other of his point of view'.

But there was no showdown. When Henry pressed for a service contract, Deloittes advised postponing until March, but 'if Henry insisted on a choice between Australia and a service agreement, he should be allowed to go to Australia'. (Henry had, of course, already served in Australia, from which he had returned to become Sales Manager in 1945.) In June he was duly appointed Managing Director but he did not hold the office for long.

The summer of 1964 saw interminable discussions on the implementation of Deloittes' recommendations, about many of which Henry was lukewarm. When he went on holiday in the autumn of 1964, he was exhausted. Before he came back he had decided to accept the managing directorship of the Australian company which would become vacant a year later, on the retirement of Bill Nichols.

In February 1965 Millett records having a discussion with Henry about 'his proposed resignation and taking over in Australia', but nothing was in black and white. In the same month Henry booked his passage for October. During the summer Henry was selling his house and Millett was looking for a new managing director.*

In August the terms of the move were finalised, and Harry Henry left in October 1965 for Sydney, from where he continued to do battle with Millett. He tried so to organise his correspondence as to limit the control of Australia from London; indeed he informed a colleague that he intended to tell London as little as possible. Millett retaliated, when he visited Australia to find out for himself the state of affairs, by ensuring that no-one revealed his journey to Henry. He arrived unheralded at the Sydney office – at a time when Henry was out.

While Henry was deciding, or being urged, to go back to Australia, the search went on for the Financial Controller and Sales Director that Deloittes had recommended. Many exhaustive interviews resulted in the appointment of Ian Dickson, a chartered accountant who was Company Secretary at Penguins, as Financial Controller in January 1965. He was an Executive Director from the start, and was put onto the main Board in June 1965.† On Henry's departure Ian Dickson was made General Manager – but not Managing Director.

David Kingham was another recruit of this period, who responded to the higher profile that Millett was giving to the company. Kingham, joining in February 1966 from Leonard Hill, a small technical publisher, embarked on a programme of books in commercial education, but was quickly seconded to Washington, as described in Chapter 8, to supervise the closing of that office.

Alan Roberts and Stan Hall, who became respectively Chief Accountant and Order Service Manager, also joined the company at this time as a result of the Millett – Deloitte reforms.

In 1966 Millett made a public declaration of his search for new blood, by telling shareholders in his Chairman's Statement:

'It may at one time have been thought that promotion in Butterworths, as in some other publishing companies, was difficult to obtain, at any rate in or near the Board room, in the absence of the right background, e.g. the right blood relationship, the right tie. I do not say that such a criticism could have been justly made of Butterworths but I fear that

* He saw Barker of the Publishers Association on 5th April to ask his advice. Gordon Graham, who was to become Managing Director ten years later, was one of the people he approached.
† One other Executive Director was appointed to the main Board during the Millett period, namely K.J., when Whitlock, who was becoming increasingly infirm, resigned his non-executive directorship in June 1966. Whitlock died in 1968.

it was not made sufficiently apparent that promotion was not only open to all but was open at a sufficiently early age. In consequence some ambitious young men were apt either not to join us or, if they did, to become discouraged and leave. Be that as it may, when I came to Butterworths I found an unduly large proportion of our Executives were over fifty years of age, and that there was a singular lack of the younger generation either in, or being groomed for, executive office.

This is being remedied so that the wealth of experience of the older generation may be blended with the new. One consequence is that today Butterworths can offer the prospects of unusually rapid promotion to those of the younger generation – whether they are already with us or wish to join us – who can prove themselves worthy of promotion. So as to make this policy clearly apparent the Board have resolved that no one should be taken on by the Company in any capacity so long as a relative of that person is a director or employed in high office in any Company in the group.

This rule may exclude, or at any rate defer, the acceptance of the occasional promising candidate but I think it is sound and is already producing results. Recruitment is also being helped by an improved pension scheme and free life cover equal to three year's salary, which is particularly attractive to the young married man.'

Recruits may not have flocked to Butterworths in response to this invitation, but the staff liked it. When Millett joined the Board three of his colleagues had sons employed in the business. The son of a fourth (Niekirk) had just finished a six-year stint. Lord Leslie, the son of the then Chairman, was in charge of the Scientific and Medical Division. His departure coincided with Millett's appointment as Chairman. David Whitlock worked for some time in the Sales Department, for a time on the editorial staff of the *Law Journal*, for a time in the Production Department, and finally became House Manager. He moved to Pergamon Press in 1968. Richard Emery, after a period of training at head office and in the South African company, was sent to Chichester to help run Acfords, the printing business there, ending up as Managing Director of that company. He joined Heinemanns in the summer of 1967.

Millett's chairmanship was catalytic rather than innovative. No new enterprises were undertaken during his four years of office. No acquisitions took place and no new major works were planned. The management had to be got right first. But a lot of things changed.

In October 1964 Deloittes produced the first five-year forecast ever to be prepared for Butterworths, covering the years to the end of 1968. Other reports and memoranda from Deloittes followed: Sales Accounting Procedures (October 1964); Budgetary Control (December 1964); Job Evaluation (August 1965); Mechanisation (October 1965). By that time Deloittes had been around for two and a half years. Their roving commission was ended, but consultants can be habit-forming, and Butterworths continued to use them. Undoubtedly the experiences of this period initiated Butterworth staff into procedures and concepts which were to become commonplace.

While new blood was Millett's constant demand, he did not hesitate to use his own muscle to clear away what he considered to be publishing deadwood. In 1966 he urged Sheila Carey to go through the list of contracts eliminating those which should no longer be published or which had not been delivered within a reasonable time after the contract date (provided the goodwill of worth-while authors was not jeopardised). Among potentially unsuccessful publications which were unloaded were the *Caxton Medical Dictionary*, the Johnson joint-venture reprints, *Nordic Clinical Odontology*, *Traumatic Medicine and Surgery for the Attorney*, and *Taxes – Around the World*.

When the Executive Directors began to meet in March 1964, they were presented by Harry Henry with his Financial Review, dividing the activities of the group into four categories: profitable and expanding; profitable but static; unprofitable due to new development; unprofitable and declining. The profitable categories were London legal, Australia, New Zealand, Canada, and South Africa. The unprofitable were Butterworth Inc. (U.S.A.), Medical and Scientific, and Acfords.

Acfords had never made a return on capital remotely approaching that of publishing, and the fluctuations of small profit (or even small loss) were not significant in the context of the group activities. But medical and scientific publishing and the U.S. company were the very areas in which expansion was sought. The U.S. company had always been under Henry's jurisdiction, but medical and scientific had formed an autonomous division, responsible direct to the Board, from 1960 to 1963. They had been brought back to Henry's jurisdiction under the Deloitte proposals, and it was his task, aided by the Executive Directors, to put them in order.

Henry commented in his Review that medical publishing 'over the years presents an erratic course with some good years and some poor'; that scientific publishing 'was showing a steady improvement during the years 1953 to 1958. Since 1958 there has been a steady decline, without any break in the downward trend.'

After allocating overheads *pro rata* to sales, medical just broke even from 1956 to 1963, making a net profit in the years 1957, 1958 and 1961. Scientific made a net profit in one year only, namely 1958. Butterworth Inc.'s aggregate net loss over the four years 1960 to 1963 was £136,000.

The Executive Directors recommended continuation of all three operations. They won their way on medical and scientific. Their proposals were to strengthen the sales organisation, to consider expansion into university and sub-university books, and to accept the revised publishing programme in the five-year forecast. During the whole period from 1964 to 1967 the management made repeated attempts to define the policy so as to make for a coherent list. Projects were looked at more critically than before, in the hope of producing books with an international sale, and of avoiding over-printing.

Forecasts produced by Deloittes showed a net loss on medical and scientific of £47,000 in 1964, improving to a net profit of £137,000 in 1968. Deloittes made it clear that these forecasts were based on information provided by the Executive Directors. The forecasts reveal the unlikely prognosis that turnover would increase by 76%, cost of sales by 42%, and overheads by only 16%. In 1964 the loss was actually £92,000, due to a very heavy write-off of stock. In the following four years the aggregate profit amounted to £30,000, compared with an expected aggregate of nearly £200,000.

In regard to Washington, however, as described in a previous chapter, Millett had *his* way. All except one of the other main Board directors supported him. Harry Henry alone voted for continuance.

There was nothing in the first two years of the 'Millett intervention' to indicate any but the simplest of motives. The Bond family and their advisers were dissatisfied with the progress of Butterworths. They hoped that with Millett on the Board they would be able to find out what was wrong, and that the company could be put on its feet. There were two things about which Mrs. Willis had particularly strong views – that the company should remain an independent memorial to Stanley Bond's enterprise, and that their sons should, if they so desired, be able to enter their father's business.

Millett's main concern developed on different lines from those originally envisaged. Small independent British publishing companies like Butterworths could be swallowed up by U.S. competitors, and must be defended, said Millett. And in any case Butterworths sorely needed new management.

Amalgamations of one sort or another could be the answer to both these dangers. He also suggested that there might be fiscal advantages from size. He often talked about 'buying management'. Two forms of development were envisaged. The proprietor of a small business, lacking financial or other facilities for development, could sell himself and his list to Butterworths. There could be an amalgamation of two or more equal groups with Butterworths in a merger. Either of these could bring additional management strength (and incidentally reduce the 'threat from America').

Millett was given to using his Chairman's Statement to reach a wider audience than the shareholders. In May 1965 he wrote:

'While it may not have been the Government's intention deliberately to harm small companies, they are adopting a system of taxation which will inevitably have that effect. Your company has been established for over 50 years from small beginnings and has every sympathy with those who wish to keep their independence and not be swallowed up and become part of some vast book factory, or, on the other hand, merge with a company which, while its advertisements rightly called the new taxation measures penal, nevertheless is directed by one of the Government's most vocal supporters.

In my opinion there are too many firms of publishers in this country, many of whom are trying to cover too broad a field and there is, I believe, room for rationalisation. There are no less than 68 members of the educational section of the Publishers' Association and the numbers are still increasing. On the other hand, if the Government succeeds in its apparent intention to swallow up or abolish the Grammar Schools and the Public Schools and impose a drab "Comprehensive" uniformity, the demand must necessarily be for much larger printing numbers of far fewer educational books, while the number of big buyers of educational books must be proportionately decreased.

If, therefore, there are family publishers who after serious consideration find the present trends too much for them or who feel that if this country is to withstand the growing American invasion, there must be rationalisation and concentration of effort and production, and believe that they have a contribution to make to a merger with Butterworths, I shall be happy to discuss terms with them, terms which would give them a large measure of independence and enable them to reap a reasonable reward for their efforts. Moreover, if any such merger is effected in the near future, it would appear almost certain that most of the penal effects of the new legislation on vendors can be avoided.'

The position of Stanley Bond's two sons was of concern to any would-be partner. And it certainly discouraged some potential managing directors in the 1965 search. For a long time Butterworth staff had expected that one or both might wish to step into their father's shoes. In the sixties, even those senior staff who had resented the so-called nepotism castigated by Millett did not all find it objectionable that a son of Stanley Bond should enter his father's business on a privileged basis.

The elder son, Ian, after leaving McGill University, Montreal, went to work for McGraw-Hill in England, where he started to learn publishing 'from the bottom'.* By 1967 however he appears to have abandoned his publishing aspirations. Millett's resolution against 'nepotism' may have discouraged him. The younger son, Brian, preferred to follow his stepfather and entered the firm of Willis, Faber and Dumas, the insurance brokers.

Millett's overtures attracted no small companies, but a year later one large one approached Millett.

> 'The discussions with Longmans [wrote Richard Millett in 1978] were initiated by Mark Longman not by me, after many months of vainly searching for management outside. Longman had learned of these searches and I admit that I welcomed his approach and it was he who suggested trying to bring in Penguin, but warned me this was a long shot and that Lane would probably never agree to anything. The deal would probably have been on the basis of an exchange of shares for shares in a holding company; Butterworths would have maintained its independent existence but the scientific and probably the medical would have been hived off into Longmans. The move would have been welcomed by the authorities and [the Industrial Reorganisation Corporation] would have supplied the finance.'

One great attraction to Millett was the expectation that Mark Longman would chair the new group, and Millett, even if he remained on the Board, could then have devoted all his time to his solicitor's practice. Not that being a publisher was unattractive. He enjoyed it, and in unguarded moments was known to say that, if he had his life again, he might have liked to be a publisher; but the call of a remunerative City practice was stronger. For those whom he tried to engage as managing director, the position of chief executive of Butterworths was not

---

* Gordon Graham, now Chairman of Butterworths, was then Managing Director of McGraw-Hill, and remembers Ian Bond as a 'keen and personable' young man, but Ian did not reveal to Graham his connection with Butterworths while working at McGraw-Hill.

seen as secure, either in the existing ownership or in any potential merger.

In his May 1967 Chairman's Statement, Millett was still talking in the same vein:

'Butterworths and other U.K. publishers particularly in the scientific and educational field will, apart altogether from the consequences of current legislation, have to face increasing competition from the U.S.A. There are about 1,000 publishers in this country, although some 95 per cent of the books published come from 376 members of the Publishers Association.

Increase in size by no means necessarily results in increase in efficiency, but 376 publishers is, in my opinion, far too many, and sooner or later business economics, aided by the anti-family legislation, will, I believe, overcome family pride and indeed family selfishness and lead to much-needed rationalism in British publishing with attendant benefits to those engaged in publishing as a fulltime occupation, to the shareholders and to the National Economy. If this does not come about soon, it may well be too late and British publishing may be dominated by foreign interests, particularly in the export market, as has happened in several other trades in consumer goods. The heavy Brigade from the U.S.A., and not only the heavy Brigade, are moving in fast. Butterworths are one of the largest British publishers, and our sales last year were £3.6 m. The book sales, excluding magazines, of one U.S. publisher alone were over £30 m. in 1966, and I estimate that the sales of their U.K. subsidiary were in excess of £1.5 m. as against an estimate of £750,000 three years ago.* In case there may be any misconception on this point, let it be stated that, in my opinion, the first duty of the board of every company, public or private, lies to the company, i.e. to the staff and shareholders as a whole, and not to any particular section or interest.'

Richard Millett had a dramatic effect on Butterworths and its image. He galvanised the company after its long sleep, and made the rest of the publishing industry take notice of a company they had previously taken for granted. For those who had grown old in the service of the company it was a traumatic experience.

Millett never tried to court popularity, but did what he believed to be his duty to the company regardless of the

* He was referring to McGraw-Hill.

consequences to others. He foresaw that he would be called 'this terrible fellow, Millett'.

He had a very agile mind, darting from one subject to another and from one aspect to another with a rapidity which could be disconcerting. One colleague said that he was a master at finding 'complicated solutions to simple problems'. Sometimes the very agility of his mind prevented him from making up his mind quickly, or caused him to change his mind afterwards.

His remarks were sometimes rude, sometimes humorous, occasionally both. One day he was complaining about dust on the books in the showroom window. He pointed to a long-haired office boy and said: 'Tell him to get his hair cut and with what comes off he can make a little brush and dust the books with it'.

He was in the habit of suddenly asking for figures (of which the relevance might not be immediately clear). There were three techniques: plead ignorance; say I'll find out, and take hours laboriously producing exact figures; or give a prompt guesstimate. Those who followed techniques one and two fared worse than those who had the courage to adopt the third.

Millett enjoyed the whirlwind approach to problems. Once, when Butterworths wished to withdraw from a joint venture with a continental publisher, there had to be a flight at short notice to brief a foreign lawyer, numerous long-distance phone calls and insistence on express post. A day in London with the foreign lawyer (starting first thing in the morning and ending in time for others to catch their last train home, when Millett went off to give the lawyer a midnight supper) produced illegible draft after illegible draft, each one fair copied by Millett's secretary, with Harry Henry, Ian Dickson, David Jollands, Sheila Carey and K.J. on constant call.

To the City, Millett was seen to be improving Butterworths' profit record, and the shares were increasing in value. To the City press, he was the author of pungent Chairman's Statements. He was always good copy, and enjoyed attacking government legislation – corporation tax, selective employment tax, and the disclosure provisions of the Companies Act, 1967, were among his Aunt Sallies.

His 1965 statement devoted two pages to the affairs of the company and five pages to the iniquities of the Finance Act. Particular attention was given to the provision that any copyright royalty paid to a shareholder in a close company was not a deductible expense for corporation tax purposes. An amendment deleting the provision was tabled forty-eight hours after *The Times* and other newspapers had drawn attention to

Millett's outspoken comments. He was thanked by the Publishers Association.

Millett had discontinued Board room lunches for VIPs fifteen months before the 1965 Finance Act made entertainment non-deductible. He wrote in his May 1965 statement:

'Monies spent in this way are disallowed as an expense for corporation tax. Your Company does not possess and never has possessed any grouse moors, fishing rights, Rolls Royces or West End flats, palatial or otherwise; it does not give away turkeys or entertain at nightclubs. On the other hand, the management were accustomed to offering modest refreshment at a nearby restaurant to visiting authors over a business lunch, thereby extending the working day which I am told, in this country as a whole – I am not here speaking of your Company in particular – is already one of the shortest in Western Europe.'

And in 1967 he told the shareholders:

'I hope that in the light of these statistics our increased profits for 1966 do not appear to be anti-social. I am confident that you will share my gratitude to the Management and staff for their hard work in the last twelve months, but that in the light of the above figures, you may ask me to draw their attention to the Red Queen's remark to Alice:

"Now, here, you see, it takes all the running you can do, to keep in the same place. If you want to get somewhere else, you must run at least twice as fast".'

No wonder the *Financial Times* said in 1967 that 'Summer without a Butterworth annual report would be a pretty dull affair'.

During the Millett years another publisher with a talent for getting his name in the papers, and one who had once had a connection with Butterworths, was becoming increasingly interested in what Richard Millett was doing with Butterworths. By 1967, undeterred by numerous rebuffs to his overtures, he decided to make a frontal attack.

Chapter 13

Takeover

The fifth floor at 88 Kingsway, where executive secrets had long been husbanded behind discreetly closed doors, was thrown into a state of turmoil on the morning of 10th October 1967. The reason was a letter from Henry Ansbacher & Co. Ltd., the merchant bankers, intimating that they had been instructed to prepare a formal offer to buy Butterworths, and setting out the terms. Their principals were Pergamon Press, the enterprise which Robert Maxwell had built from slender beginnings in the early 1950s, when he bought Butterworth-Springer Ltd.

The move did not come as a total surprise to the Board. Maxwell had made approaches as early as 1964, and less than a fortnight earlier Richard Millett had rejected his latest communication in terms so forthright that Robert Maxwell had described the letter as 'totally unacceptable'. Millett in effect told Maxwell to 'get lost', but Maxwell was a hard man to rebuff. But, even at the moment of the Pergamon bid, a merger with Longmans was still hoped for by Millett.

Millett had known for some time that he might need to defend the company against an unwelcome takeover. He had been warned by one of the partners of Deloittes in June 1966 that if non-voting shares were abolished by law a takeover bid was likely to succeed, and that if a merger with a company with the necessary finance and expertise was rejected on the grounds that Butterworths should remain independent, Millett would be justified in resigning, his task having been made impossible. Little more than a year later time had run out. An unwelcome bid had been received; if it was to be defeated an acceptable bid must be found without delay. On 10th October, the day the Pergamon bid arrived, Millett was advised by merchant bankers that an acceptable deal should be set up before the Pergamon offer was posted to shareholders. To reject the Pergamon bid without an alternative would be unfair to the non-voting shareholders.

For three prominent Butterworthians the Pergamon bid was not the first event of that day. Simon Partridge, Sheila Carey, and David Perry* had been told first thing that morning, by Ian Dickson, of their appointments as Executive Directors. When the letter came from Ansbachers they saw their appointments as possibly of very brief duration. Indeed had the appointments been made a few hours later they would have contravened the spirit, if not the letter, of the offer.

Sheila Carey left for the Frankfurt Book Fair without knowing about the Pergamon bid. She was contacted with difficulty late that night. The next morning the news was in the British papers, resulting in a babel of speculation. Sheila, coping with her customary calm and confidence, told those who thought it was all over that Millett was 'a bonny fighter'. She was proved to be right.

Although the number of voting shares then held by the Bond family and by the trustees of Stanley Bond's will was not so large as to make the company a close company for the purposes of the Corporation Tax provisions of the Finance Act 1965, it was sufficient to make it extremely difficult for a bid to succeed which was not acceptable to the family. Including shareholdings of directors, staff, former staff and relatives of these, Millett and his directors thought they could count on 50.82% of the voting shares. The balance of the voting shares included 10.2% owned by I.P.C. (who also held 10.8% of the non-voting shares).†

The directors, however, were conscious of their duty to all of the shareholders (the bulk of the company's shares being non-voting and held by the public), and to the staff and the customers. As voting shares rose from 24s. 6d to 42s. 6d, and non-voting from 21s. 6d to 36s. 6d, the Board supported Millett's view that Butterworths had only three choices: to accept the Pergamon bid; to sell to, or merge with, a more acceptable third party; or to demonstrate beyond all reasonable doubt that the shareholders would fare better if Butterworths continued as

---

* The earlier careers of the first two have been referred to in Chapters 8 and 9. David Perry (previously Henry's P.A.) had borne the principal responsibility for dealings with the overseas companies since Henry's departure to Australia in October 1965.

† I.P.C.'s interest dated back several years. In March 1964 Millett had been invited to meet Don Ryder, who was a director of I.P.C. as well as Chief Executive of Reed Paper, becoming in 1970 the Chief Executive of the combined Reed International. (There had been earlier meetings, the first in 1961, when the trustees had discussed their policy for the future, which would depend largely on what the Bond boys would do when they came of age.) Millett was told that I.P.C. might be interested in acquiring a large block of voting shares and in drawing up a long-term management agreement. The I.P.C. shareholding was held by nominees, and the beneficial ownership only became known after the Pergamon bid.

an independent company (taking into account the likely effect of this on the share prices).

Maxwell was held in high esteem both in the City and in the press. A few months earlier he had been congratulated by the President of the Board of Trade on his successful eleven-country tour, on return from which Maxwell had announced sales of 7000 sets of *Chambers' Encyclopaedia*. When Millett was reported in *The Times* as saying 'I would want to know a lot more about Pergamon before any merger, and would be very reluctant to accept Pergamon paper under any circumstances', his doubts as to the stability of the Pergamon empire found little support in the City.

When the formal offer documents from Pergamon were posted to shareholders by Ansbachers on 23rd October, Millett sent out simultaneously a letter on behalf of the Board to all ordinary shareholders, as follows:

'I understand that Henry Ansbacher & Co. Ltd. are today posting on behalf of Pergamon Press Limited (Pergamon) an offer to acquire your shares in Butterworths. I have not yet seen the formal documents but the consideration to be offered for the Ordinary Shares will be shares in Pergamon, with an alternative cash offer of 37s. 6d for each "A" Ordinary share and 32s. 6d for each "B" Ordinary share as compared with the current market prices of about 42s. 6d and 36s. 6d respectively.

So far as the offer for exchange into Pergamon paper is concerned, your Board and their advisers, Morgan Grenfell & Co. Ltd., may have many questions to put to Pergamon. These questions may not be confined to what appears in the offer documents but may extend to the many developments affecting Pergamon that have been announced in recent months.

Meanwhile discussions are taking place with others who have indicated their interest in merging with Butterworths and as you will have learnt from my last Annual Statement, your Board is not against mergers in principle.

The outcome of these discussions will be reported to you as soon as possible and meanwhile your Directors strongly recommend that you TAKE NO ACTION in response to the Pergamon offer(s).'

All well-informed members of the staff were deeply concerned. Those who were not actively engaged in the fight watched anxiously for its outcome. The majority hoped against hope for continued independence. Fear of Maxwell was rife, though there were some who would have welcomed his drive, and discounted any danger to their careers. Rumours of other bids were eagerly canvassed. Membership of a big group is seldom welcome, but some particular bidders aroused helpless mutterings among helpless staff, a number of whom felt they were being kept in the dark.

Meanwhile typists, messengers and the lithographic department were rushed off their feet at Millett's behest, preparing communications for press and shareholders – however little they understood the contents.

Millett, with the aid of Dickson and other members of the Butterworth staff, began marshalling facts in support of the viability of an independent Butterworths, together with reasons why an exchange of Butterworth shares for Pergamon shares would not be to the shareholders' advantage.

One telling fact was that since Millett became Chairman the net profit had increased from £390,000 in 1963 to £506,000 in 1966, and was expected to reach £580,000 in 1967. These figures had been attained in spite of the write-off by the group of £503,000 worth of stock in three years (1963 to 1965). In the previous *seven* years only £341,000 had been written-off. It was argued (e.g. in the Chairman's Statement of May 1966) that this indicated an over-valuation in the earlier years. Had this not required rectification, the profits for the Millett period would have been even higher.

The net profit per employee had risen from £469 to £571 in 1966, and was expected to reach £634 in 1967. These figures were thought to compare favourably with Pergamon's figures.

As to the worth of Pergamon shares, Millett caused numerous world-wide enquiries to be made into the activities of Pergamon Press. These enquiries led Pergamon to take out a writ for libel against Butterworths.* But this did not weaken the determination of Millett and his colleagues to resist the bid.

At the same time Millett sought higher bids from more acceptable quarters, in case Pergamon should make a cash bid of an amount which the Board would find it difficult not to recommend. A cash bid would render doubts about the stability of Pergamon irrelevant. (The offer documents of 23rd October had a cash alternative, but not of an acceptable amount.)

Millett was soon in touch with numerous prospective buyers on both sides of the Atlantic. City and publishing figures have vivid recollections of the flow of visitors to Millett's office, and his hurried visits to suitors. Enquiries to Butterworths, some by transatlantic phone, were referred to Millett's City office. For

* After the I.P.C. takeover Butterworths replied to the writ with an apology.

him, even more than for the rest of the Board, let alone the rest of the staff, it was a period of unparalleled excitement.

It soon appeared that very few were likely to outbid Pergamon. These were quickly narrowed to two – I.P.C. (the International Publishing Corporation, proprietors of the *Daily Mirror*) and Crowell-Collier-Macmillan of New York. I.P.C.'s initial bid was not acceptable to the Butterworth Board, and Crowell-Collier were the first to make a firm bid of an amount which, financially, was one which the Board could recommend shareholders to accept. They had already displayed an interest in Butterworths. A visit from their Chairman and President on Christmas Eve of 1966, to discuss a possible American agency, was seen by some Butterworth executives as having something more drastic behind it. But there was a doubt as to the propriety of allowing England's premier law publishers to pass into American hands. A move to get the Bar Council to make representations to the Government is believed to have been afoot.

At this stage Millett went to see Cecil King, the Chairman of I.P.C., which was a significant shareholder. King not only made a better bid than either Pergamon or Crowell-Collier, but satisfied Millett that the character of Butterworths' business would be maintained and the interests of the staff respected. Some argued that making Butterworths a unionised house, to conform with the other companies in I.P.C., would inevitably change its character. But an independent Butterworths would not for long have been able to stand out against unionism.

The I.P.C. offer was in paper not cash:

For each voting share, 49s. 6d of $7\frac{5}{8}\%$ Unsecured Loan Stock *or* 48s. of 7% Convertible Unsecured Loan Stock.

For each non-voting share, 43s. 3d of $7\frac{5}{8}\%$ Unsecured Loan Stock *or* 42s. of 7% Convertible Unsecured Loan Stock.

If I.P.C. stock was taken at par, the offer placed a maximum total value of £6,800,000 on Butterworths.

A shareholder who bought a single 5s. share in 1947 for 36s. 6d would have found its value halved by the end of 1952. By 1959 he would have found a steady market equivalent to his original price. Eight years later, in the summer of 1967, the purchaser of one 5s. share would have had shares worth on the average 63s. 6d rising to 70s. $10\frac{1}{2}$d immediately before the Pergamon bid. The I.P.C. offer was 142s. $10\frac{1}{2}$d, about four times the 1947 price. It had been a long wait for those who bought when the company went public.

It was a term of the bid that it should be promptly accepted by the Bond family and trusts, and that no higher bids should be sought. The Bond family and trusts put the interests of the public shareholders before their own strongly held wishes that Butterworths should remain independent, and sadly accepted. The Board recommended the other shareholders to do likewise. The matter was settled on 31st October. By the end of the year the formalities had all been completed. The offer had been formally conveyed to shareholders and accepted by a sufficient number to enable I.P.C. to acquire the balance compulsorily.

Many members of the staff (and probably some shareholders) desired the continuance of Butterworths as an independent quoted public company. Many maintained then (and still do) that Millett had always intended to sell; Millett states categorically that this was not his intention. But independence became difficult once the bidding had started, unless the interests of the non-voting shareholders were to be ignored.

Although not familiar with Butterworths' business, I.P.C. were (and are) the largest publishing enterprise in the U.K. In recommending acceptance of the I.P.C. offer, the directors were not motivated merely by financial considerations, though the offer was a good one. The preservation of Butterworths in its role and style were also factors.

I.P.C. are sometimes said to have paid about £1,000,000 more than they should have done. Cynics said, groundlessly, that Cecil King wanted to be the publisher of *Halsbury's Laws*. Other members of the I.P.C. Board were enthusiastically interested in the development of an information retrieval system, and coveted Butterworths' legal information bank. King himself offers a much simpler explanation. His group was already established in various book fields by the acquisition of Odhams, Hamlyn and Ginn; it needed strengthening on the technical and academic side. Butterworths came on to the market, and met his requirements; the price to be paid depended on how the bidding went.

One can only speculate as to how shareholders at large would have fared had Pergamon shares been accepted. A successful Pergamon bid would have led directly to Millett's resignation, and probably to that of all the other directors. Millett's most remembered *bon mot* during the battle was his answer to the Butterworth commissionaire, who commented on the beauty of a bunch of flowers Millett was carrying. 'Yes,' said Millett, 'they're for Captain Maxwell's grave.'

During the two months November and December 1967 Butterworths were in a state of suspended animation. The old Board still remained, with Millett as Chairman, but it was agreed that he, together with Emery and Niekirk, should resign in due course. Millett was anxious, with the battle behind him, to get back to his practice.

The I.P.C. offer went out on 17th November, and by 4th December it had become unconditional. The same day a shareholders' meeting approved a total payment of £12,500 by way of compensation for loss of office, divided between the three resigning directors.

Cecil King held a reception in the *Mirror* building for Butterworths' executives on 9th November; he and other I.P.C. directors visited the Butterworth premises. Ian Dickson was asked to put forward his views as to the future management of the business. Among other things he suggested that Cecil King should act as Chairman, and indicated the hopes of himself and K.J. to be recognised as Managing Director and Deputy Managing Director. Butterworths waited anxiously for the answer, and speculated nervously as to which of the bright young men from I.P.C. would be put into the management or on to the Board.

Before Christmas it was indicated that Cecil King himself was indeed to become the new Chairman. This was considered an honour; he was not in the habit of chairing subsidiaries. A Board meeting was called for Thursday 28th December. Cecil King was first appointed to the Board. Millett, Emery and Niekirk next tendered their resignations. King was then appointed Chairman. Ian Dickson and K.J. were duly appointed Managing Director and Deputy Managing Director. Sheila Carey, Simon Partridge and David Perry were appointed full directors.

I.P.C. could not have chosen a better way to boost the morale of the company. The team which was to lead Butterworths in its new corporate role consisted (except for the Chairman) entirely of full-time executives, and all except one had long service with Butterworths. I.P.C. was patently honouring Cecil King's promise to 'preserve the character of the business'.

One hundred and fifty years, almost to the day, since Henry Butterworth set up in business, his company was absorbed for a sum beyond his imagining; but his name and all that it had come to mean in the worlds of law and publishing would be preserved.

The first six months after the takeover, contrary to all expectations, seemed uneventful. Cecil King adhered to his purpose of letting the Butterworth executives continue to run what seemed to him a reasonably run business. He acted as a strictly non-executive Chairman. Only Ian Dickson saw him between Board meetings. I.P.C. did not rush to interfere and Butterworths showed no resentment of their new masters. I.P.C.

executives were not involved in publishing decisions but were concerned, for example, with the maintenance of buildings; the occupation of new premises for computer and order-handling functions; and the appointment of a new Managing Director for the Chichester printing works. The 'no nepotism' resolution was rescinded. Cecil King reckoned that I.P.C. was large enough to avoid abuses. If a director employed an incompetent relative, both would be found out and dismissed. In a curious way I.P.C. and Butterworths cohabited but did not communicate. In contrast with their stormy takeover of Hamlyns, the Butterworth integration was a calm affair for I.P.C.

David Kingham was later to describe this period in more colourful terms in the *Butterworth Gazette*. He refers to Paul Hamlyn

'taking possession for I.P.C. facing the grey-suited ranks of the Butterworthians dressed in a (then) dazzling concoction of greens, liberally sprinkled with purple polka dots. Nothing could more dramatically symbolise the change which had overtaken this staid, and somewhat run-down, old family firm.'

Hamlyn may have thought he was taking over, but it was from Cecil King and other directors at I.P.C. headquarters that Butterworths took their orders. Butterworth executives of the time were determined to play the I.P.C. game without losing their own peculiar 'professional' aura – and I.P.C. were willing to let them try.

There was one small cloud on the horizon. Butterworths found themselves again, after less than five years, being investigated by management consultants. I.P.C. commissioned Tyzacks, and specifically Norman Fisher, a partner in that firm, to advise on the absorption and organisation of Butterworths. By April 1968 plans were being discussed for the formation of a Book Division, to be chaired by Paul Hamlyn, consisting of two groups – the general publishing, based on Hamlyns, and the professional and technical, based on Butterworths. It was proposed that Norman Fisher should head the Butterworth Group, and that Cecil King should withdraw from the chairmanship of Butterworths, which he had never intended to hold more than temporarily. But these plans were not generally known at Butterworths. Change was looming ahead, but it came gradually and without trauma.

Chapter 14

The Corporate Life

On 9th May 1968 Butterworths held a reception to celebrate the one-hundredth edition of *Stone's Justices' Manual*. Cecil King received the guests at Stationers' Hall, under the Caxton and Shakespeare windows presented by Joshua Butterworth. Lord Parker, Lord Chief Justice, and Lord Denning, Master of the Rolls, were on the platform. Denning and King made speeches. If King seemed to have his mind on other things, it was understandable, for at that moment his resignation from the Board of the Bank of England was being delivered to the Chancellor of the Exchequer. Next morning his scathing editorial, castigating the Labour Government, appeared in the *Daily Mirror*. His summary removal from the Board of I.P.C. and, of course, from his five-month-old chairmanship of Butterworths, followed three weeks later.

The *Stone* party at Stationers' Hall. Left to right: J. P. Wilson (joint editor of *Stone*), the Lord Chief Justice (Lord Parker), Cecil King, the Master of the Rolls (Lord Denning), James Whiteside (joint editor of *Stone*). (Photograph by H. W. Neale)

Butterworths thus experienced very rapidly after being taken over the influence of corporate politics on their internal hierarchy. With King went his master plan to develop I.P.C.'s book publishing interests. In the course of acquiring the magazines and journals of Odhams, Newnes, Iliffes and others, he had acquired their book publishing as well. To these he added the general publishing business built up over a brief ten years by its colourful owner, Paul Hamlyn. During this period the reputable schoolbook house of Ginn (an offshoot of the American house of that name) also came into his possession. Butterworths was his last acquisition.

King's departure put an end to further expansion, but not to re-organisation. Just as the magazine, technical journal, newspaper and printing interests were rationalised, by the formation of Divisions related to product rather than to antecedents, so it was planned, at the time of King's departure, to form a 'Book Division'.

The Book Division concept was not consciously abandoned. Indeed, Paul Hamlyn remained nominally head of such a Division. But the new Chairman of Butterworths, Norman Fisher, a figure as formidable in his own field as any I.P.C. director, was not going to allow any intervention in Butterworths' affairs. Under his influence the Book Division was organised in two separate groups – Hamlyn and Butterworths. The Butterworth Group had transferred to it the Newnes technical and Ginn lists from Hamlyns, and the Iliffe scientific list from Business Press.

Norman Fisher was a man of parts. He had been Director of Education for Manchester and Principal of the National Coal Board Staff College. He had been a management consultant and question-master of the B.B.C. Brains Trust. He had been director of a publishing house (Macdonalds) and was to become Chairman of the Printing and Publishing Industry Training Board. It was agreed he would devote half his time to Butterworths. He took office on 1st July 1968.

Fisher saw Butterworths as a proving ground for his management theories. Directors and managers found themselves attending seminars to which they submitted ' Key Area' papers for discussion. Performance appraisal was another Fisher innovation. Under his command, the personnel and training departments swelled in numbers and influence. He made himself highly visible, making systematic walkabouts to get to know the staff. He instituted a bonus for twenty-five years' service. Managers wondered whether he or Ian Dickson, who had been appointed Managing Director after the I.P.C. takeover, was in day-to-day charge.

During this time Fisher also found time to write a novel and spent much energy trying to develop the Ginn imprint, which was for him a special enthusiasm, though he accepted its sale in 1970 to the Xerox Corporation, who by then owned the American Ginn company.*

He also liked to travel and was a frequent visitor to the Butterworth companies overseas. By the time of his death, from leukaemia, on 1st February 1972, he had become a popular and respected figure.

In the meantime, there had been several corporate convulsions, some of which were to affect the course of Butterworths. In March 1970, the International Publishing Corporation had itself been taken over, in a manner of speaking, by its own associate, the Reed Paper Group. The new group was called Reed International. At its head was Don Ryder, who had been an editor of the *Investors Chronicle*, before becoming chief executive of Reed Paper, and who was to become Lord Ryder and Chairman of the National Enterprise Board under the Wilson Government.

Paul Hamlyn resigned from the Board of I.P.C. in disagreement with the Reed takeover. Ryder shortly afterwards brought in the man who was to succeed Fisher, a high-powered troubleshooter with experience in the fields of distribution, finance and systems (including a commission for Heinemann). Ken Stephenson was hired to sort out the troubled affairs of Hamlyn, which had not fulfilled I.P.C.'s expectations of profit after it was purchased. By the time of Fisher's death, Stephenson was in charge of Hamlyn, and I.P.C. let it be known that they would like him also to be Chairman of Butterworths.

Ian Dickson and his managers received the impression that Stephenson would not be chief executive. They were wrong. Butterworths' third part-time chairman in four years accelerated the steady old company into a bumpy ride which was to shake a few people right off. Stephenson did not aim to be popular. One of the most hurtful events of the Stephenson regime, however, was not his idea, but Don Ryder's: the dismemberment of the Australian and New Zealand companies from the Butterworth empire. Ryder believed that Reed companies in each continent should be integrated. Late in 1972, Butterworths Australia and New Zealand found themselves part of an Australian corporation (Reed Consolidated Industries) which knew little about publishing.

Stephenson opposed the concept (as had Fisher), but was

* It has since reverted to British ownership as part of the Heinemann group.

unable to withstand the removal of Butterworths' second largest and smallest companies from his command. David Kingham, the young publisher who had been persuaded by Richard Millett to join the Butterworth team in 1965, at the time of the 'no-nepotism' campaign, was by this time in charge in Australia, having taken over from the ailing Harry Henry in 1969. The company had been ailing too. Obsolete stock, bad debts, a misconceived computer system, antiquated premises and poor management had led to losses. Kingham courageously rehabilitated the company, with encouragement from Norman Fisher and financial support from Butterworth U.K. to ward off insolvency.

Kingham returned to the U.K. in 1973, to become International Marketing Director, but he was not happy and left the company in 1975 to become Managing Director of John Wright & Sons, the Bristol medical publishers. He was replaced in Australia by Peter Cheeseman, a young barrister who had been labour relations officer on the *Daily Mirror* and subsequently personal assistant to Don Ryder. Cheeseman, whom Stephenson had brought into Butterworths in 1972, was to spend more than five years in Australia and bring the company there to new levels of prosperity, building on the foundation laid by Kingham. But it was 1977 before Butterworths Australia was united operationally, and a year later financially, with the parent company.

The Canadian and South African Butterworth companies were not taken over by the local Reed conglomerates, although Ryder had this in mind. Fisher had changed the command in Canada in 1968, arranging an early retirement for Ian Mail and promoting Dennis Beech, who had recently joined the company as sales manager from Prentice-Hall. Beech, a determined twenty-seven-year-old, did not have a background in legal publishing, but nonetheless consolidated Butterworths' place in the Canadian legal market. He also looked for new avenues of expansion, including the United States in which there had been no Butterworth company since the Millett clean-up. In 1972 it was decided to give the Canadian company responsibility for the development of medical sales and publishing in the U.S., but Beech complained that the best medical (and scientific) books had been sold to U.S. imprints. Beech resigned in 1975 and was succeeded by Ernest Hunter, who had been Marketing Director of Britain's Open University and had had previous experience in Canada with McGraw-Hill.

Stephenson, however, spent relatively little time on overseas affairs. The impact of his three years as the Butterworth chief executive was almost exclusively on the British scene. Until his advent, Butterworths had, in a way, contrived to ignore the

fact that it had changed ownership. Legal publishing, traditionally a sequestered vale in which highly professional editors
pursued the even tenour of their way, was remote from the other
I.P.C. publishing interests. Stephenson saw Butterworths as
unprofitable and old-fashioned and determined to cut a swathe
through it.

He believed in the private conference as a means of stirring
the pot; and the formal Board meeting as the place to bring it
to the boil. Under him, the elaborate personnel and training
structure set up by Fisher shrank once more. The accent was
on organisational change, rather than on publishing innovation.
Stephenson frequently said that he was not himself a publisher
and he saw his role as catalytic, preparatory to the appointment
of a chief executive with publishing experience.

Stephenson's first major intervention was in the company's
relocation plans. Under Fisher, the Board had decided to move
the company outside London. A consultant's report in 1971
recommended the Bath/Bristol area. By January 1972, it had
been decided to move the editorial, sales and accounts offices
to Broad Quay in Bath and the warehouse and order service
to Melksham, twelve miles away. Fisher's death occurred as the
architect's brief was being prepared.

Stephenson, however, was keen to have Butterworths occupy
one of the corporation's existing properties. Among buildings
surveyed by K.J. at Stephenson's request was a warehouse,
previously a paper mill, near Borough Green in Kent, which
had been used by Odhams and Hamlyn. In November 1972 the
Bath and Melksham options were relinquished and the move
to Kent agreed, subject to construction of an additional 17,000
square feet of office space.

This decision was followed by Dickson's resignation, ostensibly in protest against the amputation of the Australasian
companies. He was not replaced. Stephenson was named chief
executive. K.J. remained Deputy Managing Director. K.J. had
been increasingly involved in personnel and administration,
and by 1971 was in effect Administrative Director. On Dickson's
departure he handed over personnel and administration to
George Norton.

Responsibilities in the medical and scientific field had twice
to be redistributed. From 1967 to 1969 Sheila Carey was
responsible for all publishing in this area, while a single sales
department covered the whole of the company's business – legal,
medical and scientific. Kingham was being briefed to become
Sales Director on the retirement of Jim Marsden. In the spring
of 1969 George Norton, an able administrator, was engaged,
initially as Manager of the Iliffe list. He successfully accom-

An aerial view of the Borough Green premises. The warehouse block is nearest to the camera, with the office block beyond. (Photograph by Aerofilms Ltd.)

plished the task of integrating the three lists – Butterworth, Newnes and Iliffe. In the autumn of that year, on Kingham's departure to Australia, Sheila Carey took over medical and scientific sales, while Norton took over from her full responsibility for scientific publishing. David Perry, who had been considered for the Australian post, was made Sales Director, responsible for legal sales.

When George Norton was made Administrative Director at the end of 1972, scientific publishing reverted to Sheila Carey, while responsibility for medical and scientific sales was transferred to David Perry. There was thus once again a single sales department, which it was hoped would lead to economies.

During the following year Stephenson instigated a study of the scientific list by a committee consisting of David Perry, Sheila Carey and Peter Cheeseman. This led to the proposition that medical and scientific publishing must be responsible for their own sales. Legal publishing promptly maintained that the same arguments applied to their activities. Stephenson approved these ideas, and Perry left to join HMSO. His Board-level duties were divided between Sheila Carey and Simon Partridge, who had taken over legal publishing from K.J. by stages, completing in 1971.

While sales and publishing responsibilities were being re-allocated, a succession of unsung heroes was grappling with the modernisation of Butterworths' order-processing system. Recognised as obsolescent before the I.P.C. takeover, it began to come apart at the seams when required to accommodate the Newnes and Iliffe lists. Bert Meears, who had come with Iliffe, carried the major burden. He had a heart attack in 1974 which compelled him to give up his role as Distribution Director although he continued to work part-time for several years. The order service and warehouse responsibilities were then transferred to George Norton who thus learned the hard way that companies should not try to re-locate and computerise at the same time and as a single co-ordinated process. David Jackson, who like David Kingham had been in Australia for several years, came back in 1973 and took over distribution under Norton.

The move to Borough Green took place in 1973–4, and most of the British company's 500 employees work today in that beautiful but remote site. Legal publishing remained in London at 88 Kingsway and Bell Yard, and so, for a time, did the scientific, technical and medical publishing.

Legal was the division with which Stephenson interfered least, wisely, since it is the powerhouse of the company. Under Simon Partridge, the bishop's son brought in by Stanley Bond six months before his death, the legal division was doing its traditional job as effectively as ever and also innovating. Between March 1973 and August 1974 it reprinted, in 565 volumes, the Law Reports of the Incorporated Council of Law Reporting for the years 1865–1971. The negotiations for this, initiated by Partridge, included discussions about the possibility of amalgamating Butterworths' *All England Law Reports* with the *Weekly Law Reports* of the Incorporated Council. Stanley Bond would have liked the boldness of this; he would have liked less the sale of his favourite journal, *Justice of the Peace*, to its editor, Barry Rose, in 1969. But this was part of rationalisation, and was balanced by more forward-looking publishing, particularly in the field of taxation and in the development of loose-leaf textbooks, which were to become a separate department within the legal division in 1977.

Financial management was Stephenson's own field of expertise, and he kept it in his own hands for most of his tenure. Ian

Lord Denning's *The Discipline of the Law* was published to honour his eightieth birthday. He here inscribes a copy for Leslie Whitbourn, Butterworths' legal text-book editor. (Photograph by Michael Elliott Taylor)

Dickson had appointed Tony Vyvyan (one of Millett's Deloitte team who had analysed Butterworths in 1963–65) to be Finance Director after the I.P.C. takeover; and Alan Roberts had come in from Newnes* at the beginning of 1966, to take over as chief accountant from Phil Hogger. Vyvyan found his scope under Stephenson too narrow and left in April 1973. He was not replaced at that time, but by October 1974 Stephenson was ready to delegate and brought in Don Saville from I.P.C. headquarters as Financial Director. October 1974 was also the month of K.J.'s retirement, though he was to remain on the Board for a further year and would thus serve under the eleventh Chief Executive of Butterworths since he had joined in 1934.

---

* When Roberts left Newnes, that company had been acquired by Odhams, and Odhams in its turn by I.P.C.; the acquisition of Butterworths by I.P.C. came nearly two years later.

For Stephenson had decided by this time who his own successor would be. His choice was Gordon Graham, who had been with McGraw-Hill for twenty-two years; he was the publisher that Stephenson had never claimed to be; and he also had an unusually international background, having lived for long periods in Asia and the United States.

Graham, who was fifty-four when he took command of Butterworths in January 1975, saw one of his prime tasks as ensuring management succession for all the key jobs in the Group. Another was to build up scientific, technical and medical publishing, a field in which his experience had previously lain, into a second publishing arm instead of an appendage to the legal publishing. With this in mind, he consolidated these three departments into a division under David Summers, one of several first-class young publishing executives serving under Simon Partridge in the legal division.

A third high priority on Graham's list was to re-establish Butterworths in the United States. Butterworth Inc. was re-incarnated near Boston in July 1975 under Tom Kelley, an experienced editor and sales manager whom Sheila Carey had hired in 1973 to build a U.S. medical list. Butterworths' U.S. company distributes all scientific, technical and medical books in the U.S. and Canada, while the Canadian company covers both countries for the legal publications.

Another of Graham's preoccupations was to unify the company's marketing organisation (initially under David Kingham and then under Colin Whurr, who had been hired from Addison-Wesley to be scientific, technical and medical sales manager in 1973) and to widen its international operation. As medical and scientific publishing grew in the two previous decades, senior executives and salesmen visited South America, India, Central Africa and the Far East; free-lance representatives operated for the company in Europe, the Middle East and Japan. But in none of these areas was there a Butterworth presence. There was not even an Export Manager before 1969, and attendance at trade fairs was sporadic until then.

By combining the legal and non-legal sales around the world, Whurr was able to build between 1976 and 1978 an international sales organisation comparable with the American corporations, with whom it was setting out to compete in scientific, technical and medical publishing. All of the territories where there are no Butterworth companies – Asia, the Middle East, Europe, Africa and Latin America – are now covered by Butterworth travellers or resident sales managers.

Graham sees the six Butterworth companies as a multinational group consisting of equal trading partners, a stance welcomed in Australia, New Zealand, Canada and South Africa. To this end, he established a Group Board, consisting (in June 1979) of the senior U.K. executives (George Norton, administration; Don Saville, finance; Simon Partridge, legal publishing; David Summers, scientific, technical and medical publishing; and Colin Whurr, marketing) and the heads of the other five companies – Ernest Hunter, who had taken over Canada in 1976; Derek Day, promoted from South Africa, where he had been Financial Director, to New Zealand in 1979; David Jackson, back again in Australia as Chief Executive on Peter Cheeseman's return to the U.K. in 1979; Andrew McAdam who took over the South African company from his old boss Barney Barns who retired in 1976; and Tom Kelley from the U.S. The Group Board also includes Sheila Carey and two independent directors – Bryan Hope, a senior executive of IPC Business Press, and Colin Tapper, a distinguished legal academic.

There is also a U.K. Board (expanded from what had been set up in 1974 as a Law Company Board) under the chairmanship of Simon Partridge, which includes several younger executives of the U.K. company – Neville Cusworth, Nicolas Harrison and Peter Cheeseman from the legal publishing division; Mervyn Barns,* who took over distribution on David Jackson's departure to Australia; John Carruthers, production; and Alan Roberts, accounting.

Some of Graham's innovations are controversial – e.g. open plan offices; a higher corporate profile; an Operations Committee consisting of middle managers which is invited to study the U.K. company's total operations and express its views; semi-annual forums when executives report to managers. Graham's style is open, devolutionary and delegative. A corporate animal himself, he has good relations with I.P.C. He calls frequently for younger managers and better managers, but does not discard the past, as his commissioning of this book shows. Two members of the Group Board in 1979 – Sheila Carey and Simon Partridge – worked for Stanley Bond; six more then on the staff joined while Bond was alive. Butterworths honours experience and values the stability this can bring.

However, some of the most significant recent happenings in Butterworths, as this history goes to press, are concerned with the future. Butterworths has long been aware that a new form of publishing is impending, in which the computer replaces the

---

* Son of Barney Barns, who ran the South African Company. He was the first director's son to be engaged after Cecil King cancelled the 'no nepotism' rule. He served in Durban for five years before being brought to head office.

printing press, and the visual screen the paper – a revolution in the transmittal of information perhaps as great as that brought to England by Caxton. In June 1979 the legal division formed a new company called Butterworth (Telepublishing) Ltd. to develop all forms of electronic publishing – including information retrieval, word processing, cassettes and micro-publishing. Richard Tottel, who is reputed to have used a Caxton printing press and from whom Butterworths can trace a tenuous line, would be pleased to know that the showroom where the new electronic marvels will be demonstrated to the legal profession will be at Bell Yard, to which Butterworths moved in 1899 the few steps from 7 Fleet Street, where Tottel developed the foundations of English legal publishing.

Butterworths' Financial Structure

The staff and the customers were neither informed nor curious about the financial structure of Butterworths during Stanley Bond's lifetime. The business belonged to him, and that was the end of the matter. Only his professional advisers, and those few who maintained the private ledgers and prepared the accounts, needed to know.

Until 1927 Stanley Bond conducted his main business as a sole trader under the name of Butterworth & Co.; limited liability companies (with Bond as the sole beneficial shareholder) had been formed in England to trade in Australia and New Zealand (1910), Canada (1912), and India (1910). South Africa was set up in the same way in 1934. Two of Bond's special interests were the journals – the *Law Journal* and the *Justice of the Peace*. In both cases he had personally acquired the one-publication company responsible.

He was also the sole shareholder in Butterworth & Co. Ltd. (sometimes called 'the small company'), formed in 1919,* through which he published certain books the copyright of which he owned privately. He seems to have intended this as a temporary arrangement. By the end of World War II only three books remained, and the company ceased to trade at the end of 1946.†

In 1927 Stanley Bond decided to incorporate his principal United Kingdom business. This he did by changing the name of Butterworth & Co. (Canada) Ltd. to Butterworth & Co. (Publishers) Ltd. and by increasing the authorised capital from £5,000 to £250,000. He would have liked to alter the Memorandum of Association also; he was advised in 1931 that this would involve an application to the court, but although he annotated the letter from his lawyers with the words 'I think this should be done', the change was never made, and to this

---

* As part of the strategy for preventing Mr. H. Thornton Butterworth from calling his new business 'Butterworth', without qualification.
† This is the company which it was proposed to use in 1962 as the vehicle for legal publishing in the U.K.

day the first 'objects' clause of the parent company starts with the words 'To carry on in Canada and elsewhere the businesses of law, medical and general publishers'.

So the Canadian company took over Stanley Bond's personal business, and he took shares as the consideration. For some years the company continued to operate in Canada, and kept separate accounts relating to the Canadian business. In 1931 a company was incorporated in Ontario (again with Bond as sole beneficial shareholder) to take over, gradually, the Canadian operation. This was done to ensure that the customs duty was calculated on an 'arms-length' discounted price, and not on the published price.

Butterworths thus remained a group of separate companies, with the same, and sole, shareholder in common, until his death.

The sale of shares outside the family was necessary in 1943 to pay death duties. The shares then taken up by Hambros Bank were transferred initially into the names of various nominee and investment companies. In 1944 the Prudential were registered as the beneficial owners of 10,000 shares, and the Pearl of 4,000 shares.

The years from 1943 to 1947 were spent in the rationalisation of the company structure, by making the smaller companies subsidiaries of Butterworth & Co. (Publishers) Ltd. as laid down by Stanley Bond's will.

The company went public on 14th January 1947, and on 20th January *The Times* and the *Financial Times* published the prospectus leading to an application to the Stock Exchange for permission to deal. The *Evening News* reported that 'Three large queues were lined up when dealings started at 9.45 a.m. [on

---

BUTTERWORTH & CO. (PUBLISHERS), LIMITED.

(Incorporated under the Companies (Consolidation) Act, 1908.)

This Notice is not an invitation to the Public to subscribe, but is issued in compliance with the Regulations of the Council of The Stock Exchange, London, for the purpose of giving information to the Public with regard to the Company. The Directors collectively and individually accept full responsibility for the accuracy of the information given. Application will be made to the Council of The Stock Exchange, London, for permission to deal in the whole of the issued Ordinary Stock of the Company.

SHARE CAPITAL

Authorised
£250,000 in 76,000 Ordinary Shares of 5/- each and 924,000 Ordinary Stock Units of 5/- each   Issued and Fully Paid £231,000

Neither the Company nor any of its Subsidiary or Sub-Subsidiary Companies has outstanding any Mortgages, Debentures or other Loan Capital.

DIVIDEND, CAPITAL AND VOTING RIGHTS.—The entire issued capital of the Company ranks as regards Dividend, Capital and Voting Rights and in all other respects *pari passu*.
No shares in the capital of the Company may, without the sanction of the Company in General Meeting, be issued with any preferential rights to Dividend, Capital or Voting.
BORROWING POWERS.—The Articles of Association of the Company provide

that the borrowing powers of the Company exercisable by the Directors shall be restricted so that the aggregate principal amount outstanding of moneys borrowed by the Company and of moneys borrowed by the Subsidiary and Sub-Subsidiary Companies of the Company incorporated in the United Kingdom (but exclusive of all inter-Company borrowings) shall not without the consent of the Company in General Meeting exceed £150,000.

DIRECTORS :

KENNETH ALFRED EDGAR MOORE, F.C.A. (Chairman of Trinidad Petroleum Development Company Limited), West Timber, Bucklers Hard, Beaulieu, Hants. (Chairman.)
HUGH QUENNELL (Chairman of British Lion Film Corporation Limited), 57, Cadogan Place, London, S.W.1. (Deputy Chairman.)
VIOLET MYRTLE BOND, Widow, Dycheham Park, near Petersfield, Hants.
GUY THOMAS HANMER, Lieutenant-Colonel in H.M. Army, Garden House, Westonbirt, Tetbury, Glos.
PAUL DOUGLAS ARCHIBALD NIEKIRK, Solicitor, 14, Rosemount Road, London, W.12.
FRANK WILLIAM SEABROOK EMERY, A.C.A., Park Cottage, West Dean, Chichester. (Executive Director.)
EDWARD LAWRENCE JONES, Brook Hall, Finchingfield, Essex. (Executive Director.)
JOHN WILSON WHITLOCK, 7, Woodcote Park Avenue, Purley, Surrey. (Executive Director.)

23rd January]. Small lots were being handed out at 35s. and by 10 o'clock the price had risen to 36s. 8d easing later to 36s. 6d. The market had been expecting an opening price of 34s. 6d to 35s.'

The *Financial Times*, commenting on the effect of the 'unequivocal and depressing terms of the Government's 'White Paper', said of Butterworth shares: 'In more favourable circumstances they would have gone higher in recognition of the company's strong position, progressive record and promising prospects'.

In June 1949 a rights issue – the only instance in Butterworths' history when new capital was sought – was fully subscribed, the purpose being to 'provide adequate working capital for the company's expanding business which is largely reflected in the substantial increase in the stock, debtors and work in progress'. Opportunity was taken to repay the existing bank overdraft of £100,000.

A total of 76,000 shares of 5s. each were offered to existing shareholders in the proportion of 1 for 14 at a price of 10s. (the market price being approximately 34s.). The Capital Issues Committee of the Treasury queried the profit element (nearly 2s. for each share held), but were satisfied with the explanation that 'the proposed issue of ordinary shares is small in relation to the existing issue of ordinary capital and, whilst it is appreciated that there is an element of bonus involved at an issue price of 10s. per share, the Directors consider it fair and reasonable to the shareholders to include this element of bonus, having regard to the profits which in the past have been ploughed back into the business, and to the amounts of taxed profits (the total exceeding £75,000 in four years) which have been applied exclusively for the benefit of the staff.'

At the same time an issue of 250,000 $4\frac{1}{2}\%$ Cumulative Preference Shares of £1 each were offered at the price of 20s. 6d per share on the basis of one share for each four ordinary shares held.

By 1955 the company's reserves were such that a scrip issue was justified in order 'to bring the ordinary share capital into line with the capital employed'. In the previous year the trustees, some of whom felt that they had too many eggs in one basket, had been in negotiation with two groups for the sale of considerable blocks of shares. One of the interested parties was the Drayton group (with which the Chairman of Butterworths, Lord Rothes, was associated, and to which the company's landlord belonged). The family being loth to see voting control pass into other hands, Richard Millett devised a proposal to divide the existing 5s. shares into two 2s.6d shares, one voting and one non-voting: and to capitalise £125,000 of reserves by the issue of one 2s.6d non-voting share for each existing 5s. share. 'If the resolutions are passed', Lord Rothes wrote to shareholders, 'the final result will be that an original holder of one 5s. ordinary Stock Unit will end up with...one "A" share of 2s.6d voting and two "B" shares of 2s.6d each non-voting.'

The Chairman's letter went on:

'Approximately 46% of the issued Ordinary Stock of the Company is held by the Trustees of the Estate of the late Mr. Stanley Shaw Bond who died in 1943 and the Trustees of the Estate are therefore in a position, if they so desire, to exercise *de facto* control of the Company. The Trustees consist of Mr. P. D. Niekirk and Mr. P. H. B. O. Smithers, M.P., both of whom are Directors of the Company, and B.V.W. Investments Limited, the latter Company, of course, acting through its own Board of Directors. Serious disagreement exists between the Trustees as to the policy which should be adopted in regard to this very substantial holding of the Estate in the Company. The view expressed on the one side is that the late Mr. Stanley Bond, who built up the business of this Company and of its Subsidiaries, would have wished that the holding and control should be retained in the Estate. The view expressed on the other side is that this holding, which at present market prices is worth about £500,000, is far too large to retain in the Estate and that by doing so the Trustees are retaining too many eggs in one basket.

The Company is not, of course, concerned with which of these views is the correct view but it is very much concerned to see that the general management and conduct of its affairs shall not suffer as a result of them. I regret to say that the dissension in which two of your Directors are concerned on one side and B.V.W. Investments Limited on the other is such that I see danger of the Company's business being affected if the situation is not remedied. The proposals set out above have accordingly been designed to meet so far as is possible both views so that the Trustees of Mr. Bond's Estate, if they so desire, may, by selling the non-voting Ordinary Shares, be able to realize up to two-thirds of their investment in the Company without affecting their voting rights at General Meetings.

Since the proposals are designed to a considerable extent to solve the problems of a single Stockholder, the Company has submitted them for the consideration of leading Counsel who has advised that they are fair and proper for submission to the Stockholders, inasmuch as they are of benefit to

Stockholders as a whole and designed to bring to an end a disagreement which is becoming embarrassing to the Company.

All the Trustees of Mr. Bond's Estate have expressed themselves as in agreement with the suggested proposals and have given me an assurance that if the Resolutions are duly passed at the meeting, they will use their best endeavours to dispose of any "B" Ordinary Shares which they may wish to sell in such manner as to cause the least disturbance to the market in the Company's Ordinary Share Capital...'

The scheme was accepted by the majority of the shareholders and was passed at an Extraordinary General Meeting.

Four years later a further proposal to capitalise reserves was frustrated by the institutional investors. The intention was to do this without changing the balance of power established in 1955. The directors therefore proposed to issue to 'A' shareholders two new 'A' shares for every five held, and to 'B' shareholders two new 'B' shares for every five held – in each case like for like. A letter to shareholders of 8th May contains the following discussion of the merits:

'Your directors consider it both equitable and desirable that, upon any capitalisation in the form of Ordinary Shares, both "A" shareholders, with a vote, and "B" shareholders, without a vote, should receive like for like so that the proportion of voting and non-voting shares will remain constant. The only alternative would be an issue entirely in non-voting Shares which would mean that every such capitalisation would result in a further reduction of the proportion of voting Shares to non-voting Shares in the total issued equity capital and this they consider would be undesirable. They are advised that in order to give effect to the proposal to issue Ordinary Shares on the basis of like for like it will be necessary to alter the Company's Articles of Association to that effect, since under the existing Articles both "A" (voting) and "B" (non-voting) Ordinary Shares are entitled to the same rights upon a capitalisation. This change involves a variation of the rights attached to the "A" (voting) and "B" (non-voting) Ordinary Shares and accordingly it is necessary for the proposal to be sanctioned in accordance with the Company's Articles of Association by separate meetings of "A" (voting) and "B" (non-voting) Ordinary Shareholders.

Notwithstanding this variation of rights, your Directors are of the opinion that the proposal is in the interests of the

Company and of each class of Ordinary Shares, and they recommend its adoption.'

Lord Rothes knew that the 'A' shareholders would receive shares which were worth on the average 6d a share more than those to be issued to 'B' shareholders. He knew also that proxies against had been received from sufficient 'B' shareholders to prevent the scheme. At the crucial meeting of 'B' shareholders the necessary resolution was passed by show of hands; the Chairman then demanded a poll. Three hundred and forty holders cast 919,850 votes for the resolution; sixteen holders cast 516,882 votes against. The resolution had not obtained the three-quarters majority needed.

At the Extraordinary General Meeting of all the shareholders which followed, the Chairman said (in reply to a question) that the sixteen shareholders who had opposed the scheme were mainly insurance companies.

The opponents polled 25.84% of the *total* 'B' shareholding, so that the resolution was not lost merely because of abstentions.

Accommodation

Moving house was practically a hobby at Butterworths. 'I was located in 11 Bell Yard, Whitlock in 227 Strand, Emery and Henry in 4 Bell Yard, Hutt near St. Paul's, the *Research* people in the Strand opposite Charing Cross, and the warehouse in Newington Butts.' So wrote Ron Watson in 1978, recalling the Butterworths of 1950. He could have added that the Advertising Department was in Bream's Buildings.

Much of Butterworths' locational history could be a case study of bad planning. To make an accurate list of all the properties occupied, the terms on which they were held, and the departments which occupied them would be wearisome. What follows is a rough sketch.

The original business, which had started at 7 Fleet Street (the historic 'Hand and Star'), moved to 12 Bell Yard in 1899, and overflowed into the 'house next door' in 1905. The expansion in 1912 into the far larger premises at 4, 5 and 6 Bell Yard was a milestone. Within ten years it was necessary to house the *English and Empire Digest* editors at 228 Strand (the building of which the ground floor is now a watchmaker's shop, L. Caplan).

Owen Elliott, the only conscious historian among the staff in the first half of the twentieth century, wrote in a letter:

'In the early part of 1912, a removal was made from 11 and 12 Bell Yard to the "new premises" at Nos. 4, 5 and 6 Bell Yard, which had recently been vacated by the Law Union and Rock Insurance Company. The change-over was a masterpiece of organisation, and in one night we were all transported from the old to the new. Whereas in the old premises we had all been cramped and confined into small corners caused by the constant and steady expansion of the business, when we got the new premises we found infinite space, or so it seemed. However, that condition did not last very long, and bit by bit the space was filled up, until Nos. 4, 5 and 6 became as crowded as Nos. 11 and 12 had previously been. The Central Hall with its beautifully

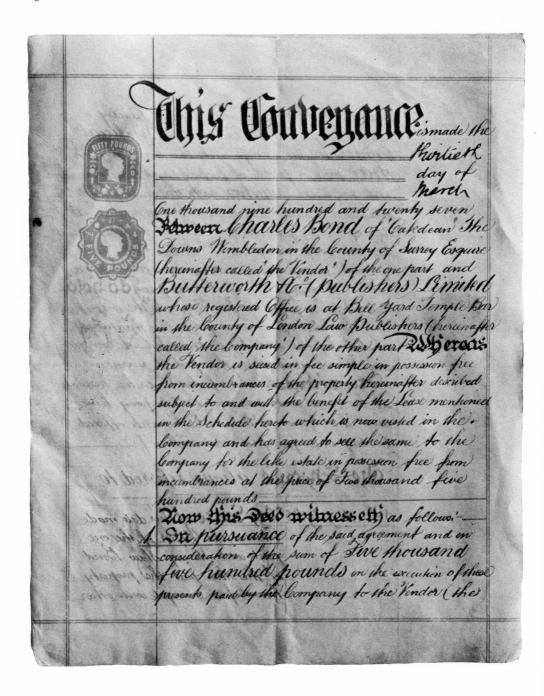

Assignment of the freehold of 11 Bell Yard by Charles Bond to Butterworth & Co.
(Publishers) Ltd., who were till then his tenants

polished floor* began to be laid out in offices. Then the overflow started; annexe offices again appeared, this time "up the Yard" and on one occasion across Fleet Street.'

About 1936 Butterworths took over part of Clark's College in Chancery Lane, to which access could be obtained down a long tiled corridor at the back of 4 Bell Yard. This annexe housed the Accounts Department under E. C. Leader in the years up to World War II.

The evacuation to West Dean Park and neighbouring locations during World War II was an unavoidable, but irrelevant, break in the company's long succession of premises in the square mile surrounding the Law Courts. The company grew during the war, and the directors had the foresight in 1944 to rent premises at 227 Strand, just opposite Bell Yard, and over the Temple Bar Restaurant. This building was fitted out to house the Publishing Department, who moved back to London in November 1945. The Sales and Finance Departments followed to occupy 4, 5 and 6, and 11 and 12 Bell Yard (and a suite in Bream's Buildings). The showroom was where it had remained since 1912 and throughout the war, at 6 Bell Yard.

The final evacuation of West Dean Park involved delicate questions of dilapidations. A social historian would revel in the twenty-six page 'Schedule of Dilapidations accrued at the above during the tenancy of S. Bond, Esq. and Messrs. Butterworth & Co. 21.6.35 to 15.7.46'. In the end Emery reached a very satisfactory settlement of £1750 (of which the company bore £1450 – for seven years during which eighty to a hundred people were working there, and sixty to eighty actually resident).

At this period the Publishing Department was growing fastest. An increasing amount of work on the legal side was being done by internal staff. Expansion of the medical department and an entry into scientific publishing were planned. The first step was to buy 9 Bell Yard (now demolished), a building containing only one room on each floor, previously occupied by a little old stationer wearing a skull cap. The circular iron stairs leading from ground floor to first floor did not please the female staff of Butterworths. Inadequate though it was, the second edition of *Halsbury's Statutes* was started there.

Meanwhile the neighbourhood was being scoured for bigger premises. J. W. Whitlock, travelling down Ludgate Hill on the top of a bus, spotted St. Paul's Chambers, a block of offices let

* Stan London recalled that as an office boy he received a rise of one shilling a week, when he polished the floor of the central hall on his own initiative.

4–6 Bell Yard. Head
office from 1912 to 1953

out in suites. *Halsbury's Statutes*, medical and scientific were the
first to go there. Others moved there over the next six years,
as leases fell in, relieving the congestion at 227 Strand.

During the late forties an insurance company, acting for
Quennell and Butterworths, was steadily buying up properties
in Bell Yard with a view to building a new Butterworths
building which would have extended through from 4 to 12 Bell
Yard. Architects were engaged to draw up plans, which did not
prove easy due to the shallow site. Plans were finally abandoned
when the L.C.C. required a turning circle at the foot of Bell
Yard, which would have reduced considerably an already
restricted site. (At a later date it might have been permissible
to put the building on stilts.) The abandonment of these plans
was a great disappointment at the time, but the building would
have been too small.

By 1952 the inconvenience of the scattered offices had become
intolerable, and it was decided to start looking for a single block
to house the whole company. This was found at 88 Kingsway.
Butterworths' landlords were British Electric Traction of which
Butterworths' Chairman was a director. The Showroom and
certain offices (e.g. the *All England Law Reports*) remained at 11
and 12 Bell Yard, in the heart of London's legal world.

In 1976, when 88 Kingsway was reconstructed on an open-
plan basis, the premises seemed dingy and old-fashioned, but

in 1953 people thought it was not 'Butterworths'; it was not 'Dickensian' enough. The list of equipment offered by the landlords included 100 coal scuttles, 44 shovels, 32 pokers and 12 pairs of tongs, together with hearth dogs, fire-guards etc., valued in all at £25. Butterworths did at least install central heating in the rooms which lacked it.

Straightaway an additional suite was rented opposite Charing Cross Station (in the Coutts Bank 'pepper-pot' building); this housed scientific editorial and *Halsbury's Laws Supplement*. The old head office at 4, 5 and 6 Bell Yard was sold.

Soon the Charing Cross offices were threatened with demolition (they subsequently remained empty for nearly twenty years). It was learned that, the purchasers of 4, 5 and 6 Bell Yard

88 Kingsway.
Registered office since
1953

having divided the building, Nos. 4 and 5 were available for letting. So the Scientific Department moved in 1955 into part of the building which Butterworths had deliberately abandoned two years earlier. They stayed there until 1964. Chambers were taken in Essex Court for the *Law Journal* and *Halsbury's Laws Supplement*, and suites of offices were taken one by one in Windsor House, Kingsway.

In 1961 after the establishment of the Medical and Scientific Division it was decided that in three or four years (when existing leases expired) the Division 'should be housed together in one modern building', but this plan did not come to fruition.

From then on the situation becomes more and more confused, and it is difficult to say who moved into what building when. Some of these movements were attributable to differences of opinion as to whether the business should be organised by product or by function. Should scientific Sales, for example, go with scientific editorial or with legal Sales? Broadly speaking legal publishing remained in 88 Kingsway; and legal sales and accounts (including order handling) had no major move until they went to Drury House in Russell Street in 1968. There were exceptions too numerous to mention. These involved not only the buildings already mentioned but suites of offices in Sardinia Street, Africa House (Kingsway), 125 High Holborn, and even as far afield as Bedford Row.

It would be impossible to estimate the management time devoted to the search for accommodation, and the number of buildings, suitable or unsuitable, which were inspected, negotiated for and rejected.

The books moved almost as much as the people. During the war much Butterworth stock was taken to Wendover in Bucks, where all sorts of unlikely buildings and rooms in farms and public houses were rented at minuscule rents. These were given up after the war when a warehouse and packing store was occupied at Barking. Scientific books were stored for a time in Newington Butts. In 1959 the whole operation was moved to brand-new premises at Chichester, alongside the printing works of R. J. Acford Ltd. which Butterworths had purchased. The Chichester warehouse was doubled in size in 1971, only to be vacated three years later.

There was a possibility in 1963 of obtaining premises at Chichester to enable the order-handling functions to be housed within easy reach of the warehouse. Some of those who had been at West Dean during the war looked nostagically at their old haunts in West Sussex. But from 1963 the possibility of a move of all or part of the offices outside London was never out of the minds of the directors, even if it was not always under active discussion or investigation.

In 1970 an independent report on relocation was commissioned. Its recommendations as to exactly which departments should be moved were not acceptable to all. The differences of opinion as to the relation of organisation and location, already referred to, became acute. The year 1972 was marked by a series of meetings designed to reconcile the arrangement of staff with the location of the directors supervising them, who would nevertheless need to be in touch with one another.

But the suggestion of Bath as the target location was universally welcomed. At that time the site of the old Midland Railway Station at Green Park, near the centre of the city, was likely to become available, and Butterworths understood that the City Council would permit the building of an office block facing the city, with a warehouse behind on the site of the platforms.* Unfortunately conservationist pressure developed, which would have caused long delays even if it could not have prevented the scheme entirely.† No alternative site could be found permitting Butterworths' unusual mixture of warehouse and offices, which did not suit normal zoning plans.

Other sites and buildings were examined. It had been provisionally agreed to rent an office block in Bath and to build a warehouse and order-handling block at nearby Melksham, when it was decided by I.P.C. that Hamlyns should vacate their premises at Borough Green in Kent. These were found to be suited to Butterworths' physical needs, even if Borough Green was less glamorous and less convenient than Bath. The developments at Borough Green have been described in Chapter 14.

One by one all the outlying offices in London were vacated during 1973 and 1974, leaving only 88 Kingsway, and the offices in Bell Yard. Plans were next discussed for long-term accommodation in London. It was finally decided to use the top four floors of 88 Kingsway for legal publishing, production and advertising, and to erect a purpose-built block in Bell Yard for the Showroom, and those editorial functions which needed to be close to the Law Courts.

I.P.C. Properties had by then acquired the outstanding

---

* Butterworths undertook to incorporate the classical booking hall in the design for the new development.

† The use of the Green Park site was not settled until January 1980, when the Department of the Environment granted planning permission to Sainsburys for a superstore and car-park.

The Showroom at 11 and 12 Bell Yard before demolition. (Photograph by Bishop and Stray)

freeholds from 9 to 12 Bell Yard.* All in those buildings were moved temporarily to 4 and 5 Bell Yard, or to 88 Kingsway, while the buildings at 9 to 12 Bell Yard were demolished and rebuilt. The new building was opened by Lord Denning on 19th October 1977. Meanwhile those in 88 Kingsway played musical chairs while the floors were gutted one by one, and refitted in a modern open-plan style.

At last Butterworths were housed on only three sites, in buildings specially designed.

* No. 9 was bought for immediate occupation in 1946, and No. 11 in 1902 (subject to an existing tenancy expiring in December 1904). No. 10 was not occupied by Butterworths until after its demolition and rebuilding. No. 12 was occupied leasehold from 1899 till its purchase by I.P.C.

Butterworths and the Book Trade

For much of its 160-year history Butterworths dwelt in isolation – even from its fellows in the law-book trade. It was 1947 before it joined the Publishers Association. It was the 1960s before there was any real dialogue with booksellers, and then it was hostile.

In 1822 a body called The Associated Law Booksellers was established. It included six of the eight principal law booksellers. The two odd ones out were both Butterworths – Joseph Butterworth & Son, and the newly established Henry Butterworth. An attempt in 1848 to interest Henry bore no fruit. When under-selling caused difficulties in 1853, the Association decided that stock should only be sold to Bond and one other 'at the prices sold to gentlemen'. The Bond who was causing difficulty to his fellow-traders was probably Charles Bond senior, the grandfather of Stanley. The tradition which Stanley Shaw Bond inherited, both from his father and from Butterworths, was to have nothing to do with the book trade.

The isolation was deepened by the kind of publishing undertaken by Stanley Bond in the twentieth century. The strength of his business was in multi-volume works designed for a unified, easily located readership. The high revenue from each sale – compared with the revenue from the sale of a single book – and the concentrated nature of the market made it not merely possible but advantageous to set up a sales organisation dedicated to selling Butterworth books, and nothing but Butterworth books, to lawyers and to nobody but lawyers. The direct sale technique facilitated also the sending of Services and supplements to subscribers by name.

This direct selling organisation, in parallel with the publishing concepts themselves, enabled sales to be maximised at a cost per unit which compared favourably with the discounts which other publishers, with their more diffuse product lines and markets, gave to booksellers.

Butterworths demonstrated its independence by having its own Showroom which was a bookshop in which their salesmen were trained. In the early days of the book trade (the days of

Richard Tottel) publisher and bookseller had been one and the same. As the centuries passed publishing and book-retailing became separate trades, *except* in the law-book business.

Booksellers naturally believed that they were being excluded from profitable business to which they were entitled, but their attempts to establish the same type of relationship with Butterworths that they enjoyed with other publishers were rebuffed. Academic booksellers handled student text-books, but only a few specialists such as Wildy, Solicitors' Law Stationery Society, and Sweet and Maxwell (also a bookseller as well as a publisher) handled all legal literature. Discounts were given only on text-books, and rarely exceeded ten per cent; sixteen and two-thirds was reluctantly conceded as an incentive to sell more students' books. Booksellers handled Butterworth books only when they could not avoid doing so.

Bond had set up offices in the major Commonwealth countries, and they conducted their business on the same lines as London. Smaller territories, where English law applied but which did not justify the existence of a local office, were supplied through a local book dealer or by a British company active in that territory. The arrangements were usually exclusive, which held the local bookseller at arm's length.

These arrangements worked admirably while publishing activities were confined to works for a discrete readership mainly resident in a territory served by a Butterworth office. Diversification into medical and scientific publishing brought problems. Although medical publishing had been initiated with a multi-volume work which could be (and was) sold direct to practitioners, the Butterworth system was not suited to the medical list as a whole with its preponderance of single-volume publications and its considerable market in countries other than those served by a Butterworth office. The conventional outlet – the bookseller – was needed to achieve sales both at home and abroad on an effective and economic level.

On the scientific and technical side, there was no real equivalent to the multi-volume encyclopaedia or to the private practitioner, such as gave medical publishing some superficial resemblance to legal publishing. The need for retail outlets was, therefore, even greater.

At the same time, in the early post-war years, more legal student text-books were published, but the opportunity to sell through booksellers, even if only in university towns, was regarded lightly by the Butterworth management. To them the student of today was the practitioner (and direct customer) of tomorrow.

In 1955 a 'Report on Sales Methods' commented that 'no

one knows the booksellers as Bill or Fred'. A slow thaw began in 1960 when the medical and scientific activities were separated from the legal. H. F. Roberts was appointed Sales Manager. His career started with J. & A. Churchill, the medical publishers, and he had also worked as a medical bookseller for Lloyd-Luke. David Jollands, the Editorial Director from 1964, made Butterworth history by attending the annual conference of the Booksellers Association. Mutual antipathies melted slowly, especially as Butterworths continued its traditional selling methods unabated. Booksellers found Butterworths Janus-faced.

A noteworthy diplomatic advance during those years was the appointment of John Keep as European representative. A freelance publishers' representative, handling lists of many British publishers, he was liked and respected by European booksellers and did much to improve Butterworths' standing in his territory.

By the mid 1960s, Butterworths' direct distribution system was obsolescent. The absorption of Iliffes in 1968 brought it within sight of total breakdown. Iliffes also brought two managers experienced in relations with booksellers – Ken Maclennan on the export side and Bert Meears who joined as Trade Sales Manager. They *did* know the booksellers by their first names. Their attempts at detente were hindered by poor deliveries, and by the booksellers' long-held suspicion that their orders were processed separately from, and more slowly than, orders placed direct by lawyers.

Gradually the service improved, discounts were put on a more generous basis, and a degree of cordiality ensued, both at home and abroad. No single event could be said to have brought this about, but the arrival of Gordon Graham in 1975 must have been greeted by the book trade as final proof that the isolationist days were over.

A similar aloofness marked Butterworths' relationship with other publishers (except for the special relationship with Sweet and Maxwell – Butterworths' 'friendly rivals'). Butterworths did not join the Publishers Association until 1947, and in the early days there was little active involvement. 'We don't get our money's worth', and should economise by withdrawing, it was frequently asserted. Bond, Whitlock and Emery all took part in public life outside Butterworths, but never in the activities of the Publishers Association.

When the Association was planning its defence of the Net Book Agreement in 1956–7, it approached its illustrious law-publisher member in search of support. Butterworths produced an elegantly reasoned opinion that the Net Book Agreement was not in the public interest and was, therefore, indefensible.

History does not record the fate of these papers in Bedford Square, but the Association briefed Counsel who convinced the Restrictive Practices Court of the innocent nature of the Agreement, which Butterworths signed along with all other publishers in 1962.

In the mid-1960s Butterworths, through David Jollands, began to take a regular part in the affairs of the Association. Gordon Graham had been elected to the P.A. Council in 1973 (before joining Butterworths). Sheila Carey has been Deputy Chairman of the University, College and Professional Publishing Division for several years, and is Chairman of the Medical Group within that Division. Colin Whurr, Marketing Director, served as Chairman of the Far East Working Committee of the Book Development Council.

Butterworths had finally joined the industry to which it belonged.

Butterworth Colophons

Richard Tottel's premises had a sign hanging out, bearing a
hand and star, and his imprint usually mentioned this. The
fullest form is 'dwelling in Fleet Street within Temple Bar at
the sign of the hand and star'. He seldom used a device or
colophon. When he did it looked like this*:

An even more rudimentary form appears occasionally, as in
this imprint*:

* From Year Books, Henry vi, year 4 (published 1556) and year 3 (no
  date) respectively. Reproduced by permission of the British Library
  Board

Another form appears as the watermark in paper used by Tottel for a number of his books:

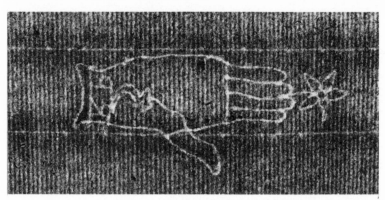

Joshua Butterworth, in the mid nineteenth century, revived the Tottel device, adding words of his own in Victorian 'olde-worlde' English:

After the Bond family acquired the Butterworth business in 1895 one of their first actions was to register the Hand and Star as a trade mark. A trade mark consists of a device, but not words, and therefore the colophon was (and still is) registered in this form:

A simplified form of the Hand and Star appeared in the early years of the twentieth century, and was in limited use up till about 1930. It was blocked in gold on the spine of the books (or blind blocked on the back cover), and occasionally appeared printed in the preliminary pages. Though the general form of the device was always the same, there were variations of detail in the different cuttings of the brass. The address does not always appear, and the usual 'Butterworth & Co.' is changed in India to 'Butterworth's' (with an apostrophe) or 'Butterworth'.

In the 1930s a new colophon was designed. It appeared on the new major work of that period (*Atkin's Court Forms*) and came into general use on the covers of legal works – with the exception of *Halsbury's Laws of England*. The letter B was shown against the background of the scales of justice, and the full name of the company (whether 'Publishers' or a subsidiary) appeared in the surrounding ring. By this means the group as well as the particular company could be identified.

With the development of medical publishing just before and scientific publishing after the war, variants were produced substituting the snake of Aesculapius, or a pair of laboratory scales, for the scales of justice. In the scientific version the distinctive B was omitted.

In the 1960s the current colophon was criticised on the ground that its detail was unclear when blocked on a book. Unsuccessful attempts were made to design a simpler version.

With the incorporation of Iliffe, Newnes and Ginn into the Butterworth Group in 1968–9, Norman Fisher caused a new device to be designed, to act as a link between the different imprints. This took the more modern form of a logotype. This device was accepted without enthusiasm by the publishers, particularly in the legal department. Subsequently, it was stylised by Hilary Norman, who became company designer in 1976, and today appears in books and letterheads, as on the right:

In the case of Newnes Technical Books a deliberate exception has been made to the concept of the 'Group' image. A plain capital N is now used, but from 1974 to 1980 a device based on the letter T was employed:

Butterworths in New Zealand favour a Kiwi:

But the Hand and Star still survives in the Australian Company:

thus linking Sydney in 1980 with the London of 1580.

Index

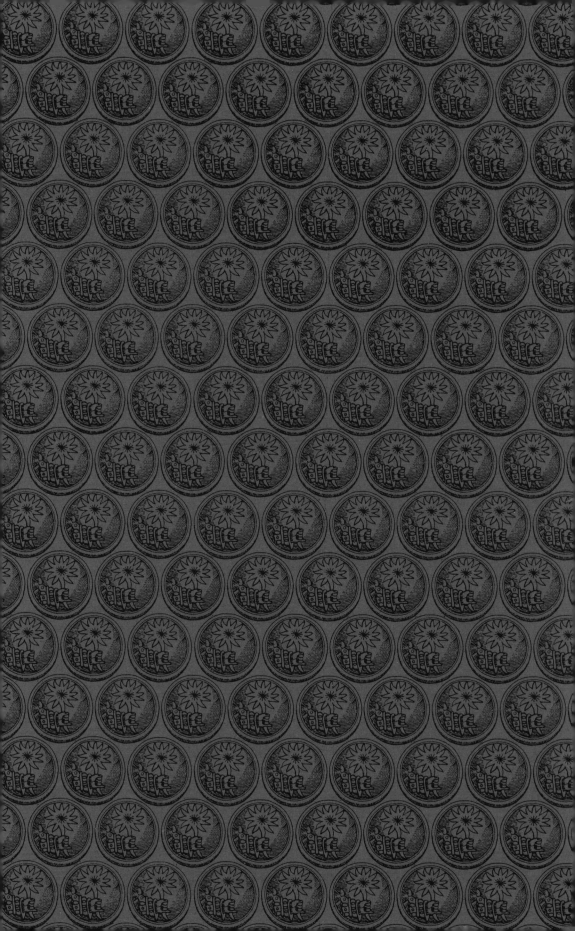